sort your career out

&

make more money

**Build your dream career, showcase your strengths
and unlock a money-making mindset...**
it's the most practical career book you'll ever read!

sort
your
career
out &

make more money

FROM THE TEAM AT **my millennial money**

SHELLEY JOHNSON
GLEN JAMES

WILEY

First published in 2023 by John Wiley & Sons Australia, Ltd

Level 1, 155 Cremorne St, Richmond Vic 3121

Typeset in FreightText Pro 11pt/15pt
Printed and bound by CPI Group (UK) Ltd, Croydon, CR0 4YY

A catalogue record for this book is available from the National Library of Australia

Cover design by Jess Pearson
Cover design concept by www.askjasonknight.com
Back cover and candidate portrait photos: Caitlin Schokker
Front cover and internal image (money in the air): © Cammeraydave/Dreamstime.com

Car boot image: © DreamStockIcons/Shutterstock
P227: Live Laugh Love image: © Christal Steele/Shutterstock

Disclaimer
The material in this publication is of the nature of general comment only, and does not represent professional advice. It is not intended to provide specific guidance for particular circumstances and it should not be relied on as the basis for any decision to take action or not take action on any matter which it covers. Readers should obtain professional advice where appropriate, before making any such decision. To the maximum extent permitted by law, the authors and publisher disclaim all responsibility and liability to any person, arising directly or indirectly from any person taking or not taking action based on the information in this publication.

C9781119899556_090223

We acknowledge the Awabakal people, Traditional Custodians of the land on which we build our careers, and pay respects to their Elders past, present and emerging.

We extend that respect to Aboriginal and Torres Strait Islander peoples who may read this book.

contents

Career Book Authors—
2 positions vacant

Location: flexible

Pay: blood, sweat, tears and a packet of Tim Tams

Must be able to:

- write lots of words

- *not* bore people to death with human resources (HR) jargon

- help people maximise their career opportunities

- use their (extensive) experience to deal with messy career problems, like how to work out if it's just a bad day or if it's a bad boss, or if it's a complete career crisis and it's time to make a big change, to go and study something new, to change industries, or maybe it's time to go on a holiday to Tahiti *breathe*

- help readers build a career they love

- focus on practical over theory.

Final shortlist—internal HR use only

Candidate 1:

Shell Johnson

Candidate 2:

Glen James

Qualifications and criteria suited to role:

☑ HR consultant & business owner

☑ hates HR jargon

☑ has had multiple career crises

☑ has read way too many books on work, careers and employment

☑ Masters of Human Resource Management

☑ explains things clearly (co-host of the *my millennial career* podcast)

☑ keen interest in helping people build careers they love

Also enjoys:

☑ her super cute family

☑ sci-fi and fantasy fiction

☑ fine dining and eating out as much as her bank balance allows

Qualifications and criteria suited to role:

☑ business owner

☑ employer of people

☑ has been a tradie, financial adviser and now runs a media business

☑ has career crisis experience

☑ explains things clearly (host of the *my millennial money* podcast)

☑ keen interest in maximising careers for maximum financial benefit

☑ author of *Sort Your Money Out & Get Invested*

Also enjoys:

☑ his cars and boats

☑ starting his day nice and early at 11 am

☑ filter coffee

how to
read this book

Well, we got the job! Guess we'd better write all those words now (hehe).

If you read the HR memo on the previous page, you know we're here to help you build a career you love.

So, let's do just that.

Glen in the driver's seat

Think of this book as your career handbook. It's just as much for career newbies as it is for those looking to optimise their current career situation. The system we've created is applicable to all career situations because it's driven by strategy first, and practical activities second. At the beginning of each chapter we've included a TL;DR (too long; didn't read) to provide a summary of what to expect in the chapter so you'll know before you dive in.

I write this as a business owner, an employer of people, someone who has had to change their own mindset and break away from societal norms. As Shell lives and breathes all things careers, has managed plenty of people of all ages and has almost seen it all, she will offer her own strategic and practical insights that will enable you to apply what you learn right away.

In my book, *Sort Your Money Out & Get Invested* (I will refer to it as *SYMO* moving forward), I shared an illustration of building your financial life like a house: starting with solid foundations before you worry about the walls like your lifestyle goals or investing. While *SYMO* could be read in any order, it is highly recommended that you read this book in chapter order.

I honestly believe this book is the prequel to *SYMO* as the best investment you can ever make is in yourself. That's investing into your mindset, your confidence, your health, your relationships and of course your career (the list does go on .... can you think of anything else?). The best investment return you'll likely make will be in your own career and ability to earn an income.

It is also so important that you're moving in the direction of a career you love. We all have bad days, so ask yourself: on balance, do you like your work or career? Whatever the answer is, this book will help you. If you love your career or job, you will be able to learn strategies and one percenters that will take you further, faster. If you love your career but hate your job, you will get the tools to make that move. If you have just left school or commenced university, this book will equip you with setting things up in the right order.

To get the most out of this, lean into the exercises, challenge your own thinking and write all over it. It's a workbook and a space for you to brain dump. Only feel guilty about writing all over this book if you have borrowed it from the library!

And, just as we have here, we will make it clear at the start of each chapter or section who is writing.

Shell in the driver's seat

This book was born out of a career crisis .... mine.

I'd worked in human resources (HR) for over a decade, mainly in large, not-for-profit organisations. After having my second baby, Bowie, I decided to quit my full-time role leading an HR team, and start a new job as an HR specialist in a small business. Despite being in the same industry, it was a very different role from anything I'd done previously.

It was about 4 months in when I realised the job wasn't right for me. I'd always been such a confident and decisive person when it came to work. I was hosting a successful careers podcast. I was the person who solved everyone else's weird work problems. And yet here I was completely lost, stuck and confused.

I had no idea what the heck I was doing with my career. But I knew I couldn't stay where I was. So I quit my job.

No job lined up. No plan of where-to next. No cards up my sleeve.

Well, except for one. I called my friend Glen James.

> *Shell: Hey, I quit my job.*

> *Glen: Yeah right. What are you going to do now?*

> *Shell: I'm winging it. I have no idea. I'll probably take a few months off to figure it out. Maybe do my own thing, freelance. Who knows?*

> *Glen: *long pause* .... I've got an idea .... Let's write a book.*

> *Shell: On what?*

Glen: On careers. We'll call it Sort Your Career Out. The prequel to SYMO.

Shell: Hahaha. But, I'm unemployed and having a complete career meltdown right now.

Glen: Perfect time to write it.

Glen was right. It was the perfect time to write this book.

It was born out of a real-life career crisis. I was the first beneficiary of the book. Through the process, I sorted my own career out. I can't wait for you to do the same.

Maybe you've picked up this book because you've got a career problem you're trying to solve right now. You want to land a promotion, need to earn more money or you're looking for a totally new career. Wherever you're at, we'll help you sort it out.

Over the years working in HR, and through the *my millennial career* podcast, I've helped thousands of people win at work and build a career they love.

This book is your career guide. Each chapter is jam-packed with practical advice to help you clarify your strengths, brainstorm your goals and map out your next move. It isn't about finding a job that doesn't suck—we've got big goals—it's about building a career you love.

I'm excited to be a part of your journey as you Sort Your Career Out. Forget what everyone else is doing: this is about you, your life, your goals, your version of success.

The career car

Many of us are visual learners and the educators out there understand this all too well. That is why I developed the 'sound financial house' to illustrate the importance of doing things in the right order. There is no point investing if you have not paid off your personal loan, nor if you have some goals in the short term that you need money for, as investments should be for the long term. Therefore, foundations are things like being consumer debt free.

Shell and I wanted to do a similar type of illustration for our careers and the best way to think about it is the concept of the 'career car'. You park your career car next to your sound financial house. And just like you journey your way through your career, you head out on a career road trip. Driving off into your career is also what provides you with the money to bring back home to your sound financial house.

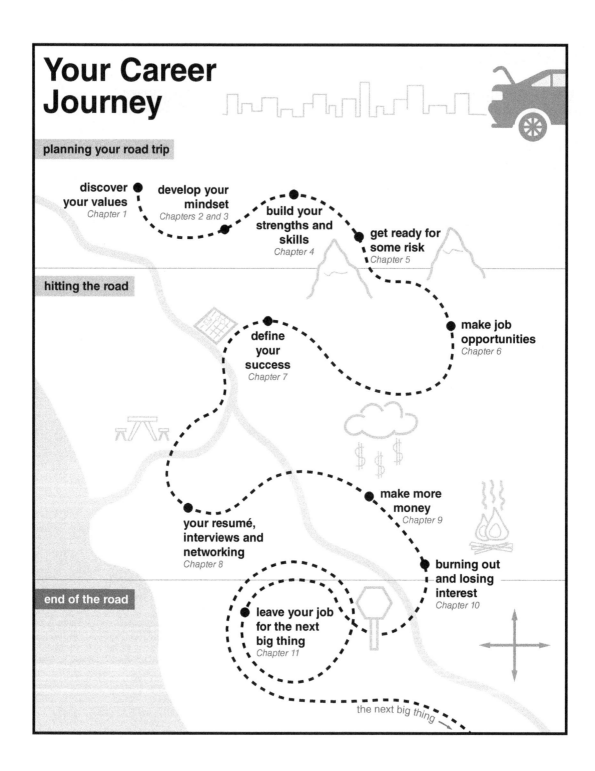

Your Career Journey

planning your road trip

discover your values
Chapter 1

develop your mindset
Chapters 2 and 3

build your strengths and skills
Chapter 4

get ready for some risk
Chapter 5

hitting the road

define your success
Chapter 7

make job opportunities
Chapter 6

make more money
Chapter 9

your resumé, interviews and networking
Chapter 8

burning out and losing interest
Chapter 10

end of the road

leave your job for the next big thing
Chapter 11

the next big thing

The best road trips require some planning. There are foundational parts to your career road trip you need to prepare for before you hit the road. You need to pack your bags, find your route, service your car and make sure you've got fuel ready to go.

This is part I of our approach: the strategic decisions you need to work through. What do you value? What's your mindset? What are your strengths and skills? What risks are you prepared for?

Once this stage is complete, we hit the road. This is part II of our approach: the tactical aspects of building your careers. We can drive forward, left, right, around the roundabout, backtrack, re-route, u-turn—there are so many directions we can go. These practical things are centred around building career opportunities, goal setting, mastery in resumes, interviews and networking. And getting that pay rise! But we also talk about tackling the more difficult aspects of your career journey, like career changes, career crises, burnout and redundancy. Learning how to process what's happened, get the car towed to a mechanic for repairs and get back on the road.

Then, in part III, Shell will walk you through how to know if it's time to leave where you are, and do it well.

The book is sectioned into these three parts, and it's best to read them in that order.

The importance of the sound financial house and the career car is that the logic can work at any age or in any situation. This isn't just for Millennials: this is for everyone who wants a career they love.

Here's a run-down on the three parts.

Part I: Planning your career road trip

Preparing for your road trip is where any great journey begins—we have to start with your career strategy. By skipping this step we risk just changing the font on your resume and ending up in yet another job or career you hate. If your strategy isn't set to the right route, you'll end up in the middle of the desert. Again. These areas are the preparation you need to know yourself. Know what you're looking for in a career and have your career car refuelled and ready to go.

Values

Your values influence the way you like to work. They are a crucial aspect of building a career you love (and are hugely beneficial to understanding life outside of work too!). When we are not aligned with our values, our life and career can quickly get out of sync.

In chapter 1, you'll figure out your own values and reflect on your job, workplace and career to see how they align (and potentially change course, if needed). This may be the first time you have heard or considered values as part of your employment. Your values guide how you work, whether you are aware of them or not. They can help you make great career moves, and avoid the bad ones. We'll walk you through a step-by-step process to define your values.

Mindset

Nailing the mindset piece to your life and specifically your career and career goals will honestly change your life. In chapters 2 and 3, I will share some of my experiences and challenge you to assess your own mindset, and how it could be affecting your career. Mindset is the origin of a lot of our career problems.

Strengths and skills

Working to your strengths and building your skills means your chances of performing better in a role are much higher—you'll be aligned to the right kinds of careers and roles. Working to your strengths makes your job more engaging and energising, but often people don't know their unique strengths. By discovering them, you'll find your genius zone where you perform best. We'll also share how to build skills that make you stand out.

In chapter 4, Shell will help you uncover your strengths and develop your skills, so you can hit your goals.

Risk

Taking risks is an inherent part of your career journey. And maybe it's the reason you aren't where you would like to be in your career: the fear of risk. Usually our minds associate risk with loss—that taking a risk means that loss could occur. Either financially, physically, emotionally or in any other area you can think of. However, this isn't always true, and we'll highlight that with risk comes the reward you've been hoping for.

In chapter 5, Shell and I will help you prevent the risks of owning too much real estate in your head, and we'll help you reframe how you assess risks (whether they're 'good risks' or 'bad risks'). We'll look at taking a risk with your career because it's a muscle that many people seldom use, and it could be the only thing preventing you from finding a career you love.

Part II: Hitting the road

Once we've nailed your strategy in part I it's time to hit the road! We get super practical here and focus on the things you can do to make your career journey meet your definition of success.

Creating career opportunities

Want big career opportunities to come to you? Here we talk about the habits that create career opportunities. It's the practices you do on repeat that bring opportunities to you. In chapter 6, Shell will outline the key habits that act as an opportunity magnet. Do these things and watch the doors swing open.

Success and career goals

So many people measure their own career success based on what other people think. This is a sure way to end up in a career you hate. You need to define what success means in your life, and it may not mean always moving 'up'. And that's okay. In fact, that's perfect. We don't want you living your life according to someone else's goals. Your life and career goals need to be yours and yours alone. This is your journey, not someone else's.

In chapter 7, Shell will help you tease out what on earth your goals actually are! She digs deep and prompts you to own your career with both hands on the wheel.

Resumes, interviews and LinkedIn

In chapter 8, Shell will outline exactly what you need to include in your resume, and everything you need to save for the script of your biopic (no life stories please). She will explain the recruitment process, what to expect and how to prepare and practise now. And she'll highlight why networking is a thing, what it achieves for you and others, and how to master it (in person and online using LinkedIn).

Making more money

Doesn't everyone want a pay rise?! In chapter 9, I will highlight the key ways you can make more money by increasing your earnings, and how to approach your manager for the pay rise you have earned with your performance track record. I'll also spend a bit of time talking about negotiation from a macro level and Shell will share her top tips for how to ask for a pay rise.

Career crises, career changes, burnout and redundancy

The number of people who listen to our podcasts and have hit one of these speed bumps in their career is huge. If you've hit one of these, then take heart: listeners of the *my millennial money* and *my millennial career* podcast community are right there with you. Shell explains what to do if you find yourself on the side of the road, waiting for the career tow truck to turn up, along with some great community testimonies which show you that you are not alone and you will find a way forward.

Part III: Reaching the end of the road

So you've reached the end of the road in your job. It happens. Sometimes it's a toxic workplace or it's just not the place you feel is right for you, right now. Shell will walk you through how to know whether it is in fact time to leave your job, and how you can develop an exit strategy that allows you to depart on the best possible terms.

Apply now

In each chapter you'll see some 'Apply now' sections. These are designed as points of reflection and exercises for getting super practical and taking charge of your career. It's all well and good to listen to what we have to say, but it means nothing without action. So warm up your muscles, turn your brain on and prepare to workshop your own situation.

Stories from the community

We've also harnessed the power of the *my millennial money* and *my millennial career* communities by including first-person accounts from listeners of the shows. People who have been in your shoes and found a way forward. We love our community, and they love us back by sharing their experience, guidance and advice. So please enjoy what they also have to share! We will also make comments on these stories.

Downloads and resources

Throughout the book we'll provide some additional content that you can download by visiting links connected by QR codes at the end of some chapters. There are templates, further reading and links that can help you journey through the stages of this book.

So what next?

With the help of the words we've written, and the experience of the *my millennial money* community, we want you to be able to prepare your career strategy, before mastering the practical things that will help you craft a career that you'll not only love, but thrive in—and give you the best shot to make more money, if this is a goal of yours!

Get in. Buckle up. And hold on.

Let's go!

planning your career road trip

values: where it all begins

1

tl;dr

- Determining what you *value* is critical to building a career you love.

- Often if something feels 'off' at work, it's a values issue.

- You need your values and career to align: if things are out of alignment, it gets painful, quickly.

- In some cases, communicating a values issue with your manager or boss can prevent the need to look for a new job altogether.

- We provide a long list of values to help you decide which are relevant to you and your career.

Shell in the driver's seat

I hate small talk. The label 'chit-chat' captures the drudgery of the act perfectly and it doesn't help that I'm woeful at these conversations. I forget to ask the socially acceptable 'ease-in' questions. The truth is, I don't care what you're watching on Netflix. And I'm sure as hell not interested in your weekend workout routine. Zero care factor. I want to know the deep things in life. What are your big regrets? When do you feel most energised? Oh, and are you still using those breathing exercises your therapist gave you?

Any job where I have to make small talk for extended periods of time is probably not going to work well for me.

I was at my friend's engagement party a few months back and, like at most parties, it's customary to engage in tedious small talk for hours on end. I checked the time. Ugh! It was only 7.30 pm. I'd already exhausted my repertoire of go-to questions. It was time to park myself at the grazing table. No-one will expect me to talk with a mouth full of camembert, right? Or at least, that was my plan, until I spotted my friend Beck breezing through the door. I saw my moment. She was my escape from monotony. I made a beeline for her.

Beck and I hadn't seen each other in months. And just as she went to say hello, I jumped in with a banger: 'Hey, I heard you burnt out and quit your job. What happened?'

Beck's eyes went wide. She laughed, which sounded more like a choked kind of cough. Yeah. Not the best lead-in. But within minutes, we were into a full-on deep and meaningful about how her desire for achievement led to fatigue, exhaustion and, ultimately, burnout. She shared her story of recovery and told me about the boundaries she's put in place to rebuild her health.

Deep, authentic conversations are the ones that really matter to me. They're the ones we remember. They peel back the facade, exposing the raw truth and insight hidden beneath. I guess that's why I'm drawn to them. Why waste time on shallow small talk when you can go deep?

In the same way conversations can skim the surface, our careers can hover in superficiality. I've seen many people stay in the shallow end. They focus on the external aspects of their career. The job titles, the money, the qualifications. Of course, these things matter, but they're just the surface—the exterior. It's easy to linger here, in the shallows where it's comfortable. But in choosing to do so we risk missing out on the deep things within us that we actually want in our lives. The deep end is where the real action is. So that's where we begin.

In this chapter, we'll dive into the deep end of your career. Instead of focusing on what you do for work (another cringeworthy small-talk go-to), we'll focus on who you are and what you *value*.

These values are the beliefs that guide and inform you in your life. We'll align these values with the other key aspects of your career road trip planning as we continue through this book. Screw surface. Dive in!

Sorting your career out starts with your values

It's Monday morning and you're driving to work. You've downed two coffees already, but there's zero buzz to speak of. To say that you're dreading your day would be a huge understatement. Your boss freaks you out with their fake smiles, whisper-shouting and passive-aggressive feedback.

Your teammates are as miserable as you, and no amount of happy hour beers can improve the vibe. To top it all off, the 'just checking to see where this is up to?' emails in your inbox have you considering throwing a u-turn and driving home to bed.

Except you don't, because you have no idea what you want to do with your career. So you keep driving and keep hoping that this week will be different.

Sound familiar? We've all been there.

Tick the boxes that apply:

☐ You're in a job where you're not challenged or growing but you don't know what to do next.

☐ You've spent $40000+ on study only to end up in a career you hate.

☐ You work in a toxic culture but you're afraid to put yourself out there for another role.

☐ You've seen a role advertised that really excites you, but you're not quite sure if you have what it takes to do it.

☐ You work for a terrifying boss who could star in their very own true-crime podcast.

☐ You're fresh out of uni or college and have zero idea what to do now.

☐ You've returned from parental leave and realised you want a change.

☐ You know you need a new challenge, but you're afraid of rejection and clam up in interviews.

☐ You desperately need a change, but you're scared out of your mind to make a change.

First, I want you to feel validated. These are common problems people face in their career. But just because they're common, doesn't mean you should accept them.

You deserve a career you love. I'm going to repeat that in case you skim read that sentence:

You deserve a career you love.

And no, we're not saying your career will be easy. Any good career has its challenges, its share of highs and lows. But overall, your career should be energising, fulfilling and meaningful. Unfortunately, many people settle for less.

Values keep you on the right career road

I looked down at my phone. There were three missed calls from Hayley and a text message: 'Shell, I just quit my job. I need to talk to you. Call me when you're free.'

Hayley, one of my clients, was running a large communications team in a fast-growing business. She's a confident, high-energy, vibrant person. But her work seemed to drain her spark. She was feeling unmotivated, depleted and frustrated. After years of ignoring how her job was impacting her life, it finally caught up with her.

I called her back and she answered the call on the first ring. 'Hey Shell, I don't have much time, but I'd love your advice. I have to start applying for jobs ASAP. Could you review my LinkedIn and resume for me?'

My answer? 'No.'

Hayley was in a tough situation. She'd quit her job without having lined up the next gig. And in high-pressure situations like these, it's tempting to go straight to quick fixes. We look for the easiest solution (i.e. getting a new job ASAP), but it's not always the right one.

When you're facing career problems, you might feel the urge to jump straight onto LinkedIn and find your next opportunity. You start googling how much you can be paid elsewhere, hoping that if you get more money, you will magically feel happier at work. Maybe you distract yourself from the underlying problems that got you here by finding a new course to study.

Let's be clear: these are not bad things. I mean, who doesn't want more money or to learn new things? The problem occurs when we look for quick fixes without doing the deep work first.

When Hayley reached out, she was in crisis mode. She was focused on the immediate problem and finding a short-term solution. While she was in that headspace, she wasn't able to look at her career strategically. It was like she had her destination in mind: get another job. But no clue how to get there.

She needed to take time to slow down. To breathe and go back to her career strategy. Before she started applying for new jobs, she needed to take time to reflect on what wasn't working for her in her current role, so she could avoid it in her next role.

On your career road trip, you need a map of where you want to go. It's a direction you can follow time and time again whenever you want to change things up or need to remind yourself of where you want to be heading. If you've started to turn off course, a map will bring you back.

That's what our values do for us: they're the key element that brings us back on track with what we really want.

Uncovering your values

Knowing your values sounds simple in theory, but many people struggle to identify their values. Sometimes we don't realise what our values are until they are challenged, or aren't being met.

Think about a tough situation you've gone through at work. And no, I'm not talking about the annoying things that happen in every workplace, like when Joel parked in your favourite car park again (but also, please stop that immediately, Joel). I'm talking about the critical moments. Often, there's a 'values conflict' at the heart of our challenging career experiences. And it's in these moments that you figure out your values.

Here's an example.

Luke got a big promotion into a director of accounting role. He'd worked his butt off to get to this point. The new role came with some decent perks. He got a $45000 salary increase, big bonuses and some exciting new responsibilities. It was all the things he was looking for. There was just one catch. It came with a new manager, Abbie. And *spoiler alert*, Abbie was going to become a big problem.

At first, Abbie seemed like a pretty cool boss. She was dynamic, had a fun sense of humour and had loads of experience. In the interview, she spoke about the endless career opportunities at Luke's fingertips. It sounded like the dream job. Luke jumped at the offer.

But five months into the role, Luke wasn't sleeping. He was working late every night and most weekends. And he couldn't switch off from work.

In the early days, it seemed like the ultimate career move. So how did Luke end up here?

In the first month of starting, Luke noticed strange dynamics in his and Abbie's working relationship. Abbie would express her complete trust in Luke, but then closely scrutinise each decision Luke made. A few months in, Luke overheard Abbie criticising his work to other team members. But Abbie wouldn't share her feedback with him directly. Luke was already irritated, but it only got worse when he watched her take credit for the team's wins in front of other leaders.

Within a matter of months, Luke's confidence had completely deteriorated. He was constantly worried about what Abbie would think of his work. The lack of trust caused him to question every decision he made. It was a painful but important experience. It's where Luke uncovered his values. He learned the non-negotiables needed for him to thrive at work.

Luke's first value was 'trust'. It was not enough to simply be told by a manager 'I trust you'. Luke needed to experience trust through action. He wanted independence and autonomy to deliver his work as he saw fit. Abbie's controlling style and failure to provide direct feedback was a breach of trust for Luke.

The second value for Luke was 'recognition'. Luke wanted the team to be recognised for the work they delivered. He wanted his team's creativity, wins and progress to be acknowledged and respected. Each time Abbie took credit for their work, he felt devalued, undermined and sidelined.

What we see in Luke's story is a values conflict. Luke's values were not met because of Abbie's management style. And when there is a clash of values, problems follow.

So what did Luke do from here?

Luke identified the gap between his values and his work environment. Once he clarified what wasn't working for him he met with Abbie to share his values and communicate what wasn't working for him in the role. He articulated the changes he needed to thrive at work.

Ultimately, he was evaluating whether the values conflict could be resolved before making any decisions, like resigning.

Communicating honestly about your values is essential. While it's daunting to have this kind of conversation with your manager, it can be a catalyst for positive change, or help you to determine if it's time to move on.

What can we learn from Luke's story? As Luke began to understand his values, he was able to articulate what wasn't working for him and identify the changes that needed to occur.

What are values?

Now that we know why values matter, let's clarify what we mean by career 'values'. There are a lot of definitions out there. But to keep it simple, we think of values as the 'non-negotiables' to you in your life. They are deeply held ideals, or the beliefs that matter to you personally. They shape how you live and how you work, and influence the type of work you love doing.

My four values are:

- *Growth.*

  I need to be continually growing and learning at work. I want to feel challenged and stretched in my job. If I'm not challenged, I get bored quickly and become disengaged in the job or work I'm doing. My value of growth has meant that taking a step back into a role with less responsibility or less challenge doesn't work for me.

- *Autonomy.*

  Over time, I've realised how important autonomy is to me. I want to work when I want, where I want, how I want. My family is my priority and so having autonomy enables me to do school pick-ups and be at important family events. Learning this about myself has been very helpful in my career decision making. It led me to start my own consulting business because my version of autonomy was better suited to self-employment.

- *Fun.*

  When work is boring, I feel like I am dying a slow and painful death. That means fun at work is non-negotiable. Fun fact: HR is hilarious because people are weird. It's a career filled with fun, drama and stranger-than-fiction moments. My desire for fun and a bit of weirdness is what drew me to this industry, and it's what's kept me here.

- *Authenticity*.

  I have an amazing BS radar. That means I want my workplace to keep it real, say it straight and tell the truth. At times, when I've worked in a team that has felt fake or inauthentic, it has caused me to feel anxious or unsettled. If I haven't been able to resolve the clash of values, I've ended up opting out.

Glen's comments on values

Values are hugely personal and I'd imagine every single person has their own values based on where they grew up, how they grew up, their influences, their exposure to basic life needs and their chemical makeup.

In my own life I am acutely aware that in the scheme of the universe I am not here but for the blink of an eye, if that. So given this fact, why would I want to put up with rubbish, toxic middle management (hi), being told what to do all the time or not having a sense of my own destiny? Sure, there is a bit of a control freak in me and for those who also live in their heads—like I do—it might be easy to fall into these deep thought patterns.

But ultimately for me, my values are really a reflection of who I am. I say what I mean and mean what I say. Let me build my own life and destiny my way. With this comes risk, which I am accustomed to, and that's why when we talk about values, risk may be part of this discussion and is so important to acknowledge.

In my book *Sort Your Money Out*, I talked about LOOT (life on own terms) as a differentiation from a money movement out of the United States called FIRE (Financial Independence, Retire Early). I challenged the notion of working at a job you don't love for a long period of time, grinding away to amass wealth to then retire early from that job. I believe we can live life on our own terms now. By 'now', I mean applying the teachings and thought starters in this book and putting a plan in place to get you moving.

Living LOOT does not mean you need to be self-employed or an entrepreneur. It is just being aware that you are in fact intentional with your life, career and vocation, ensuring these things align with your values. If you value security, a 9-to-5 government job could in fact be like living in heaven for you, whereas when I compare that against my own value set it is more like living in hell. The key here is to be aware of who you are and what you value, and then work out what you want to do. Wherever you land on the value or risk matrix of life, you still need to be in the driver's seat and not a passenger.

My top four values:

- *Autonomy.*

  I work best when I'm in control: my personality is one that needs to be in the driver's seat. I see an opportunity and I feel the need to go hard at it. That's part of the reason I chose to become a business owner: I operate best when I can make the calls. I guess you can say LOOT for me!

- *Flexibility.*

  I work best when I have the power to control how, when and where I work. Sometimes it's in a café over breakfast and a coffee; sometimes it's at home in the evenings. I need to be in a settled headspace to work effectively and those times of feeling settled for me aren't at a consistent time of day or place: I need the power to choose when I drop into the deep work zone.

(continued)

- *Honesty.*

  I am a truth seeker—always. Honesty helps me understand where everything and everyone stands so as a team I know for sure we're moving forward in the right direction. This is also a weakness of mine. In fact, in the past (a steep learning curve) during some business negotiations, people have said certain things that have not been true, and I've walked away disappointed. Not everyone says something and means it—I can't assume everyone is like me on this. So to protect this weakness of people not dealing in the same value currency as me, I need to make sure things are in writing (which is best practice anyway!).

- *Communication.*

  I'm a strong believer that communication is often the problem and solution. It's one of the most useful tools to keep going at goals at a good pace, so for me, clear and concise communication is a critical aspect of my business and my team. 'Just tell me how it is!'

apply now

Now that you know why values are important, and how they work in your career, it's time to choose your own values. Here, you'll work out what you value most from your job, workplace and career.

There are over 100 values in the list that follows for you to choose from. We know it can be overwhelming to pick your values when you're looking at a long list. You might be thinking 'all of them are important'. Yeah, they are, but not all of them are important to you.

Look for words that jump out at you. Think about what is non-negotiable for you to thrive at work. Look for those 'must-haves' in your life, work and career.

Values

Achievement	Confidence	Flexibility
Adventure	Connection	Forgiveness
Ambition	Consistency	Freedom
Authenticity	Courage	Friendship
Autonomy	Creativity	Fun
Balance	Curiosity	Generosity
Beauty	Determination	Grace
Boldness	Discipline	Gratitude
Bravery	Drive	Grit
Care	Empathy	Growth
Career	Encouragement	Happiness
Challenge	Entrepreneurship	Harmony
Change	Equality	Health
Clarity	Excellence	Home
Collaboration	Execution	Honesty
Commitment	Fairness	Hope
Communication	Faith	Humility
Community	Family	Humour
Compassion	Financial security	Inclusion

(continued)

Independence	Openness	Service
Individualism	Optimism	Simplicity
Influence	Patience	Speed
Initiative	Peace	Spiritualism
Innovation	Perseverance	Status
Integrity	Pleasure	Strategy
Intuition	Poise	Strength
Job security	Popularity	Structure
Joy	Positivity	Success
Justice	Power	Team
Kindness	Presence	Tenacity
Knowledge	Quality	Time
Leadership	Recognition	Trust
Learning	Relationship	Understanding
Legacy	Reliability	Vision
Lifestyle	Reputation	Wealth
Love	Respect	Wellbeing
Loyalty	Responsibility	Willingness
Minimalism	Risk-taking	Wisdom
Money	Safety	

List eight values that you feel resonate with you. These are the things you want to have in your career and job.

1 _____

2 _____

3 _____

4 _____

5 _____

6 _____

7 _____

8 _____

Would you rather...

Now, let's start to narrow it down. It's time to play a game of 'Would you rather...'. This will help you to shortlist your values and select your final four career values.

How to play:

- Review the eight values you've listed; group similar values next to each other to help you compare them.

- From there, you can narrow it down by picking which one is more important to you.

- It's important to reduce the number of values as it helps you clarify the things that are essential. Your job or career won't always be able to meet every value, but you want to be clear on the most crucial ones, in order to have them met.

(continued)

Would you rather ...	
e.g. Authenticity	e.g. Integrity

My final four values

Now list your final values and outline why they matter to you, or what each value looks like when it's being met.

Example

Influence: to me, this means that I get to influence and contribute to key decisions and help shape the direction of the team, business or strategy. I'm listened to and heard by the organisation I work in, and my input is valued and brings about change.

1 _____

2 _____

3 _____

4 _____

Putting your values to work

If you love your job, employer and career, you've found a values match. This is worth celebrating. If you are looking for a change or a new opportunity, or you're not loving your current job, this is where your values become crucial.

Your values will guide you and lead you down the right path. But before you make any decisions or pursue a change, you need to weigh up the opportunity against your values. This isn't just true for the big decisions, like 'should I leave physiotherapy to become an engineer?' Our values matter in both the big changes and the small changes.

Maybe you've been offered a 3-month higher duties role while your manager is on extended leave. Or a 12-month temporary role has come up in a different department and your manager thinks you should go for it. Before you say yes, stop and consider the opportunity. Weigh it against your values. Even when it seems like an easy or natural decision, it's important to evaluate the opportunity against your values to check for any potential conflicts.

Before accepting a new job

Use these simple steps to weigh up a new opportunity:

1. *Review the job advertisement, core duties and any information available about the business.*

   Ask yourself:

   o   How do the duties in this job match my values?

   o   What areas in the job don't align with my values?

   o   What parts of the job will energise me?

   o   What parts of the job will drain my energy?

- How does the business brand or values align with my values?

- What areas might be a deal-breaker for me?

2. *During an interview, ask the interviewer questions that relate to your values.*

   Here are some examples that may help you design your questions:

   - One of my values is learning. That means I love to try new things so that I can be continually growing and challenging myself. What are the learning and development opportunities in this role?

   - I love spending time with my family. What does flexible work look like for employees here?

   - Being trusted in a role is important to me. It helps me to thrive at work. Can you tell me what trust looks like in this role?

   - Having autonomy helps me do my best work. What level of discretion will I have over my goals and work?

   - I thrive at work when I get to have an influence over the strategic direction and goals. What level of influence does this role have in the strategic activities?

Will my values change over time?

The short answer is yes. Your values do change over time. Life changes can cause your values to shift. However, I'd argue they don't change very often. For me, between the ages of 18 to 28 years my values were fairly consistent and aligned with being in the early part of my career. They were 'growth', 'fun', 'authenticity' and 'achievement'.

After having kids, my values changed. Achievement became less important. Instead, I wanted more autonomy. The need to have ownership over how I worked became essential to me. I wanted complete autonomy so I could work in a way that suited my family.

So, it's worthwhile reviewing the list of values every few years and reflecting on them when you're considering making a change.

Asher, 31
Central Coast, NSW

I left school and found myself in the general workforce, just doing the things that I thought everyone did. I ended up getting a job with a national company in their head office and was doing a 3-hour total commute each day. Soon enough, early rises, constant travelling and consistent late nights became normal and I slowly entered the rat race.

I worked my way through the ranks, finally ending up in a well-paid people management role. The money was amazing, but I soon realised that it came at a cost. The role and the environment that surrounded it were not something I could learn to enjoy—even after 12 months of trying. As a result, I began experiencing anxiety and increasingly felt that I wasn't where I wanted to be.

I knew I needed to get out, so I made the decision to leave that world and do something completely different. I needed to spend more time doing things I loved and one thing that's always been important in my life is music—I'm a bass player. So I found a job in a local music shop, a complete shift in the kind of work I'd been doing, but one where my responsibilities weren't suffocating me. I was close to home and I was doing something I cared about.

Changing to a role that offers far less money might not make much sense to many, but I now look forward to work each day and I get to spend more time at home with my family.

I decided that my quality of life is more important than money and have not regretted my decision since.

Asher knew something was up. He was experiencing a clash in values. With a bit of time and assessment he figured out his non-negotiables and the values that truly mattered to him in his life (not just his work), and he took proactive steps to build his career around those values.

How do you know if you have a values conflict?

Not every work conflict and problem relates to your values. It's important to work out whether you're dealing with a clash of values or if it's one of those normal (albeit irritating) work issues found in every workplace.

The following examples will help to demonstrate the types of values conflicts you might experience:

- *Annoying work issue:* Josh is playing his Foo Fighters Greatest Hits playlist without headphones because he thinks it helps the whole team get into a state of flow (ummm, sorry Josh, it's not working for me).

- *Values conflict:* you value flexibility and choice in where, when and how you work. You want the option to work from home or a café or the train. And, you want to work hours that suit your personal life. But your workplace has just announced that all employees have to work from the office 80 per cent of the week.

- *Annoying work issue:* your manager is slow to respond to your queries and emails, and sometimes forgets to get back to you.

- *Values conflict:* you value inclusion and want all team members to feel they belong. But your team is cliquey and the boss fosters an 'us vs them' culture, pitting team members against each other.

- *Annoying work issue:* your teammate is a loud talker, louder typer and even louder eater and it's equal parts irritating and gross.

- *Values conflict*: you value kindness and care, but the organisation you're working in tolerates bullying, gossip and cutthroat behaviour from its employees.

The difference between an 'annoying work issue' and a 'values conflict' is defined by impact. Is the problem something you can address, work through or compartmentalise? Or is it pervasive and systemic—that is, an issue that's not easily resolved? Is it the type of problem that impacts your health? Does it keep you up at night or cause your engagement, performance and motivation to decline?

As much as your teammate's loud eating is seriously irritating, it probably won't rattle you to your core. But seeing a teammate thrown under the bus in a meeting because of terrible workplace culture will. It will stay with you. You'll be thinking about it tomorrow. And when it happens again you'll be keeping a tally. This, friends, is a values conflict.

Annie, 29
Broome, WA

I was working in the landcare/environmental sector as I had a degree in this area. I was casual and my boss had promised full-time, but that never happened. I didn't realise how much I was struggling till he made me work on my birthday for a job that was not  urgent. I got talking to the other worker there and realised I needed out.

I messaged my uncle, who was always looking for workers—I didn't know anything about the job. Ended up in north WA driving around on a quad bike digging holes for 8 months.

I got my head back in the game with the environment sector. I landed some amazing opportunities but then ended up in a similar situation where the promise of full-time work never eventuated.

(continued)

I needed a change. I was either thinking of agriculture or tourism. While I thought through my options, I quit and went to work on a remote cattle station, which is when I started to listen to podcasts, *my millennial money* included.

I worked a year there, loved it, but realised I wanted to be involved in the research side of things. I managed to secure a job as a technical assistant in irrigation research. Not long after I applied for a development officer role within the same organisation and officially started this year.

I now live in the most amazing place, with my horse, in a secure job and thanks to the *my millennial money* podcast I am getting ahead of the money game.

Some of Annie's core values were safety, reliability and consistency: the stability of knowing she had a permanent job. But she also found a great balance between her overarching lifestyle goals (like where she lives and being able to enjoy spending time with her horse) and her career goals.

So, once we know we may have a values conflict, what next?

How do I deal with a values conflict?

In most cases, the best step is to have healthy and honest conversations with your manager. If you're rolling your eyes or shuddering at the thought of having one of the conversations, we get it. They aren't easy discussions to have.

So, here's our 'three-step values framework' for how to have conversations about a values conflict. It will help you prepare for any difficult conversation you need to have at work.

1. Value	The first step is to identify the value conflict for you. What specific value do you feel is being challenged or not being met? Communicate it.
2. Situation	Next, describe the situation or give an example that supports the concern raised.
3. Impact	Finally, communicate the impact this situation has had on you or others.

Let's put the framework into action by walking through an example conversation with your boss.

1. Value	I want to chat with you about a challenge I'm working through at the moment. For me, one of my personal values is growth. I've learned that I do my best work when I'm growing and learning in my role. I love having opportunities to stretch and try new things.
2. Situation	I've been doing this role for two years, and at first it was a big learning curve, but over the past 6 months I feel like I've stalled in my growth and development. When I look at the core skills in the role, I feel like I've mastered most of them, and I'm no longer challenged. I'm also not getting any development opportunities or feedback either, so there's not a lot of on-the-job growth or learning happening at the moment.
3. Impact	As a result, I'm feeling my engagement is dropping and I'm not as energised by the role anymore. I feel like I'm not progressing towards a goal and challenged in my work. I would love to explore if there are any other roles within the business or if there's scope to adjust my job description so I can have more learning and growth in my role.

I'm a big advocate for having healthy conversations at work. Using the three-step values framework will help you have healthy and honest conversations at work. But more than that, the ability to have difficult conversations is a vital career skill to master and they can have an incredibly positive impact on your career.

apply now

Reflect on any previous roles you've had, or perhaps a current role. Where were/are your values aligning well?

_____

_____

_____

_____

Where were/are your values clashing?

_____

_____

_____

_____

If you're facing values-based issues in a role you're currently in, what options are available to you to communicate the issue and find a solution?

_____

_____

_____

_____

What things are just annoyances at work, and not complete value-breakers?

_____

_____

_____

_____

_____

(continued)

Practise placing any relevant values within the three-step values framework so you can move into discussions about the issue/s in a prepared way.

1	**Value**	The first step is to identify the value conflict for you. What specific value do you feel is being challenged or not being met? Communicate it.
2	**Situation**	Next, describe the situation or give an example that supports the concern raised.
3	**Impact**	Finally, communicate the impact this situation has had on you or others.

A final word

So, you've uncovered and defined your values. In chapters 2 and 3, we'll work through your mindset and how we can align it with your values to craft a career you love.

---

resources

Scan the QR code for these resources and more.

- Download the values longlist.

- Download a blank template of the three-step values framework to keep workshopping your values issues.

what's all this talk about mindset?

2

tl;dr

- Our mindset is a key force behind our life choices—positive or negative.

- We often default to a negative mindset, which restricts us without us even knowing it!

- Mindset is not 'manifesting' (sorry to offend so early).

- Our upbringing and experiences can direct our mindset too much if we aren't paying attention.

- Having a 'growth' mindset combined with a bit of effort and action on our part brings about the best results in our lives.

- Having a mentor can be a great way to challenge your mindset.

A note on this and the next chapter.

I'm not a professional psychologist or counsellor. The words in these chapters might feel as if I'm leaning into these roles, but I'm leaning in more to my own experiences: my personal story of a change in mindset, career and life.

I focus on being enlightened to the fact that anything is possible with your life and career. I hope you skip many years of struggle and frustration after reading my story and learning from the principles I have uncovered so far in my life. Working through my own mindset has been a critical aspect of my own career road trip, and I hope you find it helpful.

In the words of Napoleon Hill (author of *Think and Grow Rich*): 'Whatever the mind can conceive and believe, it can achieve'.

What is mindset?

Mindset is a funny thing, isn't it?

We all have one, we all use it, we rarely talk about it as a society and the minute you do it's like you're at a property moguls sales conference where an 'expert' is talking about a 'millionaire mindset'.

But mindset is another key part of our career road trip preparation, along with the values we've previously established.

This very moment your own cognitive bias is probably kicking into gear in relation to your career, dictating your response and action.

Your thought process might jump straight to:

- 'No way can I get a job working for that business.'

- 'I can't leave this job; it will look bad on my resume.'

- 'I'm stuck in an industry I hate, and there's just no way to get out.'

- 'There's no way on earth I could be successful quitting this job and starting a business.'

- 'I've studied for 4 years for this; I have no choice but to get a job in this industry.'

- 'I could never do that job; I'm not equipped.'

To be fair, I hate the use of the word 'mindset', or more so a 'growth or money mindset' when it's linked to such things as private jets, expensive cars and gold watches. Seems self-indulgent.

I prefer to reframe mindset as more active than passive when we face up to decisions that can impact our own life. Mindset guides the steps we take next: if you're approaching your situation with a defeatist mindset, you won't be motivated to even *try* and make a positive step forward in your career.

Our mindset can also be shaped from the experiences we have had growing up—good or bad. Like cognitive bias, our mindset can also be irrational and unconscious.

Here is a question for you: is anything possible with your own life, and career, if you go after it?

It might be a hard pill to swallow for some, but the answer is actually yes. Not because I can personally say I overcame adversity and achieved greatness—the answer is yes because I have seen others do it.

You, too, have seen this.

Take for example Ahn Do, who barely survived a journey to Australia. After his family started with nothing, he built an amazing career.

Or Liesl Tesch, who became an Olympic medallist of two different sports, after a bike accident left her with incomplete paraplegia, and is now a member of the New South Wales parliament.

And I'm sorry to disappoint you, but I'm not talking about manifesting. I'm not into this pseudoscience, which leads to you receiving a new car because you thought positively enough about it and *tada!* ✦ new car ✦ I think you'd call that luck, chance or coincidence.

I have a small problem with 'manifesting'. I have heard of people 'willing' something into being. They manifest a new job, car, relationship, or whatever it is that they want. My issue with manifesting and those who do it is that I haven't seen many people manifest a meal for someone in need of one or a shelter for a person without a home.

I'm being a little over-the-top here, but I want to point out that this type of behaviour can seem self-indulgent and selfish.

A good mindset alone isn't going to make all your problems go away, but it's a great start and a really healthy part of your life to have in check. We'll be pairing your healthy mindset with the other key career road trip essentials before we hit the road.

Instead of the predominantly negative phrases listed earlier, a healthy mindset might look like any of the following statements:

- 'Just because someone else succeeds, doesn't mean I won't.'

- 'I am actually qualified for this role because of my experience.'

- 'I'm okay with the outcome as I gave it all I had.'

- 'Even though I'm the first in my family to attempt this, it doesn't mean I will fail.'

- 'I can absolutely get there—it might just take some training, experience and sacrifice.'

- 'By doing this in my career I'm taking a risk, and risk is a necessary part of progress.'

This chapter is my guide to helping you change your mindset. If you already have a solid mindset, is it encouraging you on your own career journey? It'll be practical and fun. Think of it as the street-smart guide to mindset.

Childhood will never leave you

Think about the music you like and your favourite band or group. Most of the time these tastes were developed in the most influential years of your life. I remember growing up listening to the band T00L on many afternoons after school with my friend Ricki Cook (hi Rick) at his house in Berkeley Vale, New South Wales. We were in our early teens. Can you guess what my favourite band still is?

Your childhood and teenage years remain with you. So do the memories—good and bad—trauma (which can't be understated), taste in music and sometimes fashion (lol, hope not) but also your worldview and mindset. Gosh, humans are complex.

Growing up in working-class Australia has its opportunities and challenges, relatively speaking. While I grew up well fed and sheltered, we were a working-class family. I went to a local government high school (Berkeley Vale Community High—shout out!) and most students, as in most working-class suburban high schools, were, on balance, all cut from the same cloth. After all, the simple rules of economics and life are such that not everyone is a multi-millionaire and the majority of a country's citizens form a nice study for those who like looking at bell curves.

So yes, there were some outliers of underprivileged students and some 'new money, rich bogans' popping up. It was a continuous conveyor belt of learning as much as possible, remembering it, regurgitating it to get high test results and going to university or starting your career after your final year of high school—if indeed you made it that far! I didn't.

I left school after completing year 11 and the first term of year 12. But I was only allowed to leave school because I had lined up an apprenticeship. My parents knew that I would have relatively more success than the average bear in life with a trade qualification under my belt. They were not degree or trade qualified themselves, but they still did great. They lived within their means and Dad's self-employment provided much fruit to complement Mum's fixed wage. With no disrespect intended—only reflection—growing up, none of my immediate family or extended family were, or are, degree qualified. So the mindset I was surrounded by growing up wasn't about aiming for a university level education or anything other than a trade that would give you a good income and a skill that would set you up for life. And that's not a bad thing at all.

My two apprenticeships

And so I left school, and started an apprenticeship in telecommunications, which was a wonderful opportunity for a 16 year old—being thrust into full-time work and working with a variety of people every day in the real world. This wasn't a construction job where I was just on sites with other workers; I visited offices all around town installing and programming phone systems. It was a very 'white collar' trade, if I'm being honest, and I was thankful for that because it meant there weren't too many days where I came home filthy from working in construction-type environments. But long term it wasn't for me, and I wanted to double down on my real passion: finance.

When I finished my apprenticeship, at the age of 20, I resigned and embarked on a Diploma of Financial Services, Financial Planning course. I figured I would enrol in the diploma at a private college and try to get a job in financial planning—an industry I knew nothing about, where I knew no-one and that I didn't think I was really equipped for because I wasn't great at maths and numbers. In fact, before I dropped out of year 11 at school, maths was my least favourite subject—and my report card proved it.

> FYI, a good financial adviser is a great project manager who understands the goals of individuals, can work backwards and can put financial strategies in place to achieve those goals and keep clients on track as time unfolds. It's not really about sitting there crunching numbers. It's a people business. Sure, knowing about all the legislation and financial instruments is important—but that's considered hygiene.

Going for various jobs and being declined was soul crushing. At one point, I tried to get an entry-level job in the mailroom at Macquarie Bank. I thought all I would need was some practical thinking and a bit of 'go' to land the role. After three interviews, I didn't get the job. They didn't provide any feedback, but I guess I must have failed the psych test.

After numerous other rejections, I decided to go for an interview at an office that had multiple jobs on offer. I didn't really understand how it all worked at the time, but it was a recruiting firm that focused on financial services.

I was driving my 1997 Mitsubishi Mirage to the city for an interview (with the recruiter) for an entry-level position in a financial planning office when I received a phone call. 'The role you're coming in for has just been filled. Sorry.' The caller continued, 'But another role actually just fell through, so, if you're interested, continue your way in as we think it would be perfect for you.'

I agreed to go for the interview, even though I was 100 per cent convinced that I would do the interview, not get the job and then somehow go back to telecommunications. It wasn't my finest hour because I was so deflated and didn't really care. Have you ever been to a job interview without any motivation? Well, that was me. Have you ever been late to a job interview? That was me too.

'You seem very relaxed,' I heard the interviewer say. I was thinking, 'Sure, relaxed/don't care.' Same thing.

It turned out that I was exactly what they needed. A junior, someone keen on the industry, someone already studying (though they didn't know I was studying as the recruiter hadn't mentioned it) and someone just ready to lean in and learn. I ended up doing an apprenticeship at this firm, moving up through various roles—and, best of all, it's where I was when I met my 'rich dad' mentor. Funny how things work out.

> If you're keen to get in the door of a new industry or role, it can be easier (if possible) to look at the private sector and small-to-medium businesses. These have fewer layers of bureaucracy and sometimes business owners and managers of smaller businesses can be a little more practical with their recruiting. In short, you can probably be more raw and honest with them in person as opposed to coming up against yes/no tick boxes with electronic type forms and applications.

My own 'rich dad' experience

Fast forward to age 24. I was still working in the same financial planning practice, and had worked my way up, becoming registered and licensed as a financial adviser. At the time, I knew I wanted to do something bigger with my life, but I felt like I didn't really have any skills to offer and wasn't good at anything. I didn't feel I had my future life set up. I was still living at home with my parents and commuting to work each day for an hour or so in each direction.

I worked mainly in a support role as an associate, which was great as it gave me real-life exposure to being a financial adviser but I was also under the shelter of the partners of the firm. It was a bit of a blended all-rounder role as I was still doing some paraplanning work (creating the strategy and formal advice for the partner).

I'm not sure if it was an age thing, a mindset thing or just something that everyone goes through, but I was seriously having an internal crisis. I didn't think I was good enough to be a financial adviser; I didn't want to keep commuting to the city each day or move closer to the city and uproot myself from my friends, family and networks (I have a conservative personality in this regard). These thoughts had been going on for a while. I felt I was at a dead end in my life and career, if I'm being honest. As I'm writing this and looking back, I had the self-confidence of a doormat compared to now.

Then I heard there was a new adviser joining the team. He had moved from country New South Wales to Sydney, having recently changed careers. He happened to sit in the open-plan office next to me as there was no spare office for him at that stage. He was about 15 years older than me.

There was something different about this guy. He had been a farmer and sold the farm, done some other investment projects in the property and medical spaces and was now in finance. He also had significant wealth behind him from his hard work and the opportunities over his career so far. It was such a random and foreign journey for me to hear about—something I hadn't experienced before. A mix of the country upbeat attitude, glass-half-full vibes and the world full of opportunities. What was going on here?

I had only ever experienced this worldview, for want of a better word, in a book I'd read years earlier called *Rich Dad Poor Dad*, where the author (Robert Kiyosaki) compared his own dad—a working-class, job-for-life 'poor dad'—with his friend's father, one who took risks, made money work for him, invested for the future and was a happen-to-life—not a let-life-happen-to-you—type of 'rich dad'.

My new work colleague seemed to be well 'connected into the social pipeline' (and that's a nod to my favourite movie, *Dumb and Dumber*, IYKYK) as he had some serious friends. He would share stories of having a friend with a private jet who would take him to events and also to view different projects around Australia. He shared stories of running into household-name Hollywood directors and drinking with them in Sydney bars, and sitting next to international celebrities at the theatre. He was also surprised this stuff happened to him, but looking in I could see how things in his world were big thanks to his mindset, which was open to growth and connection (in a genuine way!). For the money nerds, he and his family were the first people I ever met who were living (renting) in a house they didn't own, in a premium suburb, while investing elsewhere (rent-vesting).

Every morning he would send me an email with an inspirational quote, or similar, and when I read it I'd look over and he would say, 'How true is that?' or something to that effect.

There were also some practical lessons I picked up from my new colleague. I asked him, 'Why do you take your blazer with you every time you go to lunch or out to coffee?' He replied, 'No-one will ever wonder whether you're going out for a work meeting or a personal matter if you're always dressed for a meeting when you leave the office.'

When he moved to Sydney, he reached out to senior leaders at the big four banks just to introduce himself and say hi. I had never witnessed this type of behaviour before. I was attracted to it. It really did set the scene for his own life that anything is *actually* possible. There are always challenges and barriers, but anything is possible.

You may be thinking, 'This type of behaviour and attitude sounds like manifesting stuff to me!'...but I would point out that it was not just positive thoughts for the sake of a new material item or opportunity for self-gain. It was linked to action and hard work.

One day at Greenwood Plaza (for those North Sydney workers who know this location), after we'd had lunch, we walked up to the counter at a newsagency because the day before we had each purchased a $20 million Powerball ticket for a bit of fun. I scanned my ticket…beep…not a winner. He scanned his…beep…not a winner. He shrugged his shoulders as we walked away and said, 'Oh well, we'll just have to earn it!' I'm not sure what it was about that statement, but it has stuck with me all these years. You see, I believe a positive growth mindset applied with action and ambition is where we start to see things really change in our lives.

Can you see why this type of mindset was completely different from what I had known growing up?

Is there any downside to having a mindset that does not default to the negative?

apply now

What was your own mindset growing up? Is it different now? If so, how has it changed? Write your thoughts here.

_____

_____

_____

_____

_____

The value of a mentor

Over the next year, my new work colleague mentored me in a passive way. I mean, I'm sure he was just being him, not even thinking he was actually *actively* mentoring me. I was gleaning everything I could. I wanted his mindset. I wanted his way of seeing the world: that anything is possible and you can work for any results you wish for.

I shared my frustrations with him around feeling like I didn't know what I was going to do with my career and life. It was he who really encouraged me to 'just do what you're doing now, but for yourself. Financial advice is easy, you just need to ask people what their goals are and help them achieve them.' Hmmm...he had a point. It's a given that this was our industry and it's 'taken as read' that we had the book knowledge. It's so funny that we can be good at what we do and enjoy it, but think we suck and get caught in our own head. We would get lunch together fairly regularly and I would always bounce my thoughts off him. Looking back, I feel bad for being such a sponge, but I'm sure it was fine and he enjoyed our chats.

He encouraged me to start my own business on the Central Coast and, to be honest, he was the driving force behind my decision to step out. However, being a junior employee at the time, I actually didn't have much money, so I would have to be smart about how I did things.

To start your own financial planning business, you need to arrange a licence. It took 14 calls to 14 different companies to get one. My mentor taught me to first speak to the ones I wasn't really keen on, to practise my pitch. You see, most licensees don't charge a fee and accept just anyone; they put a lot of effort into the compliance side and paperwork with the Australian Securities and Investments Commission (ASIC), and so on. So they need to ensure you have an actual viable business and are able to get clients.

I told him after the first couple of calls that I wasn't having much joy. I was calling and telling them I was trying to start my business from scratch and with no clients. I think this, and my age, didn't go in my favour. It was opportune though, as I didn't really want to work with these companies, but I was able to practise and verbalise my pitch to a real-world person.

I started to get traction when I made a slight change to my script after a quick workshop with my mentor. It went a little like this.

Ring ring…ring ring…

Answer: Hello, this is Mark from XYZ Financial Group.

Me: Hi Mark, my name is Glen James. I'm currently an authorised representative [industry speak for financial adviser] with ABC Financial Group and I was calling to find out what the requirements are to come onboard with XYZ Financial Group.

A slight change to my own mindset about what I was trying to do, half a teaspoon of confidence, some energy in the call and I suddenly had applications, meetings and offers from about 10 different licensees.

Nothing had changed about the pitch I was giving during these phone calls. During the first few calls I asked if they would license someone starting their own business. During my later calls, I confidently said, 'I'm doing this; are you keen to partner with me?' The difference was confidence and delivery. I had learned these one percenters while spending time with my mentor. Some might think of this as 'fake it till you make it', but really, what my mentor had taught me was to align a healthy mindset with a bit of effort and action.

In my personal and business life I've always had the view that learning and implementing the one percenters can only be a good thing. I figure if I spend years implementing the one percenters into my life, surely I'd be ahead of the curve.

Mindset mentor

I'll be forever grateful for this juncture in my life, where I ended up (by chance) being mentored by someone who helped me start my own business but also mentored me in a way to enlarge my mindset and change the way I thought.

If you can't find a mentor to directly work with you or meet with you for coffee or a beer, can you find a 'remote' mindset mentor who may have an online platform, a book or a podcast to glean from? Be mentored by them without them knowing and without them ever meeting you!

I attribute my financial and business success to date on having my mindset challenged, then changed. I guess it started when I was a child doing cub scouts where they banned the word 'can't', so I had something in there...it just needed some extraction.

We'll talk more about mentors in Chapter 6.

> On a personal note, when I started my business, my mentor wrote me a cheque. He said I could pay it back whenever I wanted to. 'In five weeks, five months or five years, but I will never ever ask for it back.' Talk about someone putting their money where their mouth is. It was a little bit of seed capital to get my business off the ground.
>
> I'm confident my life would not be as it is today, nor would *my millennial money* exist, if it wasn't for that chance encounter with my mentor. Thank you for changing my mindset, then my life, Macca.

So what does it all mean?

In my book *Sort Your Money Out*, I talked about the linear pattern of society of 'yesterday', probably ending with the first of Generation X, if not the Baby Boomer generation for sure. That is, you expect life to include completion of school → having a job for life → retiring → that's the end. We are now living in a world that no longer supports a 30-year job and a pension for life. I'm sure you've heard of the gig economy, which is people doing various 'gigs' to earn an income for a life on their own terms. The number of jobs or careers we drive through now looks completely different from the past. This is leaning into a mindset shift in our society as a whole.

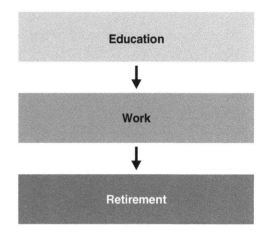

It's important to say loudly and clearly that if you love your career or job, and it has been a linear journey for you, that is amazing. I sometimes wish I was like that, but we are all different parts of one big body called humanity. This is why you need to be encouraged to double down on 'your thing'. What can you learn about your own mindset in your current career or workplace? This could be part of a mindset tweak that you need of standing up for yourself and setting boundaries, or even career opportunities for growth where you may have an inherent thought that you're not qualified to even try for that promotion. I'm here to tell you that you are.

I want to pause for a moment and have you reflect on your life and mindset right now and think back to when you were 17 years old. Are you still carrying some traits of the you of that life or mindset? Your answer doesn't matter. I just want you to think about it.

What do you want your story to be? What do you need to adjust in your mindset? Write your thoughts here.

_____

_____

_____

_____

_____

A final word

As you heard from my own story, we are left to manage and execute the cards we are dealt. For me, it was first understanding the framework of my upbringing and knowing that the way I grew up and the mindset I had grown with was not 'the way' or the same as every other situation growing up. It was easier for me doing this autopsy of my upbringing in my early 20s as I'm naturally more self-aware than most, but I encourage you to think about your upbringing and how it may have impacted your own view of the world.

The world is different now, and so we need to think differently. This could involve unlearning what we have carried from childhood and been told by parents, or reframing what has been driven into us at school.

Well, that's my story about how my mindset was unlocked and enlarged. I hope as the years go on you'll be able to write your own story about key events in your life that you gleaned from. Just as we choose to drive our favourite scenic route again and again, I hope you come back to this chapter throughout your career road trip when you need a refreshed mindset.

In the next chapter we're going to dive into where your personal mindset may be stuck and work through some challenges to keep moving forward in your career.

resources **Scan the QR code for these resources and more.**

Subscribe to the *my millennial career* and *my millennial money* podcasts to have your mindset challenged and encouraged! We chat a lot about mindset across our podcasts.

more on mindset
... this is not a tacky motivational seminar

3

tl;dr

- There are four main mindsets: cultural and societal, generational and family, institutional, and psychological.

- It's important to know where you sit in the mindset categories to ensure your mindsets aren't making decisions on your behalf.

- There are a number of mindset hacks you can use to ensure your mindset is healthy and serving you well in your career.

Glen in the driver's seat

We identified in chapter 2 that your mindset is a set of beliefs that influence how you see yourself and the world around you.

Now let's dig deeper into your mindset, thinking a bit more specifically about where your mindset could become stuck, like a car going around the same roundabout over and over without any progress on your career road trip.

I asked members of the 'my millennial money' Facebook group the following question:

'Right now, how confident are you with your mindset when it comes to your career?'

Forty-five per cent of respondents stated that they were not very confident at all.

If you're in the 45 per cent, my hope is that this chapter will get you up to a baseline confidence level or affirm that you may be more confident than you think. If you're in the remaining 55 per cent, let's refine your mindset and challenge any blind spots that might appear while reading this.

Most of my mindset anecdotes are from my own experience and observations and they will apply to many parts of your life. However, my wish is that you read about them with your career in mind because in a modern working society, most of us will spend more time with our work colleagues than with our own family and friends.

My mindset categories

I believe the four main mindset categories that influence us in life are: 1) cultural and societal, 2) generational and family 3) institutional, and 4) psychological.

I can't emphasise enough that I'm not a psychologist of any description. These mindset categories are just what I've observed in my own life and by reflecting on the people around me, particularly past clients of mine. Not everyone will be negatively affected by these types of mindsets. For example, I talk about depression and anxiety in the psychological mindset section, which could cause you to think about things in an unhealthy way but, of course, not everyone will be diagnosed with these conditions.

Consider, for example, a lounge room with a coffee table full of rubbish: take-away wrappings, cans of drink, old bills in their still-sealed envelopes and junk mail. It's a mess. In fact, there's so much rubbish and clutter that if you left your peach-flavoured Zappo wrapper on it, the householder wouldn't even notice. Compare this with a clean, windexed glass coffee table. The smallest bit of rubbish would stand out so it could be easily removed!

Your mindset may have been exposed to an environment full of clutter and you don't even realise it. Clutter from societal norms, generational and family clutter, institutional clutter if you've worked in the same role for years, and so on. If so, while reading through about the four mindsets I have identified, perhaps you can see if you need to 'tidy up your coffee table' so you have the best shot of taking opportunities and seeing things as clearly as possible.

I would encourage you to develop your own healthy mindset so that if you are ever confronted with a negative mindset, you can identify that it isn't healthy and make the necessary adjustments.

The four mindsets

During your career road trip—particularly in the early years—you might be pulled in the direction of one of the four mindset categories. For example, working in a government department for many years might pull you into an institutional frame of mind.

Alternatively, you might need to be pulled out of a negative mindset, or—as we will soon see—an unhealthy mindset.

It's important to note that I'm not making statements on what is right or wrong; rather, I'm going to provide you with examples of each of the mindset categories so that you can reflect on them in relation to your own life. I want you to learn to look at each of them from another angle and hopefully discover what, if anything, needs work.

Cultural and societal mindset

The more you live and work in a truly international world, the more important it becomes to understand where you're coming from and where the people around you are coming from.

In 2017, I landed in one of the busiest cities in the world—and busy cities mean busy airports. It was my first time in such a populated country, and my first experience of a huge volume of people was at the baggage collection carousel. *Whack.* Every bag trolley was slammed up against the carousel. This was no casual baggage collection. It was dog eat dog—every bag for itself.

Getting onto the train in the subway was just as bad. No waiting for people to disembark from the carriage—everyone just shoved their way through. This behaviour, I believe, has developed from a societal mindset that is the result of millions of people living in close proximity of one another. It's the mindset of 'everyone for themselves': no personal space, and if you don't get in the space quickly, you'll miss out. A lesson could be learned here in relation to your career: if you don't get up and do it, someone else will!

Do you have an embedded mindset from your own culture? Sure you do: we all do. I'm not saying you need to change your culture; just to be aware of it.

What about the mindset of 'I have no spare time to study or read'. Yet you're up to date with the latest series on Netflix. Society as a whole is addicted to TV, computers, phones...you name it! A bit less time spent on these would allow us time to read and study. I'm not saying this is bad, but we have so much stuff pumped into our lives that sometimes we end up immersed in life and lose perspective. As society moves away from the linear 'school, work, retire and die' mindset, you need to be acutely aware that there will be periods of time when you need to be open to doing some further study, education or learning in your field. Either formal or informal. You most likely do have time—perhaps it's just not managed well.

Generational and family mindset

This is where it gets really interesting. Think of the people you know and the families they come from. Were they expected to finish school, go to university and get a stable, professional career for life? You see, it's not uncommon for doctors to have doctors as parents, teachers to breed teachers, and so on. They say the apple doesn't fall far from the tree. While this is all fine, you may reach a point where it's not. I have met too many people who are in a career, job or lifestyle situation only because of the push from their family. And they hate their situation.

This generational and family mindset can also creep into other areas of your life. What about where you live, who you marry or even your work ethic?

Your challenge here is to step back and have a look at the mindset of your lineage. When I did this myself, it was fascinating to see that not only my father but also my grandfather was self-employed. Is this by chance? Maybe. Is there something in our DNA? Not sure. Either way, it's there.

apply now

What is a good family or generational mindset that you have inherited?

_____

_____

_____

_____

What is a not-so-good family or generational mindset that you have inherited?

_____

_____

_____

_____

Institutional mindset

I'm not cut out for this mindset. I think this started for me when I was in school, and one of the contributing factors was getting told what to do and in what way. It makes sense that I ultimately became self-employed.

It's not a bad thing that someone (even you) may want to just rock up to work, get told what to do and in what order, then take your pay and go home—all while working your way up through the pay grades. This mindset is important to identify in concert with what you want out of your career and also when considering your own risk profile and mindset.

Many organisations have institutionalised cultures. They have bureaucratic systems and behaviours that are deeply entrenched and hard to shift. When you're in this kind of environment and want to make positive changes, it can feel like you're swimming upstream. You're draining all your energy going against the current, but you're getting nowhere.

The problem I have noticed in relation to the institutional mindset is that if someone is working in a large institution or corporate for many years, that mindset can really impact the individual and stop them from taking risks or looking to expand their career, even if they would otherwise be someone who could manage that risk. I've seen people internalise the practices of a bureaucratic institution. If an organisation is rigid and hierarchical, slow moving and risk averse, over time employees can unconsciously adopt these practices in their own life and career. They fear taking good risks. They get stuck in old ways of working. They miss the moment to make a change. Ultimately, they fall prey to the institutional mindset that they are working within.

One thing to look out for with an institutional mindset is accepting a standard that would otherwise not be appropriate in the real world. This could involve lots of unpaid overtime, a lack of breaks, no acknowledgement of good work, poor team morale or being walked over. This is not always the case because many big employers are becoming employers of choice and conversely there are small businesses that have issues too. However, those who work in large corporations or government roles may need this as a wakeup call that what is going on is not healthy for them or their career.

Psychological mindset

'I just can't do it. I really want to, but I'm not strong enough.'

'If I go for this promotion, it won't be long until people will realise I'm not cut out for this job.'

'I always wake up tired, with a headache and have trouble sleeping and concentrating.'

Health Direct, an Australian Government website, states that,

1 in every 5 Australians—about 4 million people—suffers from a mental illness in a given year, and almost half the population has suffered a mental disorder at some time in their life.

This mindset category is all about mental health. It just sounds better to call it psychological mindset! This stuff is real, and while you may not have suffered a mental health event or condition in your life, it's important to understand this so you will be more aware if it does sneak up on you.

Poor mental health has definitely played a part in my life and career, particularly in my 20s when I was undiagnosed with depression and anxiety. You see, if you're not the best version of yourself, you can't be the best version of yourself. I now take daily medication, go to talk therapy when and as needed, and make sure I don't overwork.

While you may know all the concepts and benefits of a healthy mindset, if you are not mentally well, it doesn't matter how much you know—you may not be able to pull the trigger on your next career move.

When your psychological mindset is not healthy, you may find it harder to make decisions. You may be more prone to avoiding conflict or necessary risks. Your emotional energy may be lower. You might not be sleeping well, and each day feels like a struggle. General apathy can set in. This can be very challenging if you want to change or improve your work situation.

Regardless of your career, if this resonates with you, it's important to seek help and support from a health professional. For me personally, it has had a huge role in improving my mental health and helping me make good decisions.

Maybe you think you're all good here, but if there is some type of conflict or an issue at work, you may find yourself obsessing on it for hours and it can be disruptive to your day. You can't seem to get out of the thought loop. Hello! Well, I was once like you, and understanding my natural proclivity to being a 'thinker' and how I react to different situations really helped me. I saw a psychologist to help me with such thought patterns. I believe these toxic thought patterns can become a habit and can be detrimental to our lives and take our career road trip off course. As the following story from Esther shows, our past experiences don't have to govern what we do next.

Esther, 19
Brisbane, QLD

I am a young woman of Congolese descent whose family are survivors of the civil war, which killed millions of people in the DR Congo.

During the war, my family fled and sought refuge at the Malawi refugee camp. While pregnant with me in the camp, Mum built our house out of mud and hay. In the camp I experienced endless days with a starving stomach, drinking contaminated water and having infected wounds.

After being granted an Australian visa in 2009 when I was 5 years old, my family was challenged with overcoming the trauma we had faced. My early life in Australia came with a lot of challenges as my mum did not know how to read or write. I had to learn how to read government letters and know how to translate English to Swahili at the age of 5.

It was only in grade 3 that I realised my friends' parents knew how to read and write. I remember going to my friend's house and seeing her mum read a letter. I was in utter disbelief. However, despite the challenges my family has overcome, I believe that my life's trajectory will be guided by my determination to achieve my ambitions, not by the socio-economic barriers I once faced.

(continued)

I may have experienced war, poverty and famine but this is just the beginning. I know this isn't the full story of my life. I'm now studying Business (Finance) and IT (Computer Science) at university and want to one day start my own business. My current and future mindset will not be dictated by my past experience.

apply now

Can you identify if you have any issues here that you may need to speak to your general practitioner about?

_____

_____

_____

_____

Can you identify anything in your life that 'triggers' you mentally?

_____

_____

_____

_____

I just want to finish on this point by saying that you legitimately may be all good here, but if not, it's okay. ☺

My mindset hacks

Over the years of stretching and changing my own mindset, I've found what I like to call 'thought hacks', which give me perspective (and sometimes courage) in certain situations.

After reading about my hacks and experiences in this section, can you think about your work life and career and see how you might be able to apply them for yourself.

The purpose of having a healthy mindset is to be really sure you're going to flourish in your work, job and career. This will ultimately allow for money to flow and for you to put up with less rubbish in the day to day.

Acknowledge your own privilege

I'll be straight up and say that I'm a white male in my 30s and I'm privileged. Becoming aware of your privilege is crucial when we are examining our mindset.

Lou Jourdan, in an article he wrote for *Harvard Business Review*, describes privilege as enjoying certain advantages that others do not have because your demographic make-up places you in the majority.

Acknowledging your own privilege might be counterintuitive to you as you may think that you were from a working-class family that struggled and that you're not privileged at all. The thing is, this is particularly needed for those of us who are of white European descent, regardless of our living or financial situation. There is systemic and embedded privilege.

For example, when I was growing up in Australia it was very rare to see Indigenous Australians or people of colour in the media industry. At the time, to get a start in radio or television usually means that you have to do unpaid internships. As at 2019, only one in 10 Indigenous Australians are financially secure and fewer than two in five Indigenous Australians can access $2000 for an emergency, compared with four in five in the broader Australian population. How many young Indigenous Australians have missed out on these career opportunities because getting a start required unpaid work?

Privilege is not only about skin colour or heritage. There are many inherent biases that come into play in our society (within us). These biases could be gender, sexuality, disability, religion, geographic location or a variety of others. Becoming aware of your own privilege can help to actively challenge norms that disadvantage under-represented groups.

My point here is that acknowledging your own privilege is a great baseline and prerequisite for any mindset discussions and I would encourage you to run away from any mindset material that encourages you to do things at the expense of others.

apply now

What's your privilege? Write your thoughts here.

_____

_____

_____

_____

_____

Build solid financial foundations

I talked about my financial house in the introduction. You can see how it's built in figure 3.1 (overleaf). It's relevant here because finances are linked to everything we do in life and particularly to our careers. If you have solid financial foundations, you'll have more clarity to think about your career, not rush into decisions and, of course, be able to leave that toxic workplace without financial stress.

The financial foundation I'd like to focus on is foundation 2: 'Cashed up and debt free'. In personal finance I teach about having 3 to 6 months of expenses in a dedicated bank account for emergencies. This includes not having consumer debt such as credit cards, personal loans, buy-now-pay-later repayments or store cards. This means your cash flow is as lean and agile as possible, and able to adapt to whatever life throws at you.

Strong financial foundations are also important for your mindset—you'll ideally be living on less than you earn, not have any consumer debt, and have a cash buffer between you and the world. These things enable you to be more at peace, ensure you're more intentional and plugged in, reduce your consumption of 'things', and give you the headspace for the important things discussed in this book.

It's so much harder to think, dream and plan for the future when you are living week to week and worrying about your financial commitments. Setting up the practical things in your life, like your budget, and having a cash buffer will give you the best shot at the most rewarding career.

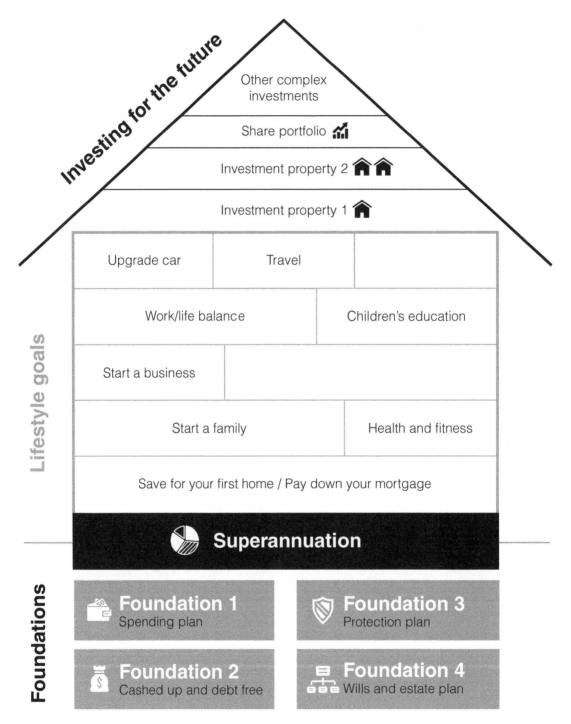

Figure 3.1: my sound financial house

Having strong financial foundations will enable you to build your life from the ground up, in the right order. There is no point buying shares or investing in property if you're not happy with your life and career. Having all the investments in the world is great, but at what cost if you have no joy or purpose in your career? Having strong financial foundations will also enable you to work towards a goal of changing careers, starting your own business, travelling—whatever you want!

Finally, if you were in a very bad work environment and you had to leave for your own mental health, having 3 months of expenses could be the difference between taking the necessary time to make the next best step and rushing into another job that isn't right because you need the money. Emergency funds are usually spoken about in relation to a broken fridge or car gear box, or emergency dental care, but the amount of mental and emotional stability and calm that emergency funds can bring is priceless.

apply now

Based on my sound financial house, what aspects do you need to work on to help support the career moves you want to make?

_____

_____

_____

_____

_____

Always run a cost–benefit analysis

I once interviewed Robert H. Frank, an author and economics professor from Cornell (in the United States), for *my millennial money* about a variety of things, but one answer to a question I asked stood out most: how does someone think like an economist? He said economists always look at the cost-benefit principle of any particular situation. In other words, take no action unless its marginal benefit is at least as great as its marginal cost.

Some mindset traits and thinking may already be ingrained in your mind. When I was about 10 years old, my grandfather asked me to pick fireweed out of the paddock on his farm in Gloucester (New South Wales). He said he would pay me 50 cents per hour. I remember that the thought of working in the heat for a couple of hours just to earn one dollar was not worth the effort to me. So I declined his offer. In short, the benefit for the cost of my time and energy was not worth my while.

The risk–reward spectrum for taking career risks is similar to this (more on risk–reward in chapter 5). The cost–benefit analysis doesn't just cover financial issues. It's a great framework to fall back on whenever you need to make a decision. Table 3.1 presents some examples.

Table 3.1:   examples of career cost–benefit analyses

Opportunity or decision	Cost (risk)	Benefit (reward)	Worth it?
Additional and relevant study for a career	$7000 Over 5 hours of study per week for 20 weeks Loss of social life in the short term	Increased income by at least $5000 Increased career opportunity Additional knowledge gained Employer will refund if pass mark obtained	Likely yes, if you have seen that doing this course will increase your income or your employer has suggested it would (they may even refund you the money if you pass!)

Opportunity or decision	Cost (risk)	Benefit (reward)	Worth it?
New job in the same industry. Very similar pay but additional commute. You were not actively looking for a job change but were approached	An extra hour per day commute $40 per week extra in tolls or travel Giving up a good work culture for the unknown	$5000 (including superannuation) pay increase May be room for promotion and growth in the new role	Unlikely worth it if you were not actively looking Could be seen as a distraction It might just be time for a chat with your current employer about career, income and growth opportunities
Change of career	Restarting at the bottom of an industry Possible pay cut in the medium term Adjusting to something completely new Perhaps not enjoying it	Happier with life and purpose Excited about going to work each day Possible income upside Meeting new people Leading to bigger opportunities	It really depends It would be worth it over the longer term. But is now the right time for you? Do you have other goals in your life that require some stability in the short term?
Reporting a serious but awkward workplace issue (may not be illegal)	Being vilified in the workplace Feeling embarrassed Overseen for potential promotion	Your integrity is upheld You may start to change the culture You did the right thing	Yes, worth it, but many people may struggle with this as their personality may not like any type of confrontation

So next time you're faced with a decision, grab a pen and paper and do a brain dump of the costs and benefits for that decision. If the benefit does not outweigh the cost, it's likely a non-starter and just a distraction!

Another activity you may wish to try is rating several components of a decision out of 5 and making an on-balance call.

For example, table 3.2 rates various impacts out of 5 (with 5 being a positive impact and 1 being a negative impact) of two example career moves.

Table 3.2: example of the impacts of a career change

Example career move	Financial impact	Career impact	Relationship impact	Mental health impact	Lifestyle impact	Average impact
Promotion to manager	5/5	5/5	3/5	3/5	2/5	3.6
Moving to regional centre	3.5/5	3/5	5/5	5/5	5/5	4.3

The ratings in table 3.2 could be summarised as follows.

Being promoted to manager means:

- a pay rise

- more career experience

- you will be dealing more with managing people

- you may be away from loved ones or need to work overtime at the last minute and this could impact your mental health.

Moving to a regional centre means:

- your salary may be the same or slightly less (though not always), but the costs of living will be lower

- career progression would be weaker than in a city

- low commute times or remote working

- spending more time with your loved ones and having a relaxed lifestyle away from the city, which is likely to improve your mental health.

I think, as an on-balance call, anything under an average impact rating of 3 is a non-starter. There will always be trade-offs in life, but what are you willing to trade?

If you did the above exercise and you had an average rating of 2.5, it's probably clear that the costs outweigh the benefits.

The thing is, while the above two examples of frameworks for you to try may not be perfect for every situation, the key message I want to get across is that you need to always consider writing things down, getting them out of your mind and giving them life so you can see them externally. A healthy mindset will require you to look at career opportunities and issues in a way that removes as much emotion as possible, as our emotions can and will lead us astray.

---

apply now

Try doing a cost–benefit analysis and an impact of career change analysis for yourself.

Start with a cost–benefit analysis of any career opportunities or decisions you're considering.

Cost–benefit analysis

Opportunity or decision	Cost (risk)	Benefit (reward)	Worth it?

Now rate the impact of your potential career decisions between 1 and 5, with 5 being a positive impact and 1 being a negative impact.

(continued)

Impact of career change

Activity	Financial impact	Career impact	Relationship impact	Mental health impact	Lifestyle impact	Average impact
	__/5	__/5	__/5	__/5	__/5	___
	__/5	__/5	__/5	__/5	__/5	___

Adopt a growth rather than a fixed mindset

A growth mindset is often touted in entrepreneurial circles as the key to a successful life.

Let me take you to the core of this mindset. Carol Dweck, in her book *Mindset*, says that 'Individuals who believe their talents can be developed (through hard work, good strategies, and input from others) have a growth mindset'. She adds that people with a fixed mindset are those who believe their talents are innate gifts.

Based on this description, what do you think your mindset is?

I know a few people who think they are God's gift to the earth, so they may have a fixed mindset. My point is, with your mindset and career, you must learn that you can grow, you can work with and as a team, and you can upskill.

Your career mindset needs to be the glass that is half full; it needs to always understand there are opportunities, even if they are not right in front of you or happening as quickly as you'd like.

For me, having a growth mindset is like playing the long game. Think of a bow and arrow. The archer draws the bow backwards slowly and holds it still while taking aim. If the bow had a conscience, it might freak out, thinking, 'what the heck? I'm supposed to be going forward, and fast!' The thing is, this perceived lack of momentum and going backwards is all part of the plan to shoot the bow forward.

In table 3.3 you'll see some examples of how a fixed vs growth mindset might assess career-based opportunities.

Table 3.3: assess career-based opportunities using a 'fixed' vs 'growth' mindset

Career issue	Fixed mindset says	Growth mindset says	Short-term cost
Starting a job out of university	'I can't get a job because they all require experience'	'I'll ask employers if I can volunteer a day a week to get experience or work in other areas of the business to get in the door'	Lower income to start with Not exact role to start with Your own expectations being reset
Wanting to upskill for further income and career opportunities	'I don't have the time or the money to put into more study'	'I can ask my employer if they can fund this, see if overtime is available or look at a short-term side hustle. I'll also ensure I watch less TV and sacrifice half a day on the weekend to study'	Less time for recreation in the short term Not knowing who made it to the next round of *The Voice* Intense time management needed
Wanting a change of industry	'I'm not good at anything and I have no connections to my dream industry'	'I will connect with industry LinkedIn groups, join industry associations and go to events'	Awkward introductions Feeling out of place Small financial investment to networking events
Loving job and career, but would like to earn more money	'There is nothing I can do; they are already paying me the award'	'I will talk to my leader about my own career progression and ask if I can take on further responsibilities to add more value'	Putting yourself out there to your team leader Risk of being turned down in the first instance Having to adjust to a greater workload

Take this opportunity to assess whether your mindset is set to fixed or growth.

What's a 'fixed' statement you might have been saying to yourself about a career situation? Think of sentences that begin with 'I can't' or 'I don't'. Then rewrite them with 'growth mindset' language. Turn them into phrases of 'I can do X' and 'I'll talk to X'.

Career issue	Fixed mindset says	Growth mindset says	Short-term cost

Kerb your jealousy

Have a think about your current workplace, social circles and other areas of life that have lots of human interaction. Has jealousy ever entered the chat? If not by you, have you been a victim?

One sure way to fast track a small mindset is to invite jealousy into your life. Jealousy, envy and covetousness (for those born in 1876) will do more harm to you than the person you're comparing yourself to.

What about these scenarios? How would you react?

- A friend of yours just got a $10 000 bonus.

- Your workmate was promoted to a new role in another part of the company.

- Your sister and her partner just purchased their first home but always seem to spend way too much money on going out and brunch.

I want to flag this with you for some self-reflection. I had to re-check parts of my life where jealousy had crept in, particularly in my early 20s. Maybe it's a childish emotion that was carried into adulthood from the playground and as we mature we don't realise this childish behaviour has no place in a functioning adult life.

The attitude of 'you have something I don't, therefore you shouldn't have it' is the ultimate self-sabotage and will eat you alive, while the person you are jealous of is none the wiser.

How can you make it a rule in your life that when you hear of someone's success, you enjoy it with them? You celebrate with them. Someone else's success doesn't detract from your own. The truth is, they are probably looking at areas of your life that are better than theirs, too. Make it a habit to celebrate other people's successes with them.

---

apply now

Has jealousy over someone else's career, or what their career enables them to do, ever been something you struggle with?

What area/s sparks this and how can you reframe your thinking?

_____

_____

_____

_____

Check for comparison

They say comparison is the thief of joy. Comparison is also the sister of jealousy. I think it's a natural human condition to compare your situation to others'. I mean, it's only natural and particularly more so for those in the same type of situation.

A 'compari-trap' is what I call a thought spiral when you find yourself lost in comparison. Have you ever been in such a trap? Savage, aren't they!

I have been watching *The Drive to Survive* on Netflix. The Formula One teams have two drivers each and all these drivers care about is beating the other person on their own team. This is because they have the same cars and basically if you can beat your team member, you are actually better because the reference point is almost identical. This could be the height of ego!

If comparison is left unchecked, it will eat at you and cause long-term damage. The issue with comparing your career or position with that of others is that you have not seen the journey or circumstances your work colleagues have been through to get where they are. On the surface it might look like it was easy for them—namely, that they had preferential treatment or they didn't deserve to get where they are.

The thing is, even if they did get into a role without any hard work and with preferential treatment, comparing yourself to them doesn't help you at all. You need to run your own race. I'm a firm believer in what comes around goes around and if your hard work, dedication and loyalty hasn't been noticed or realised in this instance, it will one day. I believe this because the truth is buoyant and always comes to the surface. Even if it takes a while!

You may be hard done by. You may not have been chosen for a role based on how you look, sound or some other blatant prejudice. You may believe you are the better person for the role, and you're probably right, but the problem is while this stuff may be true, it's not helpful to you to get in a thought spiral as resentment can find a home in your heart and this resident will be living in a newly formed gated community with its sister, jealousy. This gated community in your heart will not help you in the future. This gated community is not known by the people you are comparing yourself to and this gated community will only grow over time if left unchecked and end up making you a less than ideal person for the next promotion opportunity.

The only person you should compare yourself to is the you of yesterday.

If you ever find yourself comparing your career situation to that of someone else you work with, I want to encourage you to first identify that it's happening so you can arrest those thoughts.

Four ways to help 'un-compare' your situation to others, if you find yourself in a 'compari-trap', are:

1. Look at how far you have come.

2. Reflect on your own career ambitions and remember you are running your own race.

3. See if you can find it in your heart to be happy for the person you are comparing yourself to (this may be hard for some).

4. Remember that their success doesn't detract from yours.

Practice makes permanent, so next time you compare yourself to someone else in your workplace, or in life, can you practise some mental exercises like the four above, or some of your own?

apply now

If comparison is something you're stuck in, think, *what do they have that you wish you had?* There's probably something in that. How can you build that into your own life according to your version of success?

_____

_____

_____

_____

Now work on 'un-comparing' your situation:

What are you happy about for that other person you see achieving success?

I'm happy for them that they've ...

_____

_____

How far have *you* come? What have you achieved that you're proud of?

_____

_____

_____

_____

Deflect negative comments

'You'll never do it.'

This was said to me by someone I looked up to—someone who was a true leader in the finance industry and who taught me everything I knew. I was told this when I said I was going to start my own business. It was soul crushing to hear. Thankfully, I had resolve and momentum, and nothing was going to stop me starting my own business. I deflected this comment and although I haven't forgotten it, it didn't throw my world into pieces.

They say 'sticks and stones may break my bones, but names will never hurt me'. This may be the worst advice you received from society as a child. I understand the intent, but words can have a longer effect than a broken bone. In fact, a bone will repair stronger than before, whereas words can grow the longest roots and cause issues for years to come, particularly if they were laid on you by someone you love, care for, look up to or respect.

I've learned that most of us humans are guilty of saying stuff right off the top of our head without thinking.

Part of having a healthy mindset is learning to deflect negative comments that get thrown your way. I think it's more than 'having a thick skin'. A thick skin means if someone lays a verbal blow you can absorb it and it doesn't get through. I'd rather carry a mindset shield with me that doesn't allow words to get near me.

Teach an old dog new tricks

'You can't teach an old dog new tricks.'

We've all heard this saying before and, to be fair, it seems legit. But tell that to David Bottomley, Australia's oldest PhD graduate. Dr Bottomley graduated at the age of 94. He embarked on an 8-year journey to complete his doctorate of philosophy and once he got rolling, he knocked it off in 7 years. In an ABC News interview, Dr Bottomley said that he never really stopped learning his whole life and that the completion of his doctorate was not the end of his education.

I love this type of mindset: one of always learning and always growing. I don't believe always learning means formal education. It can be as simple as an online course on a new topic, a weekend community college class or leaning into a new podcast about a topic of interest.

I love learning about new, random things. I recently read a book about gut health and one about soil. I believe it's about being open to always learning—being a sponge. It's a normal part of growth. I don't enjoy reading fiction or listening to mindless podcasts—I enjoy reading non-fiction books and listening to non-fiction audio books. I do, however, love watching fiction series on Paramount+ or Netflix, etc. My point here is, we can't always be 'on' and learning because we also need chill time and recreation—but can you pick your battles and use your time to maximise learning?

What about you? What are you going to lean into? This habit of always learning and growing in any area can only be good for your mindset. I believe it sets a tone that you don't know it all. And to be honest, you don't. This swings around full circle to the fixed vs growth mindset that I talked about earlier. While informal learning might not make you a subject-matter expert, I believe it does make you a more interesting person and a great conversationalist.

When I was growing up, we inherited a Kelpie × Australian Terrier. His name was Jack. He wasn't a puppy but he was just out of puppyhood. This dog was a ball of energy; he loved playing fetch and was a happy-go-lucky, all-round good guy. But he wasn't trained at all. The gate opened and he would run if he wasn't tied up. He would bark at the hose if you were hosing the garden. The lawn mower would be drowned out by the sound of him barking at it.

As time went on, it was apparent that Jack's behaviour was not good. Luckily, we took Jack to the farm. No, not 'that farm', but my grandparents had a property in Gloucester, New South Wales, and they were happy to adopt Jack. The most amazing thing happened. You see, a Kelpie is a sheepdog and they are made for the farm. No boundaries, and lots of room to run, expel energy and not be bored. He was a different dog. Nan would hose the garden and Jack would just chill with her and not bark. All of a sudden, Jack was trained and would do as you instructed. He could be free without a leash and wouldn't run away anywhere. It was amazing.

What does this have to do with mindset? It's all about the environment, namely:

- *creating a mental environment where you're always learning and growing.* You'll recall I previously talked about LOOT (life on own terms). The days of school, university, job for life then retirement are over. It's now basically school, work, travel, university, work, education, career change and do whatever you want.

- *ensuring you're in the right physical environment.* Are you in the right workplace or a career that's suited to you? Maybe you're a people person but you're stuck in an office working alone all day and you're wondering why you hate work and life. Are you the opposite? You don't enjoy people all day long and wish you were in a non-customer-facing role? Maybe you need to free your inner Jack.

So, can you be taught new tricks, or is it a matter of changing the way you see the world and your career?

---

apply now

Where can you be learning and continuing to open your mind (it doesn't necessarily have to be work related)?

_____

_____

_____

_____

_____

Is there anything in your environment holding you back?

_____

_____

_____

_____

_____

Take ownership

This could be the most challenging part of changing your mindset when it comes to your career and work. How do you take ownership of your current role if you don't like it, dislike your team members or no-one else around you cares? The answer is, with great difficulty.

I've always had a philosophy that I'll do the best I can within a situation because at the end of the day my work and the things I'm responsible for are a reflection on me as a person. I'm not a lazy person. I'm proud of my work and I care—particularly if I'm getting paid for it.

A famous Nazarene once said that those who are faithful in the small things will also be faithful in the large. I love this as part of a mindset piece. It cuts so many ways. As with our money and generosity, it's hard to give $200 straight up to a charity if you've never been an ongoing giver of even $5 when you didn't have much money. It's hard to manage lots of money (e.g. a lottery win) if you have not managed what you have now. Back to the mindset of your career—the work and job you are doing now. How are you managing it and are you owning it (we will talk more about this soon)?

Taking ownership of your daily job and tasks is a valuable attribute to bring to the table with any employer or role. While it might feel like it's unnoticed, your manager or team leader will see this at some point. If not, having the attribute of ownership in your role will organically elevate you over time. But remember, you are taking ownership because you are proud of the work you do. This is because if you do something for a reason and that reason doesn't pay off, you'll stop doing it. You are taking ownership for you and only you.

If you can't find it in you over the medium term to take ownership of your current role or patch of the employment universe, perhaps a change in career, role or job is in order. I say medium term as this is a mindset skill that does need to be practised.

For me, it came somewhat naturally. Have a look at the photo of me when I had my first job. It was a cash job at $4 per hour (I was 13!) at a pharmacy that my mother worked at. I did three, two-hour afternoons per week. I was in charge of the storeroom. It was a very large pharmacy and essentially I was responsible for removing all the cardboard and making it clean and tidy. No-one really cared about the detail that I went to, but it was my storeroom and I made sure it was perfect—no matter what anyone thought, nor if no-one saw parts of that room.

The work I do today is no different from that of 13-year-old Glen cleaning a storeroom. My work mindset expects a standard of excellence in everything I do.

My challenge to you is how do you move your mindset to doing the best job possible if no-one ever sees your work?

apply now

How can you take more ownership over your career? What can you do in your current job to show you are owning it?

_____

_____

_____

_____

_____

Live a generous life

I believe a huge part of a quality mindset and life is to be a generous person. I'm not just talking about money here. While I do believe we all have a responsibility to help those who are less fortunate than us by way of charitable donations or to give to causes when there is a natural disaster, there is more you can be generous with, like your time, experience, support and wisdom.

This outward perspective is so healthy for your mindset: it will help you be less selfish, and we need more of those kinds of people!

If you have even one day's more experience than someone else, you can help them and encourage them in their life and career.

I have personally been a beneficiary of someone giving up their own time and wisdom with no expectations of anything in return. In fact, if it wasn't for my mentor many years ago, I dare say *my millennial money* and this book would not have come to life.

I encourage you to try and build generosity into your life every day—not as a transactional thing that you do once a year when a co-worker has a fundraiser that you flick $20 towards.

Ways you can start (and/or continue) to be generous in your life include:

- ongoing financial giving to a charity of your choice

- shouting your team lunch

- paying for a stranger's fuel or a table at a cafe anonymously (this one's fun)

- doing nice things for people without any strings attached (this is a low bar to reach!)

- giving blood (this is much needed and always appreciated)

- connecting with a new or junior member in your team and taking them under your wing unofficially (not everyone will get on with everyone, but be on the lookout)

- offering to mentor someone and catch up every month or so

- volunteering your time at a charity of choice

- smiling once in a while

- being polite and saying thank you (another low bar!)

- understanding that people may be going through 'things' and being nice to people you meet at a shop, hotel, when you're phoning a call centre, and so on

- not being so stingy and cheap (hehehe, did I hit someone's nerve?—hope so).

It's wild to think that I need to mention things like this (particularly just being nice and not stingy!) but I saw a comment in the 'my millennial money' Facebook group where a young man with a nice, flashy car in his profile pic commented on a post about side hustles. He said that he collects $20 per week from elderly neighbours for bringing their bins in each week. You can imagine this didn't go down well for him when other people read it and he soon deleted his comment.

The thing is—in relation to generosity and being stingy—it feeds into the mindset categories that I discussed at the beginning of the chapter. Mr Side Hustle soon found out that taking his elderly neighbours' bins in and out is just part of being nice. Growing up, $20 may have been mission critical for him and his family, but now that he is working full-time he has the luxury to actually just do the bins. I wonder if he continues to charge his neighbours now that he has been publicly called out!

What generosity can you try and make a habit of?

_____

_____

_____

_____

When was the last time you did something generous? If you can't remember, maybe it's time to do something now.

_____

_____

_____

_____

Play the long game

The path of least resistance is an easy road. Lots of people take it in different areas of their lives. While it's fine if you cut across the grass and skip the path on the way to the supermarket each time, I want to encourage you to always have long-term thinking at the forefront when it comes to your career and money.

Anyone who has ever achieved anything of significance and maintained that status or achievement has rarely fallen into it overnight. There is a reason why lottery winners blow their money within years of obtaining it. They didn't work for it, they don't know the value of it and they have not built systems of managing wealth into their lives over many years.

Playing the long game is understanding that children can't delay gratification and as adults we can (in theory). This is also a hard mindset concept to practise. In my professional life and in my career I've always played the long game and it's always worked out just fine.

Two main factors that will help you play the long game are:

- *having a clear strategy of what you want to do*. Having a career plan will enable you to keep focused and avoid any short-term distractions. A small pay rise from a new job may help you in the short term but if you're leaving a great organisation, great workplace culture and experience just so you can get some extra quick bucks, it could rob you of opportunities that may be better suited for you in the long run. This also speaks loudly about loyalty to your employer. I've seen LinkedIn profiles of people who have had numerous jobs over a short time (say, 3 years). It does make you think about what's going on (I'm not saying there aren't legitimate reasons for some).

  Jumping around from job to job could be a symptom of not having a clear strategy or trying to manufacture your career faster than within the organic time you may need in the trenches.

  Slow down, get clear on what you want to do, put in the hours and work and play the long game. As an employer, I can tell you that it does make a difference when I see quality people who have played the long game.

- *having sound financial foundations*. There is nothing worse than the stench of desperation, in any area of life. As previously mentioned, it's important to have strong financial foundations. This doesn't just mean strong so that you have a nice budget and you're kicking your own financial goals. Not being in consumer debt, having an emergency fund in place and having some savings can also take the pressure off your life when it comes to your career. It can allow you to keep a role that has a great workplace culture and amazing career development and training, even though the pay isn't amazing.

Having strong foundations can remove the sense of desperation and will allow you to consider options for career and job changes without the added pressure of 'needing to' because of the money.

Working towards a solid career strategy and strong foundations will also help you dodge mindlessly working up to a bigger income, building a life around it and then hating your job or career. You'll end up not being able to change to a job with a possibly reduced income and giving yourself the chance to retrain in it as you need that high income to support your life.

Conversely, not living on the financial edge, living week to week, being debt free and having money left over each week will also take a heap of pressure off your life and career. This will flow back to you being less stressed, more generous, happier and able to be a better employee overall.

Playing the long game will often be counterintuitive to most modern culture as you know it, to societal norms and to many people in your life. The long game isn't always about delaying pleasure as a reward until you finish a hard task or project; it's about being strategic and forward looking. Getting a job offer that seems good in the short term may not be in your strategic interest career wise.

---

apply now

How can you lock into a long game mindset in your career?

_____

_____

_____

_____

_____

Choose facts over emotions

I was sitting in the foyer of a hotel at about 10.45 pm. I had a pint of Ben & Jerry's Triple Caramel Chunk in hand and was eating in silence, but I was with my team and other people who were helping with the *my millennial money* live national tour. We like to catch up after an event to chill together and offer any comments on what went well and what didn't. After all, we're a team that has just played and it's like we're in the locker room after a game.

I'm an introvert and at times silence is my rejuvenator after meeting and greeting people and being on stage to record a live show. But this time was different. This time I was eating ice-cream, not as part of my team catch-up, but as an emotional crutch. Circling in my head were a bunch of negative thoughts and I found myself lost among them and not enjoying the moment as the team ate their own respective ice-cream flavours.

You see, an hour or so earlier I was in front of about 150 local podcast listeners and I found myself stuck in my head. It had derailed me, and I knew it.

My emotions were telling me:

- You don't actually know anything about personal finance.

- You have no value to give.

- People are not here by choice.

- They can't wait for it to finish so they can leave.

- No-one is having a good time.

Welcome to imposter syndrome. You will also have these doubts as you build your career. The worst thing is, it pops up when you least expect it. I'm not writing this with a solution, but as an acknowledgement and to tell you that you, like me, are human and we're big bags of chemicals.

What I have learned for myself, like many other of my mindset hacks, is to acknowledge when imposter syndrome is present and to try and address it with facts.

My facts are actually:

- I am experienced in financial planning and in personal finance (I have done more than 10 000 hours of financial planning and personal finance–associated work).

- I have so much value to give to my audience based on my education, training and experience.

- People paid good money to see the show and to meet me and the team.

- They don't want it to end as they are still engaged and this is visible through their body language and responses.

- People are laughing, drinking and enjoying themselves.

Emotions are an essential part of our life and work. Don't ignore or suppress them (we've all been there). Acknowledge them. But once you've acknowledged them, you have a choice to make. You can choose to let them rule or control you. Or you can choose to conquer them (easier said than done, hehehe!).

I'm learning to give more weight to the facts and recognise that my emotions can railroad me if I'm giving them too much airtime. Now before an event or a podcast recording I focus on the facts and purposely try to keep out of my head. Emotions matter. But don't let them dominate your decisions. Focus on the facts.

apply now

Write down at least five positive facts about you when it comes to your career.

If you can't think of any, ask a friend, family member or workmate.

_____

_____

_____

_____

_____

Try reading these to yourself before an interview or important meeting.

You are the professional

I was sitting in the waiting room of a medical specialist. This professor was referred to me as I specialised in business succession as a financial adviser. He needed some death cover and income insurance set up for him personally, too. He had a complex business operation with multiple employees, entities, trusts and a self-managed super fund, and he needed advice on protecting himself as a key person within the business.

We had emailed briefly before this meeting and his accountant had sent me some of his financials to go over. This individual earned close to $2 million per year and was one of the top specialists in his field in Australia. To say I was a little nervous about the meeting would have been an understatement. There was a high chance I had never met anyone as intelligent as him before in my life. That, combined with the fact that this type of client is a dream for many professional services and could be considered a 'whale' in terms of the income earned for my business.

The issue for me was that at the time I was 27, didn't yet have a beard and was a little baby faced. I had also decided to do some 'housekeeping' on my teeth. I always wanted to fix a small gap in my top row of teeth and straighten them all up. It was honestly something that only I noticed and was very self-conscious about. So I had orthodontics at the time of seeing this potential client.

My hands were sweating a little while waiting for him to finish his meeting and I was thinking that 'this guy is going to see this young, baby-faced guy with braces and write me off in his mind before we even get started' and that I was going to be useless in front of him.

Then it came to me.

This guy knows nothing about business succession, insurance structures, policy details, what types of cover needs to consider, tax consequences or estate planning considerations—and he probably knows nothing about financial planning as he has never seen an adviser before.

I am the professional here. He is not.

I was not there to try and diagnose a medical condition in his specialty area. I got up with confidence, had an epic meeting and he remained a long-term, trusting client.

This was another example of the attack of 'imposter syndrome'. I got caught in my head for a hot minute.

You are also the professional in your desired area of expertise. If you're not yet and still learning, you will be one day and I hope you will remember my story!

Check emotional expectations

While I'm on the topic of emotions, let me reiterate that having a healthy emotional mindset will enable your career to flourish. You will find other parts of your life will also benefit—from engaging in community activities, and investing to team sports and relationships with your loved ones. Part of your own mindset is to understand that everyone is pulled from different parts: cultural and societal, generational and family, institutional, and psychological. So if your workmate, colleague, boss, supervisor or manager sees the world in a different light, are you able to seek first to understand?

It's not fair to put your own emotional expectations on someone else to carry. It's also immature.

I want to talk about this in another way: how to spot when someone is trying to put their emotional expectations on you. This way you can do a sense check and perhaps call yourself out if you start doing it to someone else.

I believe someone will be trying to put their own emotional expectation on you if they:

- are vague with a point they are trying to make

- come across as passive-aggressive

- don't seem to accept anything you try to say

- seem aggravated with the way you are doing things or your view of the world.

You will also know this is happening when you feel like saying to them 'just tell me exactly what you want me to say and how you want me to act!'

We all may have been guilty of doing this at some point and if it's a habit of yours, it needs to stop.

Convince a man against his will, He's of the same opinion still.

Mary Wollstonecraft

From a macro career perspective, owning your career and mindset is a choice, as opposed to putting that expectation on your employer. You are the only one who can step up and take control of your career. Just like your emotional expectations, you can't dump this on someone else or your employer.

A final word

I hope my story of my own mindset being 'unlocked' in my early 20s and my mindset learnings and anecdotes since then were encouraging for you. What can you do today to start to improve the way you think or approach a situation?

I find it fascinating that many of the mindset topics that have helped propel me in my career are honestly like old-school common sense. The issue is that when we are so immersed in our busy day-to-day hustle we can lose sight of the small things that matter.

Let this chapter be a reminder to slow down, and to understand that much of the mindset stuff is not about you getting more stuff and the 'greed is good' type of mindset. I would also encourage you to run away from this type of mindset teaching as it's up there with taking advantage of others. In many cases where people have been exposed for making wealth illegally or by deception there is an underlying issue of taking advantage of people.

While I want everyone to do well with their respective lives, mindsets, careers and money—I am a personal finance guy, after all—it can't be at the expense of others or without living a generous life along the way.

resources **Scan the QR code for these resources and more.**

Subscribe to the *my millennial career* and *my millennial money* podcasts to have your mindset challenged and encouraged! We chat a lot about mindset across our podcasts.

strength and skills: harder, better, faster, stronger

4

tl;dr

- If you want a successful career, you need to invest a disproportionate amount of time and energy into your strengths.

- Building new skills is an ongoing process. It doesn't stop: if you're not learning, you're stagnating—or worse, you're falling behind.

- Mastering a unique mix of skills makes you stand out: it gives you an edge.

- Building skills means getting uncomfortable and trusting your ability to learn.

- Once you move past the discomfort, you'll move into a rapid growth stage, which is when you're most engaged at work.

Strengths and skills: The fuel in your career

So you've started out on your road trip. You've had your car serviced, your maps are loaded, your crispy M&M's are ready, your spare tyre checked and your RnB playlist is blaring. But, before you hit the freeway, have you remembered the number-one must-have for a successful trip? It's time to fill up the tank. Without fuel you're not going anywhere.

Your career is fuelled by your strengths and skills. They take you where you want to go.

Knowing your strengths and building a diverse mix of skills helps you go further, faster. And like the refuelling process, you need to continually top up your skills and invest in your strengths. Because we are never done when it comes to learning and growing.

Oh, give me strength!

When I hear the word 'strength', I immediately think of 'weakness'—the exact opposite of strength. What's with that? I thought my reaction was weird, but it turns out I'm not alone. In an American Psychological Association article, Rozin and Royzman call it negativity bias. Our brains, as a survival mechanism, are hardwired to fixate on negative traits, situations and events over positive ones.

Let's test it out. Think of an embarrassing moment you had at work. Got it? I'll bet it took you a total of 0.6 seconds to recall your cringeworthy experience. Like that time I dropped my handbag and out tumbled an entire box of tampons, scattering at the feet of the new head of strategy on his first day of work. Welcome to the team! Don't mind me. I'm going to pick these up while I slowly die of mortification.

Now, I want you to think of a time you were really proud of yourself at work. Chances are it took you longer to remember a moment you were proud of than the one you were embarrassed by.

Recalling your big achievements can feel like rifling through the internal filing cabinet of your mind. You have to haul out the archives, rummaging through to find your successes. Herein lies the power of negativity bias. We're quick to find the negatives and slow to remember the positives. It explains why so many people struggle to pinpoint and talk about their strengths.

At work, we gravitate towards our weaknesses. We want to uncover our blind spots and fix the things we aren't good at. But, I've learned that people have just as many 'strengths blind spots'. These are your hidden strengths waiting to be discovered.

In this chapter, we're going to focus on discovering your strengths and building your skills. To do this, you'll need to press pause on self-criticism and dial down the negativity bias. Once you've uncovered your strengths, you'll work on developing skills that fuel your career.

Throughout this chapter, we draw on Gallup's extensive research in the area of strengths and Cal Newport's research from his book, *So Good They Can't Ignore You*.

Why do strengths and skills matter, and what are they?

If you want a successful career, invest a disproportionate amount of time and energy working on your strengths.

Playing to your strengths is one of those ideas that sounds good in theory, and is even better in practice. According to Gallup, people who use their strengths at work report higher levels of performance, happiness and energy. Sign us up please!

On the flip side, working in an area of weakness can leave you disengaged, drained and unmotivated. When an employee ends up on a performance improvement plan, it's typically because they are working outside of their strengths zone. But, your work performance isn't the only indicator that you're working outside of your strengths.

You might be able to do your job with your eyes closed, yet there's no spark or energy in what you do. This is often a sign that your job doesn't align with your strengths. You have the skills to ace the job, but your role doesn't play to your genius. This is why it's important to know your strengths and assess how well your job connects with them.

Before we discover your strengths, let's define the key terms. The words 'strength', 'talent' and 'skills' are thrown around a lot at work. But what the heck does it all mean? With the help of Gallup, it's time to clear up this corporate lingo.

Strengths

We define strengths as something you're freakishly good at. It's an area of natural talent you've worked hard to develop. Over time it's become your zone of genius—one of your superpowers.

Gallup defines 'strength' as an activity or area where you deliver near-perfect performance. Their strengths equation is: talent × investment = strengths. That means, people build their strengths by investing time, energy and focus into one of their natural talents.

Talent

Talent is your natural abilities—the things that come easily to you, and that others might find challenging. It's the innate ways you think, behave, feel and act.

Skills

Skills are the competencies needed to perform a role well. They tend to be job-specific and can be acquired through practical experience, training or knowledge. By having these competencies you are better equipped to fulfil the job.

The relationship between strengths, talent and skills

There is a strong connection between strengths and skills (see figure 4.1). But we want to point out a few small distinctions.

Strengths are unique to you. They are central to who you are because they emerge from your natural talents. Skills are a bit different. Anyone can develop a skill in anything, with or without a natural talent in that particular area.

You don't have to have an intrinsic talent with words to become a writer (just ask Glen!). You can build writing skills through learning and practice. You don't have to have a natural ability to influence people to become an exceptional leader. Leadership is a skill that can be developed through experience.

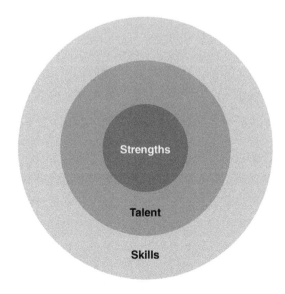

Figure 4.1: the relationship between strengths, talent and skills

Discover your strengths

There are three simple steps to discovering your strengths. Before we get into it, I want to remind you (again) about negativity bias and self-criticism. Why do I keep banging on about this? Because it's hardwired into our internal operating system. And like all operating systems, it requires regular updates and bug fixes. Consider this reminder your bias bug fix.

On an episode of *my millennial career*, Dr Amy Silver shared how self-compassion is the antidote to self-criticism. As we go through the process of discovering your strengths, turn up the volume on your self-compassion. See yourself as your family or friends see you. Basically, stop being so bloody hard on yourself. You have amazing strengths, and we're going to help you realise them.

Let's have a look at the three simple steps to discovering your strengths.

Step 1: Ask yourself (self-reflection)

If you want to uncover your strengths, you need to master the art of self-reflection.

I was about to make an important career decision, and I was struggling to know what step to take. I kept going around in circles, unsure of how to move forward. So, I called a friend of mine, Rohan Dredge, to get his advice.

Rohan is a regular guest (and a fan favourite) on our podcast. He's the type of person who asks the right (and sometimes tough) questions to get you thinking differently about a problem.

Rohan asked me three questions that he had learned from his Thought Leaders community:

1. What problems do you solve?

2. What value do you add?

3. What do you do differently from everyone else?

At first, I found these questions really difficult to answer. I was drawing a blank. So, after the call, I closed my laptop and got out my notepad. This challenge demanded old-school paper and pen. I suspended my own judgement and just started writing ideas down. Initially, I included anything that came to mind.

I thought about all those, 'Shell, can I get your advice on this' phone calls. I thought about the problems I love to solve, the ones other people dread facing. I thought about all the times I've felt energised at work and had big wins. As I answered those three questions, I watched my strengths emerge.

I started to group the themes and prioritise them into the work that I love doing most. As Marie Condo would say, 'What areas spark joy?' Using that lens, I narrowed it down to four key strengths.

This process of self-reflection is essential to discovering your strengths. Taking time to reflect on these kinds of questions can be the first step towards finding your genius zone. It requires you to think about when you've felt most engaged, motivated and inspired.

apply now

In addition to the three questions Rohan asked me, also ask yourself the following:

- When have I felt most confident at work?

- When do I feel most energised and engaged?

- What tasks, projects or activities get me into a state of flow?

- What parts of my career have I loved the most?

- What have been my biggest career wins or work successes?

- What do people compliment me on? What areas do I consistently receive positive feedback in?

- What problems do I solve easily that other people find challenging?

- What matters do people come to me for advice on?

Jot down your answers here.

_____

_____

_____

_____

_____

You should start to see some common themes. They signal your strengths. It might be a single word or a phrase. Here are some examples of what they may sound like:

Communication	Execution	Learning
Responsibility	Influence	Discipline
Leadership	Active listening	Future vision
Consistency	Building relationships	Strategic thinking
Problem-solving	Collaboration	Ambition and drive
Creativity	Diligence	Planning and organising
Empathy	Fun	

Now you've got your strengths themes clarified, it's time to test them out with people you trust.

Step 2: Ask a friend (external advice)

Remember how we mentioned strengths blind spots? We all have them, and that's why it's valuable to get external input. Ask a trusted friend, teammate or family member to be a mirror for you. They often recognise the strengths you overlook in yourself. You can also sense-check the themes you've identified in step 1 to work out if they reflect how other people see you.

Ask them the following questions:

- What would you say my top strengths are personally and at work?

- What do you think I do really well?

- Do you think I have any strengths blind spots (things I'm naturally good at that I don't see in myself)?

Then talk through the strengths you identified in step 1 and ask if they resonate.

---

apply now

What did you take away from this conversation?

_____

_____

_____

_____

_____

Step 3: Ask the internet (personality profiling surveys)

I'm not saying jump on Reddit and ask a bunch of randoms what your strengths are. Steps 1 and 2 are about gathering qualitative data through self-reflection and conversations with your friends or family.

Step 3 is about acquiring quantitative data on your strengths, personality and preferences.

There are plenty of great profiling tools and surveys out there, but here are three of our favourites. They will validate what you found in Steps 1 and 2:

- CliftonStrengths Assessment via Gallup (paid)

- Via Character Survey (free)

- Myers-Briggs Personality Type (paid).

Once you've completed these three steps, you will have clarified your strengths.

Now, you need to focus as much of your time and attention as you can on these areas. Get proactive about developing your strengths. If one of your natural talents is creativity, read as many books as you can on creativity. Get yourself a creativity mentor: someone who is known for their strength in this area who can give you advice and guidance. Complete courses and access online resources. Basically, consume as much knowledge about your areas of strength as you can.

As you sharpen your strengths you will become known for something that creates opportunities for growth, progression and recognition (more on this in chapter 6).

---

apply now

Assess your role against your strengths.

Working in your strengths creates natural momentum in your career. But not every job will align well with your strengths. It's a valuable process to regularly reflect on how well your role fits with your strengths.

Write down your top five strengths and review how often you're using them in your current job. You can also assess future jobs you're interested in against your strengths by looking at the typical duties and responsibilities. The ideal scenario is to be working in your strengths about 70 per cent of the time.

(continued)

Top strengths	How often do you use these strengths in your current role (or how often will you in future desired role)?
	Rarely/Sometimes/Often/All the time
	Rarely/Sometimes/Often/All the time
	Rarely/Sometimes/Often/All the time
	Rarely/Sometimes/Often/All the time
	Rarely/Sometimes/Often/All the time

If you selected 'rarely' or 'sometimes' for most of your responses, it indicates your current role does not align with your strengths. It may be worth having a conversation with your manager to see if the role can be adjusted to better leverage your strengths.

If your role is unable to be modified, it's not going to be engaging or energising in the long term. You might be able to continue in the short term, but we would encourage you to begin planning for a change.

How to talk about your strengths at work

Recruiter: What's your biggest strength?

Me: I can eat a family pack of Doritos in under 2 minutes and 20 seconds.

I'm not sure when exactly, but somewhere along my career journey, I became an awkward, bumbling mess when it comes to talking about my strengths.

Whenever people at work would encourage me, I would immediately undermine it. You could say my strength, at the time, was to deflect attention away from what I'm good at and recite the list of 183 things I'm woeful at. It's a bad habit I've had to unlearn.

If you're nodding your head in solidarity, we'll help you unlearn this habit too.

You've done a lot of hard work to understand and clarify your strengths. But knowing your strengths is not enough. You have to be able to talk about them with confidence.

Many of us struggle to candidly speak about our strengths. And if we do talk openly about them, we feel like we're some kind of self-aggrandising, arrogant goose.

In many workplaces, you can watch this dynamic play out. People, out of their own insecurity, subtly (or overtly) tear down those who succeed. Hacking them down to size just like the tall poppy.

This cultural norm has infiltrated how we view and talk about strengths. It's why you may feel the need to downplay your strengths and overemphasise your weaknesses. It's why you avoid garnering positive attention. And it's why you have (until now) resisted talking about what you're good at.

We want to say this loud and clear: your strengths are worth communicating. It doesn't make you a self-involved, puffed-up egomaniac if you talk about what you're good at. No, no, no. Done well, it makes you a confident, assured and secure person. And in a world of comparison, envy and insecurity, these are qualities worth having.

How to share your strengths in a non-awkward way

Don't worry, you're not going to roll out a microphone and portable amplifier and start spruiking your strengths around the office. But there are many situations at work where you need to talk about the things you're good at.

One of the barriers when talking about our strengths is that we think we're being subjective or biased. The best way to overcome this challenge is to communicate your strengths and give an example to back them up. Suddenly, something subjective (your opinion of your strengths) becomes objective (by providing proof).

Instead of making an absolute statement like 'I'm excellent at planning and organising', say:

> One of my strengths is planning and organising. I've been responsible for end-to-end event planning over the past few years. And a few months ago, I managed a two-day conference for interior designers at the QT Hotel in Sydney. We had over 400 people attend and 10 international guest speakers. The conference was a huge hit. We had raving reviews about the event and we've already sold 250 tickets for next year.

You can see how the example validates the strength. It's not self-aggrandising. It's simply telling the facts. Sharing a story to support your strength makes this conversation much more comfortable.

Bodhi had worked as a case worker for a community services organisation for 4 years. He loved the company, but he was getting bored in his role.

He'd figured out his strengths were in training and change management. He was known for running engaging team training sessions, but it wasn't a core part of his job. He knew it was time to start looking for opportunities that tied more closely with his strengths.

During a weekly meeting, the managing director let the team know they were about to kick off a big project. They were designing a brand-new app for employees to complete client reports and automate rosters and timesheets.

As Bodhi listened to the update, he knew the project would require significant employee training and change management. This was the opportunity he was hoping for: a chance to use his strengths in a more tangible way.

He scheduled a 1:1 meeting with the managing director to ask if he could join the project team. It would be a hard sell. There was no position vacant. The organisation had never employed a designated training and change management specialist. And if he was to be involved in the project, it would take him out of his casework role. But he was ready to communicate how he could use his strengths to add value to the project.

During his catch-up with the managing director, they discussed the immense challenge of change management in technology projects. He shared about how employee training can make or break projects like this.

(continued)

> Once he had raised enough concern about why training and change management were essential, Bodhi pitched his big idea: a 3-month transfer to work solely on the project and design the change management and training strategy. To show he was the right person for the job, he spoke about his strengths in delivering employee training and shared positive feedback from a recent workshop.
>
> The outcome? The managing director agreed to Bodhi's proposal. He was transferred onto the project team temporarily to lead the training and change management. And better yet, once the project was delivered, he was offered a permanent role in training and change management.

Here's what we can take away from Bodhi's story:

- He identified his strengths in training and change management.

- He saw an opportunity to better use his strengths at work.

- He proactively raised the need for training and change management as part of the project.

- He articulated his strengths and gave solid examples to back them up.

You won't always be pitching your strengths to land a new opportunity as seen in Bodhi's story. But there are still day-to-day conversations where you'll need to talk about your strengths. Here are some ways to speak to your strengths in everyday conversations:

- 'One of my strengths is my ability to _____, so maybe I can assist you with that?'

- 'I can see this challenge at the moment. I love working on _____. Can I help you solve this?'

- 'I was able to help _____ with this problem. Would you like me to take a look at it for you?'

- 'My sweet spot is working in _____ kinds of situations. If you need support with _____, let me know.'

---

apply now

Write a sentence and supporting example you can use in conversation to talk about your strengths.

_____

_____

_____

_____

_____

Practise these! Say them out loud until you feel comfortable doing so.

Whenever someone highlights a strength of yours, say thank you and own it. There's nothing wrong with saying, 'You know what? I am great at that. That's the value I bring to my life and work.' Celebrate it!

Okay, but what about weaknesses?

With all this talk about strengths, are we saying you should ignore your weaknesses? No. Not at all. We all have gaps in our skills, capabilities and knowledge. And of course, it's essential to work on those areas. But many people spend far too much time addressing their weaknesses and nowhere near enough time working on their strengths.

My final high-school mathematics exam was a bad time. I remember the day I got my exam paper back. My teacher placed it face down on my desk. I apprehensively turned it over and looked down at the result. Handwritten in the angriest red pen I'd ever seen was a total of 14 per cent. It was circled and underlined for dramatic effect, as if my poor performance needed to be made more obvious. Thanks a lot, Mrs Henderson.

As I considered my exam results, I knew I had three options (a multiple choice, if you will):

1. *Do nothing.* Continue on my current trajectory and bomb out miserably.

2. *Get a tutor.* Work really, really hard to build my maths skills and hopefully reach a mediocre level of performance.

3. *Drop maths.* Focus my time and energy on my natural talents and strengths and reach an exceptional level of performance in the subjects I actually enjoy.

Despite what my mathematics exam suggests, I consider myself to be an intelligent person. Yep, I chose option 3 (plus, isn't that what the law of averages tells you to do when you don't know the answer?). Goodbye, mathematics. It was nice knowing you.

It amazes me that as a 15 year old I intrinsically knew the power of playing to my strengths rather than spending all my time addressing my weaknesses. I chose the creative subjects that aligned with my natural talents. As a result, I excelled in my final two years at school.

Cue end credits music

Happily ever after to me. Or at least it was, for approximately 10 years. Until my mathematics shortcomings came back to haunt me.

I was in a meeting the chief operating officer (my manager) and the chief financial officer. They had decided to move payroll out of Finance and into the HR department. Uh-oh. Payroll would report directly to me...effective immediately. All those numbers, maths and data. This was not good.

I was stressing about my lack of knowledge and I spoke with my manager about my skill gaps in this area. She wasn't put off. 'Shell, I haven't employed you to be a finance expert,' she explained. 'I've employed you to lead the HR team. Your strengths in the people space are what matters most. We can work to manage the gaps.' Wise words.

From here, I developed a plan to manage my weaknesses. It was not about becoming a financial and payroll expert (I had no desire to do that). Instead, I created strategies to work around my weaknesses. It included having the right people, roles and processes in place to ensure accuracy. I got coaching to build up sufficient financial knowledge to lead the team, but I didn't spend excessive time trying to become the expert in an area that wasn't aligned with my strengths or career goals.

Being well-rounded doesn't lead to better performance. Going from a low performer at maths to a mediocre performer doesn't help all that much in my career. Moving from a good performer to a great performer is what has the most impact on your career trajectory.

You can achieve greater career success when you stop trying to be proficient at everything and instead hone your strengths. Focus less energy on improving your weaknesses, and focus more on developing your strengths.

The passion pit

For the love of all that is good in this world, enough about strengths. Where's the part where you say 'follow your passions' to find your 'dream career'?

This is not that book, and I am not that person. Passion is important. But your 'dream career' isn't built by 'following your passions'.

I am a total foodie. I am passionate about culinary experiences and spend way too much money on said experiences (I didn't choose the fine dining life. The fine dining life chose me).

Over the years, I've accumulated an exorbitant number of recipe books to satiate my obsession with food. It's a delicious kind of therapy. Yet what do all my reading and recipes and fine dining mean for my cooking skills and strengths?

Can I cook a soufflé? No.

Can I handle working in a professional kitchen? Absolutely not.

Should I open a restaurant? It's a hard no.

My passion for good food doesn't mean I should become a chef. In fact, sometimes it's best to keep these passions as hobbies so it remains something you love, and not something you have to do every day.

Cal Newport (one of my all-time favourite authors), in his book *So Good They Can't Ignore You*, highlights the flawed logic of 'following your passions'. His research found that pursuing a passion has little impact on whether a person enjoys their job or career. Rather, a successful career is founded on mastery. Cal argues that building a mix of rare and valuable skills is what makes you stand out from the crowd, creating what he defines as 'career capital' and, ultimately, leads to a fulfilling and successful career.

By leaning into your strengths rather than your passions, you slip into the jetstream of capability, fast-tracking your career growth.

Skilling it!

Skills, skills, skills. Why are employers obsessed with skills? Because skills point to your potential to perform well. If you have the skill, you may be able to do the job. Employers want to know your skillset to see if you have what it takes to smash out the job.

Skills are to the knowledge worker what tools are to the tradie. Your skills are the tool kit that helps you succeed. You'll have a whole range of them at your disposal, and you'll be constantly acquiring new ones. But the key is, you need to know how to use them.

What skills do employers expect, and what do they mean? Let's break down the HR jargon to something we *actually* understand.

~~Hard skills~~ Technical skills

Historically, they've been called 'hard skills', but we call them technical skills. These skills tend to be tangible, observable and measurable, developed through learning and practice. They are often identified as the requirements of the role. Things like:

- data analysis

- bookkeeping

- user experience design

- social media management

- payroll management

- cybersecurity

- medication administration

- business writing

- machinery operation

- instrument performance

- video editing

- foreign languages

- photography.

Your technical skills are evidenced through your on-the-job experience and also through your training and study.

It's worth noting, however, that completing the degree or getting the certification doesn't guarantee the skills. While study is important, on-the-job learning is essential for skill development. It's why many people finish up a degree and then find it difficult to gain immediate employment in the field. They've ticked the course off the list. They have theoretical knowledge, but they lack the skills that come through practical experience.

Employers want evidence of how you've practised what you've learned during your study. While you're studying, it's great to look for opportunities to gain practical exposure and experience in your area of study.

~~Soft skills~~ Human skills

Not gonna lie, I really don't like the term 'soft skills'. Why? Because they're anything but soft. They take a tonne of hard work to master. And they have a major impact on your career. So we like to call them 'human skills'. If you ask Google, they have been referred to as 'soft' because they're less measurable than hard skills, so I guess there's that.

They are interpersonal, behavioural and human-centred skills. Because they are people centric, less routinised and more nuanced, they are durable. The kind of skills that are less likely to be automated through technology, and therefore extremely valuable to you in your career.

You can see some examples of human skills and their definitions in table 4.1.

Table 4.1: various core skills and their meanings

Human skill	What it actually means...
Leading and influencing	Being able to help, show and train others to get something done, where they complete the task following your guidance
Communication	Being able to speak or write to others well and effectively inside and outside the organisation
Collaboration	Working well with others to achieve a common goal
Conflict resolution	Resolving a conflict within an organisation, or with a customer or supplier
Critical thinking	Being able to critically assess a situation, product or service and analyse what is working well, what can be improved and what options exist going forward
Innovation	Coming up with a 'new' idea to an 'old' problem
Initiative	Being the one to take a step forward to get something started or completed under your own motivation
Creativity	Doing something in a 'new' way—not just doing the 'same old, same old' to achieve goals
Flexibility	Being able to change course, adapt your approach or alter your work if something isn't working out
Resilience	Being able to bounce back from knocks or bumps on the road to achieve goals
Emotional intelligence	Identifying the emotional state of all involved (including yourself) and working through balancing these in a situation
Problem-solving	Being able to think through all of the possible solutions to a scenario
Empathy	Being able to sense the feelings and emotional states of others, and sharing someone else's experiences by imagining what it would be like to be in their situation
Responsibility	Having high levels of ownership for and accountability over activities, tasks and duties
Optimism	Tending to be hopeful and positive, and finding the good in diverse situations

takes a deep breath in

Man, that list is longer than my 5-year-old's Christmas list (which I'll have you know, she develops 9 months out from Christmas, so it's pretty comprehensive).

There are a lot of human skills out there. You need to work out what's essential and desirable for your success in your current or future role. Later in this chapter, you'll have a chance to start mapping out your skills.

Stand out by building a unique mix of skills

I went to a conference a while ago where about seven hundred people were jam-packed into a small venue. As I manoeuvred my way through the masses towards my seat, I caught a glimpse of an absolutely glorious woman. She was sparkling (literally), dressed head to toe in a bright pink sequin pants-suit, paired with pink converse high tops. Oof, it was a vibe. She was bold, memorable and different. Everyone noticed her.

Standing out is less about being better and more about being different.

In life and work, we are drawn to things that are uncommon, surprising and scarce. They demand our attention. In your career, if you want to stand out you'll need to build a unique set of skills. Skills that are difficult to replicate.

Cal Newport suggests that having a combination of rare and valuable skills gives you a competitive advantage in your career. It sets you apart. So when you're thinking about your job, I want you to think about how you can build an uncommon set of skills to stand out from the crowd.

Meet Phil Thompson. Phil is a financial adviser and runs a business called Skye Wealth. I was working with his team recently, and as I walked into his office I noticed his collection of framed qualifications on the bookshelf.

I expected to see the standard Bachelor of Business or Commerce degree (the requirement for financial advisers in Australia), but as I looked closer I was totally thrown by what I saw. Phil had his Bachelor degree in Circus Arts. Umm, what? It's safe to say I'd never met a financial adviser who'd also studied circus performance arts.

Being an obnoxiously nosy person, I had to know more. Phil indulged my curiosity, and told me the full story.

All through school Phil loved sport, creative arts and drama. At 15 years, he started a few afternoon circus arts classes. It evolved quickly. Phil began training four nights a week, and by the time he'd finished school, he had enrolled to study a Bachelor's Degree in Circus Arts at the National Institute of Circus Arts (NICA) in Melbourne, Australia.

The next three years were wild. Becoming an acrobat isn't just physically exhausting, it's a huge mental challenge. While most 18-year-old students were skipping lectures and tutorials, Phil had to attend NICA Monday to Friday, full time. It was 40+ hours a week of gruelling training in acrobatics, physical theatre, ballet, gym and the list goes on.

But Phil knew to stand out he had to do more than the expected hours. He arrived at 7 am each day, well before the rest of his class. He would use this time to practise.

'I did the same handstand exercise every single day. It was so boring and mind numbing. Some days, I felt like I was going backwards. I couldn't see the improvements and questioned if it was worth the effort,' Phil explained. But every day he kept practising. He was making infinitesimal improvements, and over time the results accumulated. Through all the training, rehearsing and practice, he mastered the skills.

Once he finished his degree, he worked as an acrobat performing across Australia and internationally. But a few years later, he realised it wasn't a sustainable long-term career option. If he was injured, he'd be out of a job, with no money and no options. It got him thinking about his next move.

Phil had been interested in personal finance for a long time, and always liked the idea of running his own business. So at the age of 24 he went back to school to build some new skills. He completed his studies and started his own business, Skye Wealth.

Phil's certainly got a unique mix of skills that have set him apart in his industry. I asked Phil if he is able to use any of the skills he learned from his circus performance days, in his finance career. I have to admit, the title 'circus performer' didn't exactly sound like there were typical 'transferable skills'. Phil's answer surprised me.

He explained that as a circus performer, everyday training involved doing the same exercise on repeat. He learned the skill of discipline. To become great at something, you need to repeat the same activity, over and over again, even when it's boring.

This skill has served him well throughout his finance career. It's helped him navigate the compliance and regulatory tedium that is part and parcel of financial advice and it's helped him be disciplined in the details.

Combined with his skills in creativity and the arts, he has built a business brand that's fun, creative and cheeky—unlike any other financial advisers I've come across. His unique skills mix has helped him stand out.

From the standard to the stand out

It's time to build skills that make you stand out. To start, I want you to look for common trends, norms and generalisations in your industry, job or career.

From here, think about skills that deviate from the norms in that particular job or industry. Look for ways to challenge the standard by building uncommon skills—things that would surprise people. Have a look at table 4.2 for some examples.

Table 4.2: building skills that make you stand out

The standard	The stand out
Role: Accountant	Role: Accountant
Typically provides financial reports full of complex data and graphs that most people can't comprehend as they don't have a data science degree	Has developed skills in graphic design on the side and used them to make bland financial reports visually interesting for everyone who reads them
Role: HR Advisor	Role: HR Advisor
Typically writes all staff emails and communication pieces that sound about as interesting as a risk and compliance policy. Nap time anyone?	Has mastered the skill of copywriting and making employee communication updates sound less like a snooze fest and more like a BuzzFeed article grabbing attention by the…eyeballs
Role: Social Media Coordinator	Role: Social Media Coordinator
Typically churns out dozens of posts per week and loses sleep over 'likes', but no-one is clear how that's helping meet the business' bottom line	Develops skills in public speaking and starts to channel their inner Brené Brown to deliver TED Talk–worthy presentations that help staff understand the strategy behind the posts—building trust, respect and buy-in

Develop new skills

Each time you learn a skill you're refuelling your career car, topping up to go further. Organisations are changing at a remarkable pace. To stay ahead of the game, your own skill development needs to outpace the change. And here's a home truth: if you're not prioritising your own learning, you're stagnating (or worse, falling behind).

Jade, 35
Central Coast, NSW

I was married with a 6-month-old child when I decided to leave my marriage and sell our family home. After being reliant on my husband's income for over 10 years and feeling like I had no control over money decisions, I essentially had to start again. I was in a job that I didn't enjoy and earning minimum wage. I knew I had to make a change, so I decided to complete a transition course, which gained me entry into a nursing degree. After completing my Bachelor of Nursing degree, I focused on my career and creating a life for my son where I knew I could support us both as the fear of having to rely on someone else again petrified me.

I loved working as a registered nurse (RN), but working shift work as a single parent was a week-by-week juggle and I couldn't sustain this long term. I knew that being an RN opened a lot of doors and there were endless job avenues to go down; it was just a matter of figuring out which way to go.

I decided to complete a postgraduate degree in cancer nursing and a postgraduate Certificate in Leadership and Management as I knew this would be beneficial whichever career path I decided to take. During this time, I spoke to my nursing unit manager (NUM) about her role and the more I learned about it, the more I realised that this was the role for me. It matched my strengths. I was able to relieve my NUM on several occasions and loved the opportunity.

Six months later a permanent nursing unit manager position was advertised, and I was successful in gaining this position. The NUM role has been a lot more challenging than I expected, but I enjoy the team that I work with, the hours are family friendly and there are more opportunities for my career to progress in the future.

Currently, I am planning to do my Master's degree in Health Management. I am really enjoying my role, but I like to be challenged and plan to progress further in my career over the next few years.

When I look back and compare who I am today to who I was when I decided to leave my marriage and change career paths, I am so proud that I made the decisions that I made, and I am so proud that I can provide the kind of future that I always pictured for me and my son.

Jade's story is a prime example of knowing her strengths and building new skills to fuel her career growth.

Jade identified her strengths were in influencing and leading. It's something she enjoyed doing. So she pursued her studies in leadership and management. Big tick. But, she didn't stop there. She also sought out on-the-job learning experiences. By acting in her manager's role while she was on leave she had exposure and experience to complement her study. Another big tick.

Working on these new skills, she was able to land her desired role. Plus she's built a career that aligns with her values of family!

Learning a new skill will feel uncomfortable at first, but this is part of the growth process. And in fact, according to Whitney Johnson, CEO of Disruption Advisors, once you've overcome the initial discomfort, you'll quickly move into a period of rapid learning, which is the time you're most engaged at work.

When I started my business, I was on a huge growth curve. Every day I'd face a new problem and new skills gaps. I couldn't find the right solutions. I was no longer just working in my technical skillset of HR. Suddenly, I was the marketer, the bookkeeper and the salesperson. Skills I had never developed in my career.

I was meeting with one of my mentors and she said, 'Shell, you've said "I have no idea how to do that" about five times in the last 30 minutes.' Umm yeah, because I've never done any of this stuff before.

It dawned on me. My self-talk was self-fulfilling. By constantly saying 'I have no idea how to do that' it would remain that way. My mentor reminded me that I may not have all the skills right now, but I have consistently demonstrated my ability to learn new things.

After this conversation, instead of saying, 'I have no idea how to do that', I shifted my language. I started saying, 'I don't know how to do that yet, but I know I can learn it.'

When you're starting a new job, a new career or starting a business or side hustle, trust your ability to learn new skills. You've consistently done that throughout your life and career. Don't be put off by the initial discomfort; it's the wobbly baby steps that are all part of the learning process.

The 70-20-10 learning model

When it comes to skill development, apply the 70-20-10 learning model as developed by the Center for Creative Leadership (see figure 4.2):

- *Challenging experiences and assignments:* this is where you'll do most of your skill development. It's the on-the-job projects and experiences. A great example is Jade asking to act in her manager's role while she was on leave and Bodhi joining the project team to lead training and change management. Be on the lookout for opportunities like these. Jump in and put your hand up. It's the fastest way to build your skill.

- *Developmental relationships:* this is learning through others. It's the coaching, mentoring and networking that helps you to build your skill and knowledge. We'll talk more about mentoring and coaching in chapter 6.

- *Coursework and training:* interestingly, like courses and training programs, this only accounts for 10 per cent of our learning and skill development. Most people jump straight to courses and study when they think about skill development, but this isn't the best move. Start with on-the-job experiences.

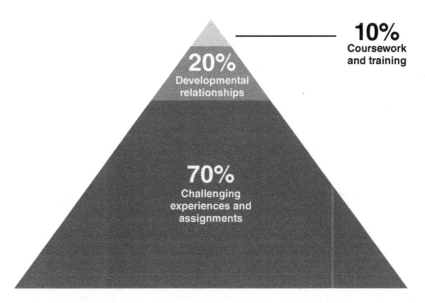

Figure 4.2: the 70-20-10 learning model as developed by the Center for Creative Leadership

apply now

I want you to consider your current role or a future role you're aiming for. Think about the skills you have currently, and the skills you need to develop to do the whole job. Next, consider what unique and different skills you could include that would help you stand out from the crowd. Write them down here.

My current or desired future role: _____

Skills needed	I have this skill	I need to develop this skill
	☐	☐
	☐	☐
	☐	☐
	☐	☐
	☐	☐
	☐	☐
	☐	☐
	☐	☐

As you look at the skills you need to develop, this becomes your career to-do list. Be on the lookout for learning opportunities and practical experiences that will help you develop these skills, keeping in mind the 70-20-10 learning model.

A final word

Discover your strengths, and assess your job or potential job options against your strengths. Aim to spend more time developing your strengths than addressing your weaknesses. Stand out by building a diverse mix of skills. Never stop learning or building your skills—they are the fuel that drives your career further, faster.

resources	**Scan the QR code for these resources and more.**	

Listen to episodes about strengths and skills on the *my millennial career* podcast.

career risks:
let's go offroad!

5

tl;dr

- To build a career you love, you're going to have to take risks. It's unavoidable. The key is to take good risks and avoid the bad ones.

- We often think about risk as a scary endeavour. But you take risks every day. It's a normal part of life. We want to help you build your risk-taking muscle.

- One of the worst career risks you can take is to avoid risk altogether.

- Before you take a career risk, you need to prepare.

- Weigh the risk against your values, strengths and career goals. It will help to inform what decisions you should make, and what decisions won't align with your broader goals.

- Remember, not every career risk will pan out exactly as you'd hoped. There will be some fails along the way and that's okay! Each time you take a risk, see it as an opportunity to learn and grow.

Risk in practice

We all experience fear when it comes to our careers. Throughout my career, I've been reluctant to take risks. My inner perfectionist is a highly strung control freak. She's left me with a crippling fear of failure and an expensive therapy bill.

A couple of years ago, it all came to a head. I was sitting at a Mexican restaurant with my sister Laura and good friend Lauren. They're both entrepreneurs who have built successful businesses. At the time, I'd made a few bad decisions and was feeling stuck in my career. I had ended up in a job where I wasn't learning or developing—I felt constrained and limited. My personal value of growth wasn't being met, which left me feeling anxious and stressed almost all the time.

I had a desire to start my own business, but I was paralysed by fear of failure. My internal feedback loop was saying that I didn't have what it takes. And it was playing on repeat. It left me feeling like I had no options. I was stuck. And I didn't know how to get myself unstuck.

A few margaritas deep into debriefing my career woes, my sister Laura leaned across the table and put her hand on mine. She blew out a deep breath and said, 'Shell, you screwed up. Accept it. Now you need to move on and make a change.'

Ouch. There it was: the painful truth I needed to hear. I sat at the table, stared down at my tacos and proceeded to cry my eyeballs out. Or maybe it was the jalapenos...who knows?

After pulling myself together from the proverbial slap that I needed, I asked, 'So how did you find the courage to start your own business?' For the life of me, I couldn't find that courage in myself. I was stuck in a rut of my own creation.

Lauren thought about my question for a moment. And what she said next is something I will never forget.

'It's not about courage. I wasn't brave; I was freaking out. I started my business because I had no other solid options. Backing myself was the best one, and what did I have to lose?'

There's a strange kind of power in stuck moments. When we're in them, we think we're out of choices. But here's the irony: stuck is a choice. Like me, you can choose to be trapped by fear of failure. Or you can choose to get unstuck by facing your fears and taking action anyway.

Your career is made in these moments. It's about weighing up all your options and making a move. It's about staring your fear in the face and making a choice to do something bold. It's about taking risks. Getting unstuck means getting uncomfortable.

In this chapter, we'll share the good and the bad career risks you can take to progress your career. We'll share how to get unstuck by taking the right career risks for you.

Why you need to think like an investor

Glen in the driver's seat

Investing your money can be risky, but it doesn't have to be. Likewise, investing in your career can seem risky, but it doesn't have to be.

Risk is the cost of entry to many pursuits, and not all risk is bad.

I find the concept of risk particularly interesting. During the countless hours I have spent talking to hundreds of clients over the years, investing risk has always been part of the conversation.

In the first part of this chapter, I'll talk about risk from a theoretical point of view; then Shell will talk about risk in practice.

Risk and investing for beginners

A rule of nature is 'the higher the risk, the higher the reward'. But a high risk doesn't mean the chances of the reward are higher—it's the opposite, actually. Before you take a risk, it's important to get a basic understanding of how risk works. Figure 5.1 will be familiar to you if you have an interest in personal finance—if not, you might learn something money related.

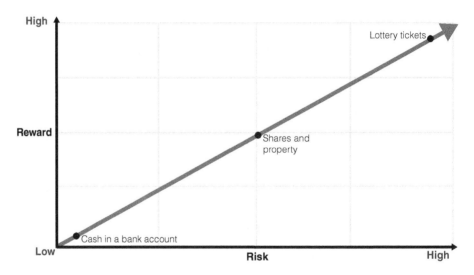

Figure 5.1: a basic investing risk reward spectrum

I want to use money and investing as a baseline for explaining risk because, just like our careers, money applies to everyone.

Generally speaking, when we look at risk charts, the following applies:

- higher reward = greater success or monetary success

- higher risk = high chance of not succeeding or failure.

When investing in shares and retirement assets (e.g. superannuation, KiwiSaver and 401k), many people have a one-stop-shop portfolio managed by an investment company that is a blend of cash, bonds, property, shares, gold and more. A basic balanced portfolio may consist of 50 per cent defensive assets (cash, bonds) and 50 per cent growth (property, shares, etc.)—see figure 5.2. This smoothes out the overall return and doesn't put all of your eggs in one basket.

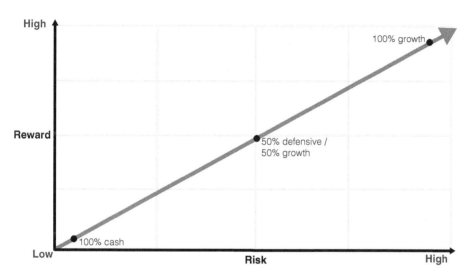

Figure 5.2: the basic risk reward spectrum for blended portfolios

When it comes to investing your money, a higher-risk portfolio will be more volatile under normal market conditions and it's suggested that you hold growth assets for at least 5 to 7 years. The reason for this is that if these assets decline in value you need to give them time to recover. Imagine if you were at retirement age and you had 100 per cent of your money in an aggressive investment...and the market declined. This would put your retirement plans at risk.

In the money world it's accepted that the older you get, the less risk you should be taking on. This way, your money is preserved ready for retirement. But I disagree with this commonly accepted notion. Here's why.

In figure 5.3 you can see a dotted line that represents that you can continue to take risks if the risks are understood. If you retire at, say, age 65, you still have a life expectancy of at least 20 years. So your money needs to be at work for you for at least another 20 years. Where I'm from, that's a lot longer than the 5 to 7 years' hold time for a growth asset. In my opinion, you can still take a risk if you understand the risk.

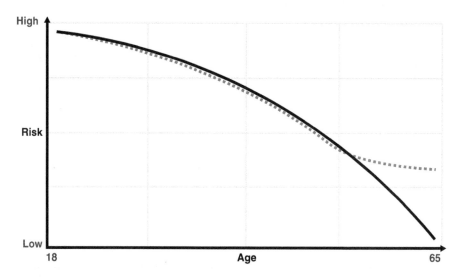

Figure 5.3:   a typical example of investment risk being reduced as you age. The dotted line illustrates that you can continue to take risks if the risks are understood

While I do agree that your financial risks should be tempered as you age, I don't believe you should move all of your money to cash (in a bank account, that is) when you turn 65. It's only a worry to be taking risks with your money if you don't understand the risks, have no solid goals or your values are not aligned. This can lead to a catastrophic outcome. Likewise, you need to understand your career risks, which means having career goals that align with your values.

Assessing your career risk

There is risk in every area of our lives: crossing the road, taking medication for an illness, going on an overseas holiday, skydiving…Many people don't even consider the downside of skydiving, for example. They only think about the joy and fun they will gain from it (unless the risk plays out, that is).

Why do people undertake risky activities on holidays with friends, while they won't ask their team leader for a pay rise because it's too risky? Maybe because there is not much resistance or buy-in for a risky holiday activity and endorphins are flowing. Any risk calculations are usually thrown out the window. But, your career is different. There is no peer pressure from excited friends while on holidays 'in the moment', but there is office politics, there is the confrontation that comes with putting yourself out there, there are awkward conversations and the chance of rejection…the list goes on.

We fear things we haven't experienced before or don't understand. We feel the pain of loss more than the joy any gain gives, so avoiding loss is a normal reaction.

When it comes to your career and the risks you take, it's about understanding that you may be 'out of shape' and you didn't even know it: you need to start exercising your 'risk muscle'.

Even the meekest of people can learn to be confident in risk assessment and taking risks; and conversely, natural-born risk takers can learn to ensure risks are worth taking.

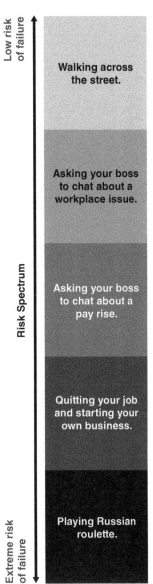

Low risk of failure

Walking across the street.

Asking your boss to chat about a workplace issue.

Risk Spectrum

Asking your boss to chat about a pay rise.

Quitting your job and starting your own business.

Playing Russian roulette.

Extreme risk of failure

Figure 5.4: example of a risk spectrum

Figure 5.4 depicts a risk spectrum: from everyday risks like walking across the street, to risks with potentially catastrophic consequences, such as playing Russian roulette. The purpose of this chapter is to help you step back and perhaps reset your risk profile. Many people feel that asking their boss to catch up for a chat regarding a workplace issue carries an extreme risk of failure. The fact is, it does not, but that doesn't change how you feel. This chapter will help you put risk in perspective and slowly start to exercise your risk muscle.

> I want to encourage you to lean into risk and start small. Walking across the street does have a low risk of failure, but the risk is still there (you could get hit by a bus). Conversely, playing Russian roulette has an 'okay' risk on paper—a 1 in 6 (16.6 per cent) chance of failure—but the failure is absolutely catastrophic and irreversible, so it should be avoided at all costs. Thankfully, in our day-to-day career life we aren't presented with such catastrophic failure risks, even if it might sometimes feel like it.

The cost of entry to cross a street is the chance of being hit by a bus, but we're happy to pay the cost of the risk of stepping out onto the street: it is second nature and so built in (because we always do it!) that we don't even think about a risk assessment. I think a healthy baseline level of career risk is asking your employer to chat about issues, salary, education and training opportunities—which are all similar to walking across the street.

Enter the workplace and your career. We're all exposed to risks at some time that we aren't used to. Talking to our boss, asking a co-worker to not floss their teeth at their desk or asking people at a team meeting, 'Whoever the lazy person is who doesn't fill up the water cooler after they empty it, please pull your head in'—these are risks because you're putting yourself out there.

The funny thing about confrontation is that we only hate it when there could be an adverse reaction. You can knock on your boss's door spontaneously with a box of doughnuts and ask if they would like one. They could say, 'Go away—you're fired', but that's unlikely (though it's still a risk). If your boss isn't hungry and is a reasonable person, they will politely decline and smile. But knocking on your boss's door spontaneously and asking them for a pay rise? That's risky, and could be awkward, so you wouldn't take that risk.

Learning the basic practical concepts that Shell teaches around situations like asking your leader if you could discuss your role and pay removes a whole heap of perceived risk and pent-up awkwardness because you have a legitimate strategy for approaching the risk. If the answer is 'no' to the pay rise at this time, at least you took that risk and perhaps have started a great working relationship with your boss for the future. By setting up the conversation appropriately, the outcome isn't as instant as what you would have liked, but you've moved a whole heap of risk from the outcome and therefore you have taken the risk by going about it the right way. You would have also worked on exercising your risk muscle!

At the end of the day, the reality is that many employers are fine with talking with their employees about workplace issues and their role. I know for many people this is a hard thing to do, but I honestly feel it needs to be the base level of risk in your career.

> Here's a task for you. Can you book a meeting with your boss to catch up about your role? Not to ask for anything. Just to say you want to come up for air to see how everything is going. If you have scheduled performance reviews, that's great, but I want you to still do this and tell your boss or leader that you would like an informal catch-up to see if they would like you to be doing anything differently.

(continued)

If you do this and it isn't something you would usually do, it's a great way to work on your 'risk muscle'. It's like you're offering doughnuts; there is no real downside. But as we know, there are risks to everything. The risk may be that if you're a slack and lazy worker, they may tell you, 'Oh, it's a good thing you asked to catch up because I want to chat to you about your lack of performance.' So be careful what you wish for. Luckily, this example is not you, as this type of person would rarely pick up a career book and invest in their own career.

Not being slack and lazy is a good hygiene factor for any valuable member of society. Make sure you are, and continue to be, skilled in your job—and don't be lazy or sloppy.

Some of the workplace examples I have used may seem like a risk to you, but I believe these smaller risks can be diagnosed as a lack of confidence. Stepping back and looking at these things through a risk lens—by, for example, arranging a meeting with your boss—will enable you to see the downside isn't all that scary and it could give you the confidence to really exercise your risk muscle!

Risks, values, strengths and skills, and goals

You can have all the confidence in the world and still be a conservative person in terms of career risks. That's totally fine. I wouldn't suggest otherwise if that isn't you. You might not want to start your own business or quit your job with no job lined up, but I'd like you to work on having the confidence to speak up and not put up with crap in the workplace.

Being quiet and shy shouldn't make you a pushover in the workplace. It just means you should have the confidence to ask to speak to someone in private to bring up an issue, or tell your manager if something is not right.

For the confident and outgoing personality types I would suggest you don't draw undue attention to yourself. Allow me to give you an example.

I was 25 years old and there was a staff meeting of 15 people at my workplace. Someone could smell and hear popcorn cooking in the kitchen (an unlikely office smell and sound) and there was chatter around this. The next minute, I walked into the meeting (late) with a bowl of popcorn. I hated office politics, staff meetings and the usual storm-in-a-teacup rubbish. As I sat down, with everyone looking at me, I was like, 'What? This is entertainment, so I made some popcorn…anyone want some?' Silence.

It might be easy for my personality type to take risks and be confident, but the skill is to learn how to control it. Don't be like me.

When we look at ourselves and our career progress, risk is only a small part of the equation. It's an important part though, because it's often the final stage of a career move. However, many people believe risk taking is the first and final part of a career move. Not so.

Consider this: an Olympic diver takes a risk by jumping off a 10-metre platform, but not before first working on the foundational things such as personal health and fitness, sessions with sports psychologists and practice dives. There is extensive work involved in getting to that Olympic dive (risk).

I want to reiterate that the risk part is only the execution: many ducks have to be lined up first to enable you to have the best shot of landing that dive (or career move).

Your own strengths, skills (including confidence) and values are the initial steps on your way up that diving board. Once you've established these, the perceived risk might not be as dangerous or scary as you initially thought. The practice of building your confidence can make you stronger and build up your tolerance and capacity for taking good career risks.

So before you take the plunge, factor in these things and it will make the jump a lot easier and less scary and you'll have more of a chance of landing that perfect career move.

You always need to factor in your values, strengths and skills, and goals as part of healthy risk taking. If I climbed up to the top of the 10-metre diving board illustrated in figure 5.5 without the correct preparation, there's a high chance I'd injure myself trying to dive. I need to start on the lower levels and make assessments before I move up to the real risk I want to take.

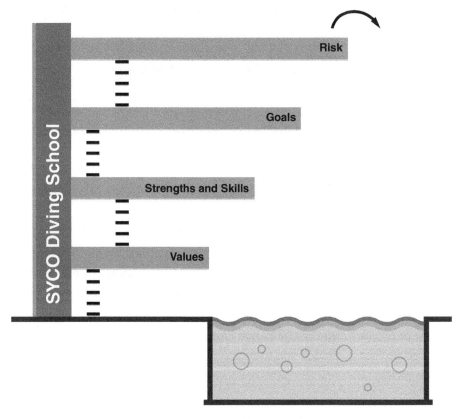

Figure 5.5: your career diving board

Creating risk because you didn't consider the known unknowns

Let's look at a scenario.

You were head hunted for a job that is closer to home, in the same industry and pays 15 per cent more than what you're currently on. It's very similar to your current role so you know what's involved. Your strengths and skills meet all the requirements, which means you're confident you have what it takes to succeed. There's also no risk of rejection because they approached you about the job. There's a lot of ticks.

The job offer meets the practicalities boxes, but it still needs to be assessed against your values and goals. The opportunity will help you achieve one of your career goals, which is to make more money. It meets your value of spending more time at home as there are no long commutes.

The only issue is that you've heard some questionable things about this company's culture and ethics. There are some interesting Glass Door reviews (Glass Door is a career website) and a few ex-employees in your network have said the culture isn't great.

In this instance, a large portion of risk has been removed because you were head hunted and it's better money. This means you need to focus on the values alignment and not be distracted by the benefits of more money.

✔ Goals

✔ Strengths and skills

✗ Values

(continued)

While the offer meets two key criteria, there's still a considerable risk involved. So wait before you say, 'Yes. When do I start?'

In this scenario, it's important to find out as much as you can before taking the risk to a level you're comfortable with. During the interview, ask questions that focus solely on the values part of the equation. Questions like:

- What is great about the culture here?
- What do you want to improve about the culture?
- What is the turnover of staff like here?
- How would you describe the employee experience?
- What leadership style works best here?

You can also ask to meet with other members of the team to hear about how they find the workplace and their roles.

The issue is that by ignoring one of the most important career aspects (your values) you may be exposing yourself to an unnecessary and perhaps reckless risk.

Let's say you accepted the role without asking these questions and it was a toxic work environment. You will end up in a world of pain. By going into the interview and resultant discussions with the known unknowns that you have identified, you can turn down the role without risk even coming into the equation.

Conversely, if you saw a job going for the most warm, fuzzy, rainbows and unicorns company and it ticked your career goals and values but you knew you'd need to work on your strengths and skills (or confidence), you might be prepared to take that risk because you trust your ability to develop the skills to perform the role.

My career risk spectrum

I'm a visual learner and teacher so I've created figure 5.6 to depict what I think the career risk spectrum may look like.

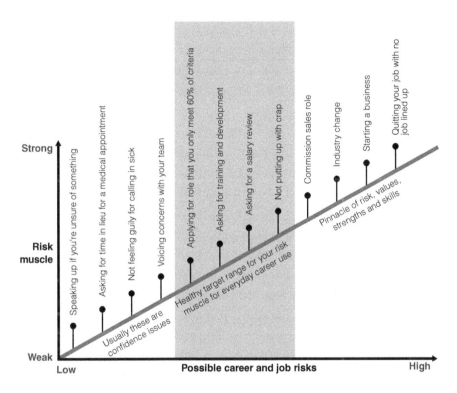

Figure 5.6: my career risk spectrum matrix

This might be confronting to look at, particularly if you're not a naturally confident person. However, I believe you have the best shot at a healthy and satisfying career if you try to get yourself into the shaded part of this matrix. While the risks described in the matrix are just examples and could differ for women, men, industry or vocation, I want to highlight that many people will have a more rewarding time at work if they can confidently approach their boss or team leader for a healthy discussion.

The cool thing is that once you learn how to ride a bike, you'll never forget. Many of us have scars on our knees from learning to ride a bike, and it does take practice, but learning low-risk endeavours such as voicing a concern with a team member will become second nature and stay with you for the rest of your career. The first time you catch up with your team leader or boss may feel sloppy or awkward, but it's just part of learning how to ride that type of bike. This is why I encourage you to practise by meeting with no agenda other than to catch up or check in outside of regular reviews, for example. It's all about practice. Practise diving from low-diving boards and be good at that before you worry about trying out for the Olympic team with a 10-metre specialty.

I hope you're starting to understand that risk, values, goals, strengths and skills are intertwined. Once you get comfortable with hanging out in the shaded section of the career risk spectrum it can be easier to progress into more 'riskier' ventures.

It really doesn't matter what examples I have used in the matrix. It's more to get you thinking about due process for your career moves to enable your career to be fruitful and to have the best shot of removing risk. You might be reading this thinking 'my friend has low confidence and is not a risk taker, but they started an online business selling penny whistles and moonpies and are killing it!' I would say that's awesome, but like gravity and the basic laws, we don't get a pass on this. I've seen countless people start a business and it's been at the right place at the right time with the right thing. The business takes off but some of the components needed to take appropriate business risks could be lacking and there may be a heightened chance of being taken advantage of by customers, suppliers or other stakeholders. This is not always the case and I just want to emphasise that this stuff is not gospel, but it's a good analogy to think about, particularly if you're just starting out on your career. So please sprinkle some salt over the matrix when you examine it!

Can you draw your own matrix, based on your own circumstances, and include some baseline hygiene factors that you may need to consider in your current role?

Keeping things tight

So what does it all mean? How do you have the best shot at looking at a job change, career change or stepping out to self-employment?

Figure 5.7 shows what could be a typical career risk line.

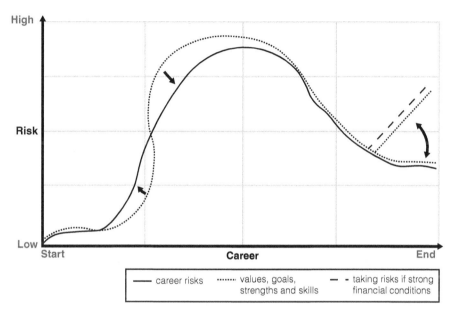

Figure 5.7: a career risk line

Here are some important points about figure 5.7:

- The beginning of your career is usually not a time when you would take big risks, so if you're reading this as a new graduate, apprentice, trainee, someone new to the workforce or even as an immigrant to a new country or culture, get settled in your job or career first. Find your flow, get the lay of the land and understand your industry culture and norms.

- Not taking career risks right away can enable you to work on the hygiene factors that are needed in your role (strengths and skills). Slow down—your time will come. It's okay because you will be developing your career goals and a plan!

- As your career progresses, taking risks will become a habit relative to your situation and personality, and be in line with your goals and values. You may never take a risk of starting your own business or quitting a stable government job, but within that role your risk muscle should be getting stronger because you are taking 'internal risks' such as asking to speak to your boss or team leader about matter-of-fact issues regarding your role.

- The dotted line represents your values, goals, strengths and skills. These need to be as tight as possible to the risks you take. If you are taking risks in your career away from this line, there is a higher chance that you will not succeed or be content in your endeavour long term. There is no need for unnecessary risk taking when these things are not aligned. You may stop taking risks if you don't take them in line with your values, goals, strengths and skills. You may have an experience that risks never pan out, but is it because they were not aligned with your values, goals, strengths and skills?

- As I've touched on already, it could be considered a commonly accepted notion that the older you get, the less risk you should take (remember the investing example?). I disagree with this for the same reasons as I disagree with the investing example. If you understand the risks and are comfortable with them, there is no reason not to take a career risk at any age—but there may be some financial considerations as you get older.

- You'll see that at the end of your career you will be at a higher baseline for taking risks because over time your risk muscle ideally gets stronger.

As you get older, you need to ensure that your financial foundations remain strong and that you have appropriate buffers in place. You can theoretically take a large risk at any age. However, the older you are, the less time you have available to recover from this if it doesn't play out.

The insurance policy for this as you get older is to have solid foundations behind you because you may not have 15 years to recover financially in the workforce if you started a business at age 62 and invested a heap of your retirement wealth into your business idea that didn't pan out. Having strong financial foundations may mean you can take that risk, and if it doesn't pan out it's not akin to a catastrophic risk such as playing Russian roulette.

In the sound financial house I detailed in chapter 3, you may choose to buy a home to live in before taking a risk and starting your own business. The key here is to keep your cash flow agile, stay out of consumer debt, get good at saving and investing, and have an emergency fund behind you. All of this can help give you comfort in taking career risks.

apply now

Practical ways to assess risk

For anything you believe is going to be a career risk, you always need to assess the risk—but you need to also look at the possible upside. We know as humans we will default to looking at the loss, because this hurts more, while failing to appreciate any potential upside.

You need to get this stuff on paper or on a spreadsheet—somewhere out of your head. Or just jot your thoughts down here:

The risk: _____

Upsides you can think of if the risk plays out:

_____

_____

_____

(continued)

Downsides you can think of if the risk does not play out:

_____

_____

_____

How it aligns with your values:

_____

_____

_____

_____

How it aligns with your career goals:

_____

_____

_____

_____

The strengths and skills you have for this risk:

_____

_____

_____

_____

What time horizon you need to prepare for executing the risk (usually the bigger the risk the more time needed to plan):

_____

For the preparation and 'time horizon' part, it might mean you need 6 months before you execute the risk as you wish to finish a training program at work, clean up consumer debt and build your emergency fund to feel more confident. Make sure you also think about physical factors in your life. There would be nothing worse than executing a risk on the week that you need to move house. You need as much clear air as possible for risks, both in the non-tangible and the tangible factors of your life.

Spend the coming weeks going over this list and thinking of as many things as possible to add to each section. Talk with a trusted friend, family member or mentor about your risk. But first do a few drafts to get it out of your head and onto paper. You might decide it's a non-starter after writing it out. This may remove any perceived embarrassment of showing a friend, family member or mentor (although they wouldn't care either way!) and will allow it to simmer for some time before you tell others.

I also want you to ask yourself, once you have brain dumped the above, 'Would I tell my best friend to take this risk?' This can often help.

In chapter 3 I talked about cost–benefit analysis. Perhaps you can run a cost–benefit analysis of this on the assumption that the risk will work. This will also help you in deciding whether it's even worth it—particularly if everything else aligns (i.e. values, goals, and strengths and skills). Some things might just not be worth doing. Just because you can, doesn't mean you should.

What if you take a risk and it doesn't work out?

Thankfully you didn't wake up today and decide to play Russian roulette before breakfast. The smaller risks that we take in our lives have a very low chance of a catastrophic outcome.

Sure there is a risk that you could be asked to pack up your desk and not to come in tomorrow if you ask your boss if you can have a word with them about the working environment. Unlikely, but in that instance there is a risk that the issue you want to bring to your boss doesn't get resolved, but just because the meeting wasn't instantly fruitful it's not a catastrophic outcome. You have used your risk muscle and practised. The good thing about taking risks is that you get practice in taking that risk regardless of the outcome. This is the silver lining.

By following the instructions in this book around values, goals, strengths and skills and then the practical things about CVs, meetings, interviews and so on, if the risk that you take doesn't play out I do not believe it will have a net negative impact on your career. This book is the fence at the top of the hill as opposed to the ambulance at the bottom for risks.

So what do you do if you take a risk and it doesn't play out?

I'm not sure—but I can tell you that it was definitely worth taking. Welcome to life. You are now a stronger and more resilient person!

Shell and I both hope that you don't take risks that aren't considered, calculated and in line with what you want out of your life and career.

Start small, keep moving and take that risk!

Career risks: The good, the bad and the ugly

When it comes to your money, there's good debt and there's bad debt. Glen talks a lot about this in his book, *Sort Your Money Out & Get Invested*. The same goes for your career. There are good risks and bad risks.

Remember the saying 'nothing ventured, nothing gained'? Well, I hate to break it to you, but to build a career you love, you have to take risks. The key is to take the right risks—the good risks—and to avoid the bad ones.

Taking risks is the fourth step towards career road trip success (after values, goals, and skills and strengths). Think of someone's career you admire. From the exterior, it might seem like it all fell into place for them by coincidence, hard work and a bit of luck. But dig into their story, and you'll quickly learn about all the courageous risks they took to get there. The freakouts, the sleepless nights and the bold decisions.

Taking risks is a central theme of every epic career. Why? Because good risks are like rocket fuel in your career path. They propel you forward. They fast track your growth. They open up opportunities you never imagined were possible.

In our research for this book, Glen and I were surprised to learn that out of the whole career map, the area of 'risk' is the one people struggle with the most.

So many people set out to avoid career risks at all costs. They play it safe. They stay in their comfort zone. And they let fear rule their decision making. And this is one of the worst risks to take in your career. Prioritising current comfort and certainty over future opportunity and growth comes at a big cost. In our careers we want to create as many opportunities for the future as we can. It means we have to take good risks regularly.

So what are the good and bad risks? Daniel Pink's research for his book *The Power of Regret* found that over time people regret inaction—the things they didn't do—far more than the things they did do that didn't go to plan. It's what he describes as a 'failure of boldness'. A deep regret for our own inaction.

This idea is so true in our careers.

Take this common career dilemma as a case study.

You've just seen a job advertised that you really want (like, *desperately* want). It ticks all your boxes. Great role, great workplace, great growth opportunities. But you're not sure if you have the skills or experience. On paper, it sounds like a bit of a stretch. So here are your options:

1. You apply for the job you really want, and you get it.

2. You apply for the job you really want, and you don't get it.

3. You don't apply for the job you really want, and you don't get it.

Which scenario will result in the greatest levels of regret?

The answer, of course, is option 3. You have zero chance of getting the role you want if you don't apply for it. If you go for it, and still don't get it, well at least you put your hat in the ring.

We firmly agree with Daniel Pink's assertion. People regret inaction more than the actions they do take. Taking action is a central part of building a dream career. It requires you to put yourself out there. It requires you to take a risk. But no risk, no reward.

A small caveat: we're not saying all risks are good for your career. Some risks are unwise. And we don't want to downplay how challenging these moments can be. Career decisions are high stakes. When you're in the middle of a tough decision, it's easy to do nothing to avoid doing the 'wrong' thing.

We want to save you the pain of trial and error. Instead of having to figure it out for yourself, we've put together our list of good and bad career risks. You can use the list to self-assess your own risk-taking behaviour.

As you read through it, ask yourself:

- What risks do I need to start taking that I've been avoiding?

- What bad risks have I been taking without realising?

Five good risks you need to take

It's a risk to not take any risk. But, as a risk-averse control freak, I get it. It's hard to know what risks you should and shouldn't take. So, here's our list of five good risks you need to take if you want to build a career you love.

1. Acknowledge your fear and take action anyway

Fear is a powerful force. We tend to respond to fear in extremes. We either want to ignore it completely, or we let it dominate our thoughts and actions.

Instead, we need to develop a healthy relationship with fear. Acknowledging your fear is the right place to start. From here, we can recognise the fear and better understand the concerns. But, don't stop there. Once you've acknowledged fear and weighed it up appropriately it's time to take action.

Don't just take my word for it. Simran Kaur's story is the perfect example.

Sim, 25

Co-host of the *Girls That Invest* podcast and author of the book *Girls That Invest* (NZ) New Zealand

When I was 8 years old a teacher told us that we'd be different from the generation before us, and that we'd never stick to just one career in our lifestyle.

'Not me,' I thought. I loved the idea of being in one field forever. I like stability. I liked the idea of being very knowledgeable in one thing and perfecting my craft.

I also came from a background where you'd be taught to choose a career that provided security over using your strengths. Being a lawyer, doctor or engineer felt like the only options available. I ended up becoming an optometrist out of the love of a secure career that also interested me. I thought I had hit the jackpot. No work to take home, high work satisfaction (how often do you scream at your local optometrist?) and an interesting variety of work. I never thought I would leave.

I started to notice an itch I had to be creative. Healthcare is quite rigid in the way that we go about things, for obvious reasons, so I'd often go home with a lot of energy to do something that fulfilled the creative side of me. I liked to create new things and build moments. I didn't realise it at the time, but what I was truly seeking was the excitement and thrill of bringing something new into the world that was bigger than me.

Very soon I found myself creating an online community and posting content about an issue dear to my heart: lowering the barriers of personal finance. In the same way that I would spend all day as an optometrist breaking down medical jargon to everyday people, I realised I had a knack for doing the same when it came to money, specifically how I managed my money. I ended up with a huge dilemma, with one part of me wanting to stick to what I always knew, and another part of me knowing I needed to dive into this new opportunity head first. It took months of convincing from my friends, family and even my own colleagues, but eventually I transitioned into a whole new field—leaving behind 5 years of training. Was the jump worth it? Absolutely. I wish I had done it sooner.

Sim knew the risk of the jump: the feeling of free-falling in a job that is less secure and safe. She took the time to weigh up and balance her fear against the potential wins, happiness and reward in pursuing her creative plans. It wasn't simply a matter of making up her own mind either. She had to be convinced by those around her it was the right move too.

Don't let the people around you dictate how much risk you're willing to handle—acknowledge the fear, but don't linger there. Focus on the opportunities you'll be saying yes to in making that move.

2. Back yourself

How many times have you boldly declared 'Back yourself!' to a friend or family member? Now, how many times have you said those same two words to yourself? Chances are, not nearly enough.

As people, we're quick to remind others they have what it takes. We see the potential in our friends and family. We're their biggest fans. We see their genius and strengths and we remind them to trust themselves. We give them all the reasons they can do it. But when it comes to telling ourselves that same thing? Well, we kinda suck at it.

Backing yourself feels risky. We question and second guess our abilities and skills constantly. Why? Because self-trust is hard work, and self-criticism comes easy.

We focus on the few times we'd failed and use that as proof that we can't trust our own judgement. Instead, we need to remember and remind ourselves of the countless times we've made good decisions and had big wins.

Taking good risks requires you develop your level of self-trust. It's not about living in ignorance. No, you'll still need to acknowledge your self-doubt, skills gaps and negative thoughts. But it's about not letting those rule or control you. To move beyond those thoughts you need to truly listen to yourself. Create time and space to uncover what you want, to learn what's important.

3. Ask for help

There are two truths you need to hear:

1. You need help.

2. People want to help you.

I've worked in HR for over a decade. I've met with hundreds of employees in that time, and I've seen a lot of different problems in the workplace. One common theme stands out: people don't ask for help nearly enough. But more than that, they don't ask for what they want or need in their career.

Asking for help and asking for what you want at work is a good risk to take.

There are so many things we can and should be asking for at work. You'll find a few ideas in the lists that follow. As you scan each list, tick the ones you've asked for.

Role changes and team culture:

☐   A promotion

☐   Support to find a new role in the business you're working in

- [ ] A chance to redesign your job description to better align with your strengths and skills

- [ ] For your boss to hire additional team members to make the workload more sustainable

- [ ] A higher duties role while your manager is on long service leave

- [ ] More team-building activities to improve engagement and connection

- [ ] A team workshop focused on culture and team communication.

Training and development:

- [ ] A coach or mentor to help you grow

- [ ] A training course or learning program to develop a particular skill

- [ ] Financial support towards your studies

- [ ] Paid time off for study and learning opportunities

- [ ] Flexibility

- [ ] Ability to work from wherever you want

- [ ] Ability to choose your own hours and work schedule

- [ ] A four-day work week

- [ ] A career break (extended leave) to travel

- [ ] Pay and benefits

- [ ] A pay rise

- [ ] Benefits like extra leave, corporate fitness program, flexible public holidays and additional superannuation

☐ Paid time off to volunteer

☐ Company shares

☐ Access to a wellbeing or employee assistance program

☐ A reference from your boss when you're ready to move on

☐ Better coffee because, I mean come on, Blend 43 just doesn't cut it.

Okay, time to tally it up. How many of these have you asked for? Call me presumptuous, but I think you've asked for way less than you could have.

We all need help. And most people (if they are half decent) want to help you. Good leaders know you perform better when you're engaged, fulfilled and happy at work. So it's a win-win for your workplace to help you.

If you've been waiting for a sign to ask your workplace for something, this is it! Don't put off asking for what you want or need at work. To progress in your career, you're going to put yourself out there. You'll need help and support from your boss, from your peers, from your family, from a mentor or a coach.

Ask for help. Ask for what you want. Ask for what you need.

4. Set healthy boundaries

I first noticed I had a boundary problem early in my career. One of my colleagues resigned. She was working full-time, overseeing recruitment. When she finished up, the business decided to save money by absorbing her role.

They asked me to take on her duties in addition to my full-time job. It was a big step up from what I was doing, so I said yes without thinking.

A few weeks into the role, I found out I wouldn't be receiving a pay increase. It was sold as a 'great learning experience'. And it was, for a while. But in time, I became stretched too thin. I was working too many hours, constantly stressed and delivering work I wasn't proud of. I didn't have boundaries in place to protect my own wellbeing and maintain quality performance.

When I said yes to taking on the role, my excitement had gotten the better of me. I was only thinking about the short-term wins, and overlooking the long-term impact. I forgot to ask questions that would set both me and the organisation up for a win.

If I had my time over, I would have still taken on the role as it was a great career opportunity. But I would have asked questions upfront to establish boundaries and set expectations.

Questions like:

- How will we manage the increased workload?

- What additional resourcing will be in place to backfill my existing role?

- What will the new rate of pay be?

- If there is no immediate pay change, can we schedule a review of the pay at 3 and 6 months into the role?

- What support will be available to help me develop?

These questions are designed to clarify expectations and boundaries early. It's not about saying 'no'. It's about how the arrangement will work best for both parties, and pre-empting any points of concern down the track.

When you're in the early part of your career it can be easy to focus on short-term wins. But this is short sighted. Your career is a long game. A lack of boundaries can lead to burnout. Saying 'yes' to every single thing your boss throws at you might work in the short term, but it's not sustainable in the long term. Studies have shown that an increase in workload leads to fatigue (no surprises there), but it also impacts performance. We don't perform better with more work.

Healthy boundaries are crucial for high performance and having a healthy and sustainable career in the long term.

Be smart and honest with your manager about the work you can do, but particularly the workload you know you can do well. This isn't about shirking responsibilities—this is about ensuring you do your job to the best of your ability for the benefit of the workplace. And it's also about making sure you enjoy what you do each day! If your workload is exploding, and you're drowning, you're not going to perform well at work and chances are you'll be fatigued, stressed and deeply unsatisfied in your career.

You need to set boundaries at work. If your workload has reached an unreasonable level, talk with your manager about it. If you're getting slammed with work calls or texts outside hours, talk to your manager about it. If you're being asked to do work way out of your skillset or role, talk with your manager about it.

Not all managers are supportive of your boundaries. But remember this is your career we're building—not your manager's.

If you find it hard to say no to additional work, consider this: boundaries aren't about saying no. Boundaries are about saying yes to what's most important to you. When I say no to working on Saturday, it's because I'm saying yes to spending time with my family. When I say no to rescheduling my annual leave, it's because I'm saying yes to taking a break (hopefully poolside in Fiji or something). When I say no to checking my emails at 11 pm, it's because I'm saying yes to binge watching true-crime documentaries on Netflix.

What are you saying yes to?

It's valuable to focus on common goals when you're setting boundaries. Don't make it all about you. Communicate the shared interests between you and your manager and how those shared interests will be negatively impacted without clear boundaries.

Here are a few ways to communicate boundaries to a manager or team member:

- *I would love to help you with that. For me to start working on it, I'll have to stop spending time on X project. What would you prefer I focus on right now?*

  In this scenario you're highlighting the need to make a trade-off decision. Your capacity and time aren't infinite. To work on a new project, you'll have to stop working on something else, which is the shared interest you need to bring to your manager's attention.

- *I'm worried if I say yes to this, I won't be able to deliver a quality outcome because of the other work on my plate. What can we drop to make this happen?*

  In this scenario you're highlighting that the quality of work will drop if you are spread too thin, which is the shared interest.

- *I'm not able to work on that tonight because I've got family commitments and wouldn't be able to give it the time it needs. If I rush through it, I'm concerned about the risk of errors. Is the deadline for that able to be pushed out a few days? Or can someone else jump in?*

  In this scenario, in order to do the work, you'll have to rush through it, increasing the chance of errors. This is the shared interest.

- *I'm struggling to get deep work done with the amount of interruptions and distractions in the office. When I work from home I am able to do deep and creative work and I'm much more productive. Is it an option for me to work an extra day from home each week?*

  In this scenario the shared interest is being productive and getting more done. Your manager wants you to be your most productive and efficient self so use that as the selling point for setting a boundary about remote work.

Your boundaries reflect what you value most. If you value quick wins and short-term success, say yes to everything. If you value long-term wins and a sustainable career growth, set good boundaries early.

5. Take a career break

Breaks. Can't live with them, can't live without them.

I don't know about you, but I'd always been bad at taking breaks. I'd eat lunch at my desk, I'd hoard all my holidays and leave. And I'd smash chunky Kit-Kats every other day because I thought that's the only break I had time for.

Well, I was wrong (more on this when we talk about burnout in chapter 8). Breaks are crucial for your performance and wellbeing. They are essential for doing deep and creative work.

Like boundaries, taking a career break can help you to have a healthy, sustainable, successful career in the long term. Still not sold? Let's take some notes from my friend Scott's story.

Scott was in his early 30s, working as an account director at a major Australian telecommunications business. He was overseeing a key account, leading a bid that went over 18 months. It was a very high stakes project and Scott was working huge hours to make sure they landed the contract.

He and his wife Rach had a young family, with three kids aged three, six and eight. He'd leave early in the morning and get home well after his kids were asleep at night. It was a tough time. Scott knew the project was coming at a cost, but he felt like there wasn't any way around it.

After months of work, it was finally go time. They would find out if they had won the contract. All the time and energy invested came down to this one moment.

Scott got the call: they'd lost the contract. It was a big moment for the entire business. And it was a turning point in his career.

Scott refers to it as a 'jolting moment'. A shake up. A wake-up call. 'I'd been swept up in my career and missed out on what mattered most; my family.'

Scott and Rach decided it was time for a break. A big one. 'We hatched this plan to travel around Australia. By the next week we'd looked at campervans and started getting things organised.'

Scott approached his boss to ask for 6 months of leave. It was a big ask, but he knew he needed this time with his family. Scott knew that whatever their decision, he had still resolved to go, so it was a matter of detail to him whether he would be taking unpaid leave, or ultimately resigning. After a couple of conversations, they agreed to give him the 6 months off and supported his decision.

Within a matter of weeks Scott and Rach had leased their house, bought a Winnebago and they were on the road. The mobiles were switched off and in the glove box. And it was time for a real break.

Taking a break like this comes with significant risks. When Scott decided to take a break, it was during the aftermath of the global financial crisis. The job market was looking bleak in 2009. But when I asked Scott about how he weighed up the risk, his answer was simple: 'I wasn't thinking about my career, I was thinking about my family.'

For Scott, his decision to take a career break was less about risks and more about investment. 'You choose what you invest in, and using that time to invest in my family was one of the best decisions I could have made.'

Work is not your life. And your life shouldn't be all work.

You don't serve your career; your career has to serve you.

When taking a break, Scott didn't overthink the career impacts. He knew work would always be there. He focused on his personal values and priorities. They were the guiding focus in his decisions.

And surprise, surprise, his career looked after itself. After spending 6 months on the road, he returned to his employer—to a promotion. His break had been a chance to rest, refresh and have a once-in-a-lifetime experience with his family, and it had consequently benefited his career.

This is the counterintuitive thing about breaks. We think they slow us down or mess with our momentum or goals. But often the opposite is true. They can help us to press the reset button on our priorities and lead to exciting new opportunities.

It's important to acknowledge that many people are not in a financial position to take an extended career break. It's a privileged position, so we want to call that out.

The good news is, a career break doesn't have to be extended to be effective. You could take 4 to 6 weeks off and experience similar benefits from that. When was the last time you took 4 weeks off consecutively? If you can't remember when, then it's probably time to start planning for a solid break.

Five bad risks you need to avoid

Okay, so not all risks are good. Like the one who tells you to invest in crypto... that's right, they know that out of more than 12000 cryptocurrencies 'this coin is the one'...Okay mate! Sure! You'd likely want to avoid this risk if you want to keep your money!

Here are five bad career risks you need to avoid.

1. Attaching your identity to your job

What would happen to your sense of self-worth if you lost your job today? It's not a rhetorical question. I want you to genuinely consider it. How would you feel about yourself?

I've seen many people make the mistake of attaching their identity to their job (and I've done this myself—it was a bad time). When work is going great, you're great. But when things don't go to plan, watch out. Your identity is going to take the hit.

Let's say I was at a wedding with a stack of people I'd never met before. I don't walk up and introduce myself by saying, 'Hi, I'm Shelley Johnson, a business owner and HR Consultant.'

That would be weird. HR consulting is what I do. It's not who I am.

There is a significant distinction between who you are and what you do.

So many other parts of my life come before what I do for work. Like, my role as a mum, wife, daughter, sister, friend and aunty. These roles have, over many years, shaped who I am and they inform who I want to become.

As for my job and career, well, yes, it's important, but it's not who I am. And sure, I'd be in a difficult position if I was to lose my job suddenly, but if that was to occur, I wouldn't lose my sense of self-worth.

When your identity is tied to a job, it puts you in a dangerous, high-risk position. It makes you dependent on something that is ultimately out of your control.

There's a lot you can't control at work. Your job gets restructured or made redundant. You apply for a promotion, but you're rejected. You get a new manager and they don't value your contribution. These are common scenarios that are outside your control. They are hard to navigate at the best of times, but it becomes far more challenging when your identity and self-worth rely on your job.

It's crucial to separate who you are from your work. Your value is not found in your job title, salary or career path. Of course, a good career will give you a sense of meaning, purpose and fulfilment. But it's not your identity.

What you do is always secondary to who you are becoming.

Separate your identity from your work. Focus more on who you are becoming—then what you do, will look after itself.

2. Staying too long in a toxic culture

Out of all the career problems you can face, working in a toxic culture is up there with the worst of them. And as if working in a toxic culture wasn't bad enough already, leaving a toxic culture can be extremely challenging.

I've often wondered what makes leaving a toxic workplace so difficult ... Maybe it's the corporate gas-lighting, which has left you questioning your own experience, wondering if you're the problem and causing you to buy the lie that you deserve to be treated poorly.

Or, it's a mild case of Stockholm syndrome, where you become so tangled up in a toxic culture that you don't know how or when to call it quits.

Well, consider us your search and rescue team. We are here to cut through the confusion, and remind you that you are not indebted to toxic workplace culture. A business that isn't loyal to you, doesn't deserve your loyalty.

One of the problems is we've become so familiar with the word 'toxic' over the past few years that it's lost some of its impact. So what does 'toxic' actually mean?

> **toxic [toksik]**
> *adjective*
>
> 1. poisonous material or toxin capable of causing harm, death or serious debilitation
>
> 2. extremely harsh, malicious or harmful
>
> 3. very harmful or unpleasant in a pervasive or insidious way.

A toxic culture is poisonous. It slowly seeps in. It can be so subtle that you don't notice it straight away, but its effects are obvious in time. A toxic culture erodes people's joy, wellbeing and confidence at work. And what's worse, it can take a very long time to rebuild it after you've left.

If you're not sure what a toxic work culture looks like, here are five attributes prevalent in a toxic culture according to MIT Sloan's research:

1. *Disrespectful:* people are not treated with dignity, kindness and courtesy

2. *Non-inclusive:* people are not treated fairly or equally and are excluded due to specific demographics (race, sexual identity, gender, age, disability)

3. *Unethical:* people behave in ways that are dishonest and lack integrity. There is a lack of compliance

4. *Cutthroat:* people use ruthless behaviour, backstabbing and cheating to get ahead. Those who display this behaviour get results and are often rewarded in a toxic culture

5. *Abusive:* hostile and abusive behaviours, like bullying and harassment, are tolerated and accepted.

If these behaviours show up frequently in your organisation or team, you're probably in a toxic environment. Changing a culture like this is not impossible, but it takes considerable time, investment and hard work. It requires complete ownership from the senior leadership to bring about the desired change.

If the organisation's leaders have communicated a need for culture change and they are taking action to fix it, it may simply be a matter of time before things change.

But, if there is no awareness or desire from key leaders in the business to change the culture, it is unlikely to occur. This is going to sound blunt, but if this sounds like your workplace or team, it's not an environment worth staying in. The cost of staying in a toxic culture is far too high.

3. Playing it safe and staying comfortable

I'm sure there are many of you thinking, 'Oooh, this one's for me'. I get it. Change can be scary. It feels safer where you are. But the truth is, staying in your comfort zone is far from safe.

In fact, one of the greatest risks you can take in your career is to take no risk. It causes you to stagnate and plateau. And with the pace of change, if you stagnate, you fall behind (as we talked about in chapter 4 around developing new skills).

You know the feeling when you sit down in a chair in the doctor's waiting room and you think, 'Ah yes, I'm going to sit back and rest my feet for a bit'. Thirty minutes goes by, you shuffle in your chair to shift your weight a bit. Okay, your left leg has gone a bit dead. But you can't be bothered standing up.

Then one hour goes by and now your lower back is aching from the poorly designed chair. You hit the 2-hour mark (what a wait!) and this stupid chair has become the cause of all the pain in your life and you've completely forgotten why you're even at this damn appointment.

This is what happens with safe career choices. It feels safe at the beginning, relaxing even. But long term, sitting still is not a strategy. It creates other forms of pain and discomfort. So don't take the risk of playing it safe. Find yourself a role where you're growing, learning, being challenged. Take a risk on a job that feels a little beyond your capability. The stretch is good for you. It's the kind of work where you'll feel most fulfilled.

4. Allowing perfectionism to take control

Will all the perfectionists please stand up? But wait! Before you do, make sure you stand up as quickly as possible. Don't falter. Oh, and stop slumping your shoulders. Hold your head up high, but not too high. No, not like that. Oh, don't even bother. Just sit back down.

Sound familiar? Perfectionism is the devil on your shoulder disguised as the angel. You think it's helping you, but in reality it's preventing you from making progress and taking good risks.

As a recovering control freak, I've been slowly extricating myself from the death grip of perfectionism. For most of my working life, I spent my commute home from work replaying my day. I'd beat myself up for the things I did do, the things I didn't do, the things I wish I'd said, the things I shouldn't have said, and the list goes on and on.

The first podcast I ever recorded on *my millennial money* was the perfect example of my perfectionism in action. Glen, John Pidgeon (co-host of the *my millennial money* podcast) and I finished the recording on how to ask for a pay rise. And on the drive home I started critiquing every little thing I said. I was freaking out about how I'd come across, what people would think of me and whether I was good enough.

So what did I do? I let my perfectionism take over. The next day, I called Glen and asked him if we could do the whole thing over again. He reluctantly agreed to let me re-record, despite the time, effort and cost involved.

In the years since then, I've never lived it down. At our team Christmas party, I was rightfully awarded the 'Most High Maintenance Host' Award because I am the only podcast guest in the history of *my millennial money* (400+ episodes) to ever re-record an episode. *Sorry team*

I used to think perfectionism was a strength—a sign of my desire to achieve great things. But now, I see it for what it really is: an ego problem. Oof—that hurts.

After recording my first podcast, I was consumed with worry about what people would think of me. Would they see me as intelligent, funny and engaging? Or would I be found out?

Well now you know. I'm not perfect (but hey, at least I'm honest).

It's helpful to remind yourself that perfectionism is ego hiding in plain sight. It holds you back, keeps you contained and stops you taking good career risks. Instead of aiming for perfection, aim for progress and watch what happens.

5. Avoiding honest conversations at work

You know the terrifying 'we need to talk' moments. I'm not talking about when you catch Ava stealing from your snack drawer. I'm talking about the high-stakes moments when you need to raise a concern or give someone tough feedback.

People go to extraordinary lengths to dodge these conversations, like they're a grenade guaranteed to blow up their working lives forever. Yet in most cases, we overestimate the impact of having the conversation, and severely underestimate the impact of avoiding it.

I was chatting with my friend Jack the other day. He loves his job and his team, but Jack's relationship with his manager is a bit strained.

His manager is technically capable, but seems to lack some of the people skills needed to lead, and gets offended easily. This combination has made it hard for Jack to raise his concerns.

It had been a few months since Jack and I had spoken, so I called him to see how he was going with it all.

Let me run you through the play-by-play of our conversation.

> Jack: *'Things are really bad. I don't know how to fix it.'*

> Me: *'What have you done to try to address the issues so far?'*

> Jack: *'Not much. I don't want to rock the boat, so I just work around it.'*

> Me: *'Do you think your manager knows how you feel?'*

> Jack: *'Nah. They're not very aware of how they impact people.'*

> Me: *'Do you think you're helping them by not communicating how things are going?'*

> Jack: *'Probably not. But giving constructive feedback to a manager never ends well. So I'm not going to talk to them about it unless they specifically ask me for my feedback.'*

> Me: *'And how is that working for you? Is it bringing about any change?'*

> Jack: *'Mmm. Not really, no.'*

No conversation, no change.

It's as simple and as complicated as that.

Dodging difficult conversations can be easier in the short term, but it is simply storing up the pain to be dealt with at a later date. Putting off tough discussions like this one doesn't help anyone. Least of all you.

That's why it's important to build your skill in having honest conversations at work.

In every workplace, you'll encounter problems that call for an honest conversation.

Here's our three-step guide to navigating a tough conversation at work. Similar to the three-step framework for communicating a values conflict in chapter 1, here's our framework for communicating a concern at work.

The three-step risks framework

1   *Core:* the first step is to identify the core conflict for you. What's at the heart of the issue?

2   *Situation:* next, describe the situation or give an example that supports the concern raised.

3   *Impact:* finally, communicate the impact this situation has had on you or others.

Example scenario

Your organisation has just hired a new manager, and you feel like they are micromanaging you. Your previous manager gave you autonomy and discretion over your role and the new style of leadership is jarring and frustrating.

Let's walk it through together. The core of this issue for you is trust, so we use that as the focus of the conversation.

1   *Core:* I want to chat with you about something I've noticed lately and look at how we might solve it together.

There have been a few situations recently where I've felt that I'm not trusted (core concern) in my role. I'd love to talk to you about it to see what your thoughts are.

2   *Situation:* I noticed in the client meeting I was running last week, that you jumped in and ended up leading the meeting.

In most of my client meetings previously, I have led the discussion as the account manager and key contact with the client.

Did something happen that made you feel you needed to jump in?

3   *Impact:* I know it's probably not your intention, but when you took over, I felt sidelined from the conversation. It made me feel as though I wasn't doing a good job or couldn't handle it, which knocked my confidence a bit.

I think it also could undermine my credibility in front of the client, which doesn't benefit the relationship in the long run.

In the past, I've consistently had great results in these meetings, so I'm keen for your feedback. Are there things I'm doing that I could be doing differently?

From my perspective, I work best when I feel I have trust and confidence. How might we work on building trust?

apply now

Have a go at filling in the three-step risks framework for yourself:

Example:

1   *Core:* the first step is to identify the core conflict for you. What's at the heart of the issue?

2   *Situation:* next, describe the situation or give an example that supports the concern raised.

(continued)

3   *Impact:* finally, communicate the impact this situation has had on you or others.

Your turn:

1   *Core:*

_____

_____

_____

2   *Situation*:

_____

_____

_____

3   *Impact*:

_____

_____

_____

4   What bad risks have you been unintentionally taking?

_____

---

5 What good risks could you start taking?

A final word

A good career requires you to take good risks. Build up your risk tolerance by starting small. Don't jump straight into quitting your job and changing careers.

Take small steps. You'll start to see the practical benefit of risk taking. From here, you can work up over time to the bolder steps.

Remember, as Daniel Pink suggests, the biggest regrets are the failures of boldness. So be bold and back yourself.

---

resources   **Scan the QR code for these resources and more.**

- Download the three-step risk framework.

- Download the practical risk assessment exercise.

hitting the road

i'll make my own opportunities, thanks

6

tl;dr

- Career opportunities don't magically appear out of thin air.

- You create career opportunities by building great habits.

- These habits continue on, even when you aren't 'looking' for a job. Over time, they act as an opportunity magnet.

- You need to own your career, not be owned by it.

- There are ways to create career opportunities if you're fresh out of school or university, or changing industries altogether.

Shell in the driver's seat

Grace had been in New York for about three months. She was working odd jobs at cafes, bars and a super-cute boutique jeweller called Catbird. She missed her Australian family, but she was determined to make the most out of her 12-month working visa. If you'd told her back then her 12-month trip to the United States would end up lasting almost a decade, she never would have believed you.

One afternoon, Grace was on her way home from work. She was walking up the stairs of her Brooklyn apartment building, when she noticed the door to apartment 103 was left ajar. Her curiosity got the better of her and she peered in.

She saw two guys in their mid 20s, dressed head to toe in expensive suits, sitting at office desks. It looked like something from the set of *Mad Men*. Their apartment was buzzing, fully decked out as a luxurious, upscale office. She was intrigued. So she knocked on the already open door. 'Umm hey, what are you doing in here?' They both looked up, mildly irritated by her intrusion.

'We're working.' They went back to typing away on their laptops.

'What are you working on?' Grace pressed, oozing all the Aussie charm she could muster.

'We're building a technology platform to help people sell their products on social media,' one of the guys responded.

Grace wasn't sure what it was exactly, but she was drawn to them. They were building something exciting and she knew she had to be a part of it. So each day she kept knocking on their door to say hello. She was determined to build a relationship with them.

Within the month, Grace worked up the courage to ask them for a job. They said no. And it wasn't a gentle no either. It was a hard no. They couldn't afford to employ her. But Grace wasn't easily deterred. She told them about her experience working in marketing agencies in Australia and asked if she could work for them as an intern or volunteer. She thought at least they would give her a reference she could use when she went back home.

They finally relented. She was offered an internship. Grace was finally on the books (or at least kind of, in an unpaid sort of way).

Within 6 months, the business had grown rapidly. James, the founder, offered Grace an official, paying job as an account manager. Over the next few years, her role grew and evolved. She's still living in New York. Her 12-month visa was a stepping stone to building her dream career. Fast forward to today and she's the Vice President of Strategy at Fohr, the very business she stumbled on all those years earlier.

Grace's story shows us the power of creating your own opportunities. Successful careers are built by knocking on doors that others walk by. Grace could have squashed her curiosity and walked by apartment 103 that day. She could have let self-consciousness, fear or ego stop her from asking for a job. She could have passively sat back waiting for the next thing to fall into her lap. But if she had done that, she would have never ended up where she is now.

Do you own your career or does it own you?

I don't know how to say this gently, so I'll just say it straight: stop waiting for people to give you opportunities. It's time to start creating them.

In this chapter, we'll share how you can create career opportunities everywhere you go. Using these strategies, you'll never be short on options.

Oh and spoiler alert: it's not about your goals. It's all about your habits. Good things come to those who create them.

Get ready: we're about to hit the freeway on your career road trip.

Before we start goal setting (coming up in the next chapter) we'll share the career habits that act as an opportunity magnet. If followed, they bring opportunities to your door (or LinkedIn inbox). As James Clear points out in his book *Atomic Habits*, 'You do not rise to the level of your goals. You fall to the level of your systems. Your goal is your desired outcome. Your system is the collection of daily habits that will get you there.'

The most successful people take responsibility for their career. They don't sit back hoping to be tapped on the shoulder for the next job. They aren't channelling Hermione Granger and casting 'Accio promotion' spells. They know the real magic is to make things happen.

They don't let fear stop them from putting themselves forward for a big opportunity. They are the kind of people who start doing the job before they get the job. They have mastered career habits that generate opportunities.

Emily Bowen, co-host of the *my millennial career* podcast, talks a lot about the power of owning your career. She calls it 'career self-reliance'. It's an empowering, liberating and challenging idea. It means you are responsible for your career. Not your boss. Not your mentor. Not your life coach. It's on you.

Unfortunately, I've seen so many people relinquish control of their career. They get out of the driver's seat and become the passenger. They hand control over to their employer, hoping their manager will sort things out for them. Instead of owning their career, their career owns them. Big mistake. Why? Because no-one cares as much about your career as you do. No-one will advocate for the things you want in your life, except you. No-one is going to drive your career forward like you will. So get out of the passenger seat and drive this thing.

Career opportunities: A cautionary tale

Nick stared down blankly at his box of belongings. It's hard to imagine 11 years of work fitting into a single box. But there it was. His 'personal effects'. Two framed family photographs. A bottle of his favourite hot sauce. A half-empty box of Earl Grey tea. And two packets of pens he swiped from the stationery cupboard on the way out (because after all these years, he bloody well deserved some fresh ballpoints).

Nick took one final look around before switching off his office light and closing the door. He sighed heavily as he hopped into the elevator and headed for the car park. He unlocked the car, shoved his box into the boot and slammed the door shut. As he drove out of work for the last time, he wondered how he ended up here.

8 hours earlier ...

Nick got to work early that day. Danica, the managing director, invited him to an urgent meeting. He'd heard the news already. Everyone knew. The company had lost its third contract in as many weeks. Three major revenue streams, all gone due to what the company labelled 'external market forces'.

It was unsettling for everyone. But as one of the key leaders, Nick had helped the company weather many storms over the past 11 years. Every business has its ups and downs. Today was no different: just another bump in the road.

He grabbed his laptop, made himself an Earl Grey tea and headed to his meeting with Danica. He was ready to tackle this challenge head-on.

When Nick arrived, he noticed something was a little off. Danica seemed nervous. Dark circles lined her eyes. She mustn't have slept well last night. 'Is everything okay?' he asked as he sank down into one of the lounge chairs. Danica exhaled slowly. 'No, Nick, it's not. This is going to be a hard conversation. We need to talk about your role.'

Nick's heart began to race. He glanced down, surprised to see his hands were shaking. He gripped his mug more tightly and hoped she wouldn't notice. 'Okay, what's going on?' He sounded more confident than he felt. Danica paused and looked at him, her face pained. 'We're making your role redundant, Nick. I'm so sorry.'

The rest of the meeting passed in a strange blur. Nick can't remember what was said. But he remembers how he felt. The churning nausea. The brutal finality. The overwhelming fear of not knowing what to do now.

Nick never imagined his role would be made redundant. It shattered him. He'd sacrificed so much for his job. The long nights and weekend work, kids' birthday parties and family events.

At the time, he'd told himself it was all for a purpose. He was on track to progress. The board had implied he was in the running to become managing director one day. Nick was in it for the long haul. He was planning on staying until retirement. But one meeting changed everything.

The months that followed were difficult. Not only had Nick lost his job and income, he'd lost his sense of purpose. His self-worth was entwined with his work. He wasn't sure how to move forward.

His whole working life and world was built around this one job and company. He'd failed to build a strong network outside of the business, which made it challenging to secure his next job. It took almost 12 months for Nick to land his next opportunity.

I wish Nick's story was unusual. Sadly, it's all too common. Many people become so immersed in their current role and company that they fail to create opportunities beyond it. This is short sighted. Your career is a long game. And to play the long game and win, you need to continually create opportunities for yourself.

Creating opportunities doesn't happen by accident. It requires action. But before we get to actions and habits, let's do some further analysis into Nick's story. It's crucial to understand why creating career opportunities matters and what went wrong for him so you can avoid it in your career.

There were three problems in Nick's approach to his career:

Problem 1: His goals were outside his control.

Nick had two goals. The first: to become the managing director one day. And the second: to stay with the organisation until he retired. Both of these goals were ultimately outside his control. He deferred responsibility for his career progression to the board, who he hoped would eventually appoint him to managing director when the current director resigned (again, not in his control). He'd made an assumption that his existing role would always be there, and was immune to redundancy.

When your career plan relies heavily on factors outside of your control, it's a problem. It doesn't mean you don't need help from people to achieve your goals. As we discussed in the last chapter, getting help from others is crucial. What we're saying is you need to plan for a range of outcomes and set goals that are within your ability to influence.

Problem 2: His career plan lacked diversity.

A good financial adviser will teach you to diversify your investment portfolio. The same holds true for your career. Nick failed to diversify his career portfolio. He stopped building relationships and networks outside of the business. All his career equity was tied up in a single organisation. When he was made redundant, he lost it all.

I want to be clear: staying with one employer for an extended period is not a bad thing. If you find an organisation you love—amazing! Milk it for all it's worth. What I am saying is it's invaluable to be invested in relationships, connections and opportunities outside of your current workplace.

Many people don't think about this until they've hit a crisis point. They don't have these networks in place for when they desperately need them. They are suddenly scrambling to grow their connections, build a LinkedIn network and find opportunities. Instead, you want to have developed your relationships and options slowly over time so when you need them most, they're primed and ready to go. One less stress to worry about.

Problem 3: He didn't have a contingency plan.

A great financial adviser will also teach you to build up an emergency fund as a contingency, in the event of an unexpected crisis or financial problem. You might have income protection insurance for those unforeseen events.

Likewise, your career needs a contingency plan. Your goal might be to land the managing director position, but it doesn't have to be limited to your current workplace. Be open to a range of options. Consider how various economic conditions may impact your employment, and take control by preparing for those scenarios.

Ryan Holiday, in his book *The Obstacle Is the Way*, explains, 'the only guarantee, ever, is that things will go wrong. The only thing we can use to mitigate this is anticipation. Because the only variable we control completely is ourselves.' Ouch. Tough love.

If you really want to know how you can avoid a situation like Nick's, the answer is: build the right habits.

Ten career habits that bring opportunities to your door

If you're waiting for me to tell you that a successful career requires you to wake up at 5 am, meditate for 45 minutes and have 4 hours of screen-free time each day, don't worry. I'm definitely not going to do that.

I do not wake up at 5 am. My kids are my alarm clock and my morning routine is anything but zen. It's pure chaos, covered in cereal and mixed with tears (mainly mine). As for Glen, well he doesn't function until 11 am because, well, I don't really know why. But good luck trying to meet with him before lunch.

When we say 'career habits' we're not giving you a list of prescriptive rules you must follow religiously to avoid being doomed for a working life of pure misery. We're not very good rule followers here. We're simply sharing a range of habits that act as an opportunity magnet.

As you read through the list, try them out for yourself. Test which ones work best for you.

And here's our guarantee: if you practise any of these for an extended period, they will open up opportunities you never expected. They are a sure-fire way to fast-track your career (no spellcasting required).

Habit #1: Find a coach or mentor

Professional athletes and sporting teams have coaches. All elite athletes know that great coaching is critical to their success. What's more, they don't just have one coach, they have multiple coaches, each for a specific aspect of their training.

Likewise, you need a coach or a mentor in your corner (and, realistically, more than one). You want a coach who pushes you beyond your comfort zone. Someone who helps you to overcome internal barriers and limiting beliefs. Someone who challenges you to grow.

Meeting with a coach or mentor on a regular basis can have a game-changing (no pun intended) impact on your career. A good coach or mentor will help you navigate complex problems at work. They can show you ways to build your skills. They can give you advice about how to communicate with your employer to generate opportunities down the track. In those meetings with your coach, you can reflect back on your work performance, and identify the areas you want to grow and develop.

I have three people that I consider mentors in my life. They help me in different areas, based on their unique skillset, experience and background. They are people I trust implicitly and are my go-to for independent, practical and authentic advice.

I've never actually said to them directly, 'Hey, will you be my mentor?' but it's implied. They are further along their journey, which means they have wisdom and insight that I don't have. They are people I deeply respect and I want to learn from.

It's not formal, but it is intentional. On average, I catch up with them about four times a year, but I call them more often than that to get specific advice whenever I have a challenging problem I'm dealing with.

What makes a good mentor?

Deb was my manager for about seven years (lucky or not-so-lucky Deb). Eventually, we graduated from that relationship to an even better one. I now consider her my friend and mentor. For many years, she's been the person I call when I've been in some of my most challenging work and personal circumstances.

If I asked her, 'How many times have I cried my eyes out when talking to you?' I don't think she would be able to give me an answer. Too many to count.

So what makes Deb a good mentor? Well, firstly she is one of the most trustworthy people you'll ever meet. But secondly, she could not be more different from me. She's calm, level-headed, thoughtful and considered in all she does. Her ability to listen and understand is something to behold.

So for me—as an emotionally turbulent, verbal-processing, loose cannon— she is the exact person I need as a mentor. The differences in how we think have enabled her to challenge my self-talk and limiting beliefs.

She's been the person to say; 'Hmm, do you think that's a good idea, Shell?' and equally, the voice saying 'back yourself' and take the risk. Having worked in human resources for 10 years longer than I have, she has developed a depth of skill in the field over that time. Basically, I'm saying find your own Deb.

But if that still feels a little ambiguous, here's a detailed list of what to look for in a mentor:

- They must be trustworthy, honest and reliable. If they are not all of these things, they will not be a good mentor.

- They must genuinely want you to succeed and grow, and not be threatened by your success.

- They should be respected for their knowledge and skill in a particular area that you're wanting to grow in. You don't go to a physiotherapist for legal advice. Likewise, you don't want a mentor who doesn't have the knowledge, credibility and skill to help you.

- They should have different strengths from you. You want them to see the world from a different perspective, as it will help to challenge your own logic.

- They don't have to be older than you. It's a common fallacy that a mentor has to be older than you. I looked for mentors who were 'further along the journey', not older, than me. They need to be ahead of you in order to guide and teach you, but that's not about age.

How do I find a mentor?

Informally:

- You can find a mentor in your current workplace or through networking events. All you need to do is simply ask someone you admire to meet regularly with you. Offer to shout them lunch in exchange for an opportunity to learn from them. I've seen this work really well for many people. It doesn't have to be complicated or awkward. Keep it simple.

Formally:

- You can also go through a more formal mentoring or coaching program. For example, you might engage a career coach to work with you for a defined period of time. Although it may be an expensive investment, it's one with high returns so definitely worth considering.

- Many industry groups have mentoring programs that you can pay to participate in. They have trained mentors who they can match you with based on what you're wanting to achieve.

Whatever option you choose to pursue, having a mentor or coach who you see regularly is a habit that will provide great benefit for you throughout your career. They can be your sounding board, your advocate, your cheerleader and your honest guide.

apply now

Think: who in your world could be a useful mentor for you? Write down their names and where their strengths lie for you in your journey.

Name	Their strengths

Habit #2: Diversify your career portfolio

As we saw through Nick's story, we don't want all your eggs in one employer's basket. There's too much risk involved. We want you to diversify. It doesn't mean becoming a jack of all trades and master of none. Going deep on your technical skillset is super beneficial for your career. It's about building diversity in your career portfolio.

If you're thinking, WTF is a 'career portfolio', good question. Your career portfolio is made up of six things:

1. It's your network or relationships

2. It's the roles you've performed in the past

3. It's the future roles that are available to you with your current employer

4. It's your skills and experience

5. It's your qualifications

6. It's the types of businesses or industries you've worked for (e.g. corporate, small business, charities or not-for-profit, public sector).

When your career portfolio is limited to a single employer, job or business, you rely heavily on them to make things happen for you. By building a diverse network and trying a few different roles at different organisations and in different industries, you'll open up more options.

Say you work in construction management and your career goal is to manage high-end residential builds. But, you haven't got the experience in this area as your employer specialises in commercial construction. Right now, your experience and skill is what holds you back from achieving your goal. A great way to overcome your experience gap is to build your network and relationships with people in residential construction. As you connect with people in that specific field, you can gain an entry point into that area.

Consider the six areas of your career portfolio: what areas lack diversity right now that you could take action on?

What areas of your career portfolio can you work on?

_____

_____

_____

_____

_____

Ashayla, 30
Perth, WA

I was working in logistics and admin for a medical company while studying a degree in writing and publishing online. During this time, I ran a number of successful Facebook pages and found that not many businesses in WA were running their socials with a business mindset—or just weren't on social media at all. I pitched to a few marketing agencies that they needed to provide social media services to their clients and why. One place gave me a job doing just that. While working for this company I learned about content and digital marketing—things like SEO and SEM. I read everything I could, and I was soon hired by a not-for-profit to run all their marketing.

A year later I was poached by another agency. The pandemic hit, I panicked, put my feelers out and revamped my resume. When applying for other jobs to further my career, I created a portfolio instead of a standard resume and this really helped me gain attention in my field. An offer from a school seemed interesting, so I slipped into running marketing, media and communications there—including photography and videography.

Now I work for the government and have just started up my side hustle consulting on social media, content and digital marketing for small businesses. I also guest lecture on the topic at a university.

Ashayla is the poster child for owning your career. She's built her network like a pro; she found gaps in the job market for her skills and seized those opportunities. By proactively reaching out to people to offer her services, she created momentum.

She also diversified her experience by working in a range of industries. From agency work, to not-for-profit and now in government, she gained a breadth of skill and exposure that makes her stand out. She's creating demand for her skills no matter what the industry. Ashayla has become an opportunity magnet.

Habit #3: Plan for the best, prepare for the worst

In a world that loves daily affirmations and manifesting the good vibes, I find a sick sense of satisfaction in preparing for the worst.

Seneca, the stoic philosopher, said, 'the man who has anticipated the coming of troubles takes away their power when they arrive'.

Glen regularly talks about planning for the worst on *my millennial money*. He says, 'Ask yourself: what is the absolute worst that could happen? Get specific. Write it down. If that happened, would you be okay? Will you survive? What could you do to move forward after this?'

It's not about being cynical. It's about preparation. With this kind of preparation, you won't be blindsided by an awful thing happening. It gives you power, control and agency. It means you own your career, instead of being owned by it.

Over my career, I've consistently prepared for the worst outcomes. Not because I'm some pessimistic miser (although I may be that), but because it's useful. It means that I've never been overly concerned about these things occurring as I've prepared for them.

As an example, in my early career, I worked hard to build up a three-month financial buffer in my emergency fund. This meant that if I ever ended up in a job I didn't like or if for some reason I needed to suddenly leave my employment without having my next job lined up, I could do so without financial pressure or stress. It was a strategic move that gave me choices. It gave me control.

Because I find this kind of planning fun, I've put together a little career scenario planning tool for you (see table 6.1).

This is not an exhaustive list. There are plenty more worst-case career scenarios. But, it's a great (albeit confronting) starting point.

Table 6.1: career scenario planning

Scenario	Likelihood	Impact	What can you do about it?
Redundancy or unexpected end of employment	Medium	High	• Use emergency fund to get through period of unemployment • Leverage network to look for new opportunities • Engage a recruiter to support your job search
Burn out (or needing to take an extended period of leave for health reasons)	Medium	High	• Take any paid leave available • Use emergency fund to enable extended leave • Seek out support through doctors, psychologists, employee assistance and/or wellbeing programs • Connect with a mentor/coach • Allow sufficient space to fully recover
Working in a toxic culture	High	Medium	• Have constructive conversations in the workplace to seek out improvements • If the toxic culture is limited to a specific team, look for opportunities in other roles, teams or departments • If no improvements are reached in a reasonable timeframe, look for new employment
Starting a new job and realising it's not for you	Low	Medium	• Make sure you ask good questions up front to assess if the job is right for you (this will reduce the risk likelihood) • Communicate what's not working for you to your manager • If no improvements are made, start applying for other jobs • Use the probationary period (first 6 months) to assess the alignment

(continued)

Table 6.1: career scenario planning (*cont'd*)

Scenario	Likelihood	Impact	What can you do about it?
Needing to leave your job before securing another one	Medium	High	• Use emergency fund to get through period between roles • Leverage network to find next role
Employer relocates interstate and requires you to move in order to continue working	Low	High	• Evaluate the change against your values • If the move doesn't suit, leverage network to look for new opportunities that do suit • Engage a recruiter to support your job search
Your all-time favourite manager resigns and the new manager is an incompetent narcissist who makes your life a living hell	Medium	High	• Raise your concerns in the appropriate channels, review the policies—e.g. anti-discrimination, anti-bullying or employee grievance policies • If no changes are made, or the response is not sufficient, begin looking for other employment
Working in an organisation that tolerates bullying and discrimination	Medium	High	• Review the policies—e.g. anti-discrimination, anti-bullying or employee grievance policies • Raise your concerns in the appropriate channels • If no changes are made, or the response is not sufficient, begin looking for other employment
Leaving job on bad terms	Medium	Medium	• Try your best to leave every role amicably, but where this is not possible, ensure you're able to have references lined up from previous roles • Communicate the exit to future employers in a way that doesn't bad mouth previous employer, but communicates honestly why it didn't work

Feeling encouraged and excited to encounter these scenarios? Yeah, nah. But at least you're prepared.

Planning for these scenarios gives you an element of control when most people would feel out of control. It reduces the power of those situations and lessens the stress they may have on you.

apply now

What hazards and scenarios are you preparing for? What's concerning you? What's the worst that could happen? Get your fears down on paper to disarm them.

Jot down a list of actionable things you could do next if any of these things do happen.

Scenario	Likelihood	Impact	What can you do about it?

The best scenarios can come from the worst ones

Zain was a diesel mechanic, by trade, but he worked as a fly-in, fly-out worker for a large mining company on the other side of the country.

(continued)

It was hard to be away from home so much, but the pay was next level. His plan was to keep working there for another 3 to 5 years. Financially, it would set him up for life.

Well, that was the plan. Until his worst-case scenario occurred. Zain was injured at work. He was in chronic pain and was unable to work for 6 months. It threw his well-laid plans right out the window. For months, he tried everything to return to work. He went through all manner of treatment and rehab, but nothing worked. The doctor wouldn't clear him to return.

The role was no longer an option for him. He had to finish up.

Zain had built up a financial buffer, giving him time, space and options. Not having to rush into the next gig was a lifesaver for him. He used that time as his own career break to figure things out.

And 6 months after leaving that job, he launched his own business. Within one year of starting he was making more than what he was in the mines. He didn't have chronic pain or have to do all the travel.

It's funny that out of a really tough situation, his business was born.

Sometimes your worst-case scenario leads you to your best one.

Habit #4: Build your personal brand

I hate to break it to you, but we are all in the business of sales. In your career, you're the product. You're the service. You're the marketer. You're the sales manager. And the employer is the customer. So what can you do to close the pitch and seal the deal? You need a strong brand.

I used to cringe when I heard the term 'personal brand'. It conjured up an image of a sleazy salesperson who was obsessed with perfecting their image and promoting themselves (no offence to the people in sales out there). But over time, I've learned how crucial building a personal brand has become in the modern world of work.

A personal brand isn't 'image management'. It's not about creating a facade to blast over social media. It's about becoming known for something.

I want you to think of an influencer or celebrity you love. For me, it's Zoë Foster Blake. I am a raving mad fan of absolutely everything she does (like every other millennial woman out there). I'm often sending her Instagram posts to my sisters saying, 'She can do no wrong!' Because to me, she can't. I've bought in, hook, line and sinker to her personal brand. I feel like I know her. She's fun, down-to-earth, smart, cheeky and hilarious.

So whatever she's selling, I'm buying. Her skin-care products. Her children's books. Her novels. I don't care. Sign me up baby.

This is what the power of a personal brand can do for you. It creates connection, influence and the clincher: magnetism. A good personal brand has magnetic energy. It draws people in. Instead of pushing your resume and cover letter out there, a good brand draws potential employers in.

If you position yourself well and show what you're good at, people will begin to know who you are and what you offer. They'll come to you, knowing the value that you bring.

So how do you build a compelling personal brand?

Now that I've convinced you of why you need to build a strong personal brand, it's time to create your own. Here are two easy steps to help you make it happen.

Step 1: Define what you want to be known for

What are you known for at work? Are you seen as the go-to for solutions or the go-to for office gossip? Are you known for your consistency or for your unreliability?

Whether you've thought about it or not, you're known for something. Within your workplace, you have a reputation. This is your personal brand. If you're not intentional about it, your brand may not serve you well. That's why it's valuable to define and clarify what you want to be known for.

A hallmark of a strong brand is that it conjures words, feelings and ideas in people's minds. It's easy to spot, understand and grasp. Its reputation goes before it.

When you think of a well-known brand like Nike, for example, words will immediately come to mind. For me, I think of action, hard work, motivation and, of course, 'just do it'.

A company's brand is shaped by the way it communicates with customers, its online presence and the products or services it provides. Companies have clear brand guidelines that help them to be consistent. It's the same for your personal brand. Once you've defined it, it acts as a guide, informing how you show up, engage and communicate at work.

But, I want to stress, it's not about becoming someone or something else. It's about turning up the volume on what sets you apart from everyone else. It helps you to amplify what makes you unique and distinctive.

Here's mine as an example.

	I am	I am not	It looks like
1	Bold	Abrasive	Bold truths, served up with a whole lot of love
2	Fun	Immature	Bringing fun vibes, not cheap laughs
3	A leader	A know-it-all	Leading and influencing people, but staying curious (because no-one likes a know-it-all)
4	Smart	Complex	Smart insights, communicated simply. No corporate jargon or pseudo-intellectual crap
5	Relatable	Fake	The go-to person for authentic convos over Friday arvo drinks

Clarifying what you do and don't want to be known for keeps you accountable and consistent. From here, you'll start to be recognised for these things in your workplace.

Step 2: Be genuine

People can spot inauthenticity and BS a mile off. It's like that 'lousy Vuitton' bag your mother-in-law bought you on her recent trip to Thailand. Thank you so much! *shoves straight into the regift drawer*. Your brand should be genuine. The real deal.

When it comes to building your personal brand, think like a marketer about all the ways your customer (the employer) interacts with you:

- What's your tone of voice?

- How do you show up online?

- What are your emails like? Personable or a hot mess?

- Are you late, dishevelled or disorganised?

- What are you like on the phone?

- Do you keep team morale high?

- How are you dressed?

- Do you look to connect with your teammates?

- Do you go above and beyond for customers?

---

apply now

1 Choose five words that define your personal brand.

2 Define what your brand isn't. Choose five words that oppose your brand. The things you don't want to be known for. This will help distil your brand with more clarity.

(continued)

3   In a single sentence, communicate what each area looks like in action.

	I am	I am not	It looks like
1			
2			
3			
4			
5			

How can you live this out at work?

_____

_____

_____

_____

_____

Habit #5: Encourage and support others in their career

At work, there's so much focus on becoming the most valuable player. We want to be the captain, the point scorer, the coach—but there's not enough focus on the cheer team.

Over the past couple of years, I've set myself a challenge to become the cheer captain in people's careers. I want to be that person jumping up and down on the sideline, supporting those around me in the crucial moments of the game.

In chapter 4 we talked about finding your strengths. The cool thing is, once you know how to identify your own strengths, you can become a strengths finder for the people around you.

For me, I am determined to become this person, so I wrote myself a post-it and stuck it on my laptop, to make sure I see it every day. It's my reminder to be the strengths finder and cheerleader for the people around me.

And just quietly, I think this should be a career goal for every person.

There's something immensely powerful about celebrating the successes of others. Sending someone a quick encouraging text might seem small, but it can have a massive impact. Just think about a time your boss sent you an email with positive feedback about how amazing you are. Ahhh, I love those moments.

When you celebrate the achievements of others, you don't lose out. You both win. And this isn't just an outrageous claim from me. It's known as the 'helper's high'. Research shows that selfless support of others increases your own health. Being generous with your words, actions and support helps the receiver, and it also benefits you. It improves your psychological state and decreases stress and negative emotions. The more encouragement, the more positive emotions. Legal highs for everyone!

Each week, set yourself a goal to send an encouraging text or email to one person at work or in your network. Be specific. You're not giving them a 'well done' sticker like you got in year 2 at school. The more detailed your encouragement, the more impact it will have.

---

apply now

Who can you encourage in their career? How can you do this?

_____

_____

_____

_____

Habit #6: Develop relationships

I love networking.

I'm kidding, obviously. Does anyone actually like it? Do people genuinely get out of bed in the morning and think, '_yes_, I can't wait to go to that new networking event tonight with a bunch of complete strangers and swap LinkedIn details and business cards' (does anyone have business cards anymore?)?

The word 'networking' feels so transactional and weird. But here's the dilemma: as much as I don't like the term, growing your professional network is really—and I mean *really*—important for your career. So for me, I had to change my mindset when it comes to networking.

Instead of growing a network, I like to think of it as developing relationships: a normal and strategic part of life and work. When you see the word 'network' used in this book, I want you to think of it as building connections and long-term relationships.

What's the point of developing relationships and building your network? Well there are a lot, including:

- meeting prospective employers and business partners who could become long-lasting contacts that you draw on throughout your career

- exchanging knowledge, learning and ideas to help you in your role

- growing your profile in your industry so people know who you are and they come to you for guidance or with potential job opportunities

- finding mentors who can answer your questions and offer help when you're stuck

- meeting thought leaders in the industry—learn from their journeys and apply their successes to your own.

Remember, a productive relationship isn't one-sided. It's value-adding for both parties. So when you're meeting people, show interest in them. See them as people first; don't just think of their title at work or what you can gain from the relationship. Try to find a way to connect with them as individuals and work will often loop into that conversation.

We'll dig more into networking in chapter 8.

Habit #7: Don't just build resilience, become 'antifragile'

Too often, 'building resilience' has been equated with bouncing back from a challenge or crisis—the idea of bouncing back to the same shape, role or context we were previously. 'Antifragility', a term coined by Nassim Nicholas Taleb, is a different thing entirely.

'Antifragility is beyond resilience or robustness. The resilient resists shocks and stays the same; the antifragile gets better,' he writes in his book, *Antifragile*.

The 'antifragile' don't simply endure or resist hardships. They become stronger because of them.

We live in an unpredictable, volatile and wild world where nothing is certain (much to all the control freaks' dismay, myself included). Nassim argues that instead of resisting uncertainty, we can become strengthened by the unexpected crises that come our way.

So how can you be more antifragile in your career? It's important to consider each unexpected challenge as an opportunity to become better. You were rejected for that promotion you desperately wanted. Instead of simply 'bouncing back', your goal is to become better because of it.

My friend Brendan and I worked together for about six years. He was running risk and compliance, and I was leading HR, so we worked fairly closely together. He is one of those quietly confident people—the kind of person who tells it how it is, has no time for ego and has a very dry sense of humour.

Brendan would regularly put forward business cases as to why his role should be made redundant. It happened so often, it became a running joke at work. He didn't have other jobs lined up, but he was always open to random changes like that, even if it wouldn't directly benefit him.

Looking back on it now, I can see Brendan was the definition of antifragile. We had some pretty complex crises at work, but he was never surprised by them. He'd absorb the learnings in every challenge. And more than that, he never relied on external systems for his sense of security. He was open to all manner of surprises. Eventually he left that role and became a clinical psychologist with his own practice. Funny that!

The next time you're in a crisis or challenging situation at work, I want you to consider how you will not just get through it, but benefit from it.

Put yourself in spontaneous challenging situations. For example, if you're a total introvert and struggle to speak in meetings, set yourself an antifragile growth challenge. At an all-employee meeting, if the CEO asks for people to speak up and share their thoughts or ask a question on a controversial matter, jump in. Be brave and do it.

I'm not saying 'suck it up' or become immune to hardship. In fact, it's the opposite. Becoming antifragile, as Nassim puts it, is experiencing and absorbing the difficulties in your fullness and becoming stronger through the process.

Are there any external systems or structures that you depend on? Write down ways you could healthily remove your reliance on these systems.

_____

_____

_____

_____

What challenging growth situations can you put yourself in?

_____

_____

_____

_____

Consider a previous challenging work situation you've been through. How did you respond to it? In what ways did you grow from it?

_____

_____

_____

_____

Habit #8: Be a feedback collector

I might be showing my age here, but does anyone remember hobbies? Hobbies are the things you used to do for fun with all the spare time you had before the internet. People would collect the weirdest things. Tazos, Tamagotchis, Pokémon cards ... ahh the simple times.

I remember back when I was in primary school, kids were obsessed with collecting postage stamps. I always thought it was an odd hobby. Students would find rare stamps from who knows where. They'd place them neatly in a special red binder, sealed in plastic, ensuring they would not be damaged by the grubby mitts of their fellow classmates.

They would bring their treasured stamp collection to school for show and tell, sharing how many rare stamps they had amassed. And they would be the envy of everyone in class.

For me, I couldn't care less about stamps. Like honestly, why? But, I did learn something from the stamp enthusiasts. They were like treasure hunters (or bloodhounds) on the prowl, searching high and low to find their prized stamps.

Like the stamp collectors, we need to become feedback collectors. The kind of people who search for feedback everywhere we go. Why? Because feedback is the gateway to growth. It's something we need in order to become exceptional in our roles. But unfortunately, it's not something that's readily available. In fact, according to *Forbes*, many people indicate they do not get enough development-focused feedback. This is why you need to make a habit of collecting feedback. Don't wait for people to give you feedback; ask for it.

How to ask for feedback

If you have a regular 1:1 meeting with your boss, make a routine of asking for feedback. But please, don't simply ask, 'Do you have any feedback for me?' Ugh! This is a terrible question that I've heard more times than I care to count. It's far too general and broad, which is why it fails to generate meaningful feedback.

Instead, be more specific and targeted. Try these questions in your next meeting with your manager:

- How could I have supported the team differently over the past month?

- Was there anything you needed from me this month that you didn't get?

- Over the past few weeks, how could I have communicated better with you?

- I'd love to know your thoughts on the report I did this month. Was there anything I could do to improve it for next month?

- I'd love to learn more from you about solving X. Can you give me some advice on how I should approach it?

If you're still not getting results, be direct with your manager. Tell them you want more feedback to help you grow and improve. Ask them if they are able to give you monthly feedback on a specific skill you're trying to master. For example, if you want to grow in your presenting capability, ask them to focus on that single skillset. This will make their job of providing feedback easier as they will be focusing on one particular thing.

One of the ways I developed my public speaking and communication skills was by asking a range of people to provide feedback on my presentations before I ran them. I remember running a workshop with about 60 people. Two of the participants in the workshop were exceptional speakers and communicators. So I approached both of them beforehand and asked them to give me feedback. But I didn't want general feedback; I wanted specific, actionable feedback, so I asked them to provide me with answers to these questions:

- What did they love about the workshop?

- What would they do differently?

- What would they cut from the workshop?

You can see by being specific it gives the person clarity about what to look for. You can do this with your team and your manager.

How to deal with critical feedback

Over my career, people would regularly give me feedback about my lack of attention to detail. Has this bothered me? Not really. I've always known it was a weakness. I was never offended or upset by it. It's a skills gap I know I've needed to continually work on.

But some feedback hits differently. There's one time I'll never forget. I was in an important meeting with an executive team and I made an offhand, sarcastic comment at someone's expense. It was careless, jarring and rude. As soon as the words left my mouth, I felt instantly sick. I knew I'd said the wrong thing and upset one of the people in the room.

I remember sitting down with my boss Deb afterwards and talking about it. She reminded me of the power of words and how I needed to be more considered, careful and kind in how I speak in those moments. Ouch. Yep, this one hurt.

So why do some kinds of feedback feel more painful than others? It's all about the impact. In this scenario, my words had a significant impact on another person. It was an issue of integrity. It was emotionally charged. It made the feedback all the more painful. When you receive critical feedback that is linked to your values and character, it can hit harder than usual. Unlike a typo in my report, my careless behaviour held a much greater impact.

Dealing with critical feedback like this is never easy. I've found it helpful to reframe tough feedback as a gift. It might not be a very nicely wrapped gift. It might not be the gift that was on your Christmas wish list, but it's a gift all the same. When your manager gives you feedback about your actions or behaviour, remind yourself that it is a gift. It is something that will help you to grow and improve.

A final note on feedback: it's important to embrace critical feedback. But don't wallow in it. Don't replay the humiliation and embarrassment on repeat. This is unhelpful. Find the learnings in it, and move on from it.

---

apply now

Ready to collect more feedback? Try the following questions in your next catch-up with your manager:

- How could I have supported the team differently over the past month?

- Was there anything you needed from me this month that you didn't get?

- Over the past few weeks, how could I have communicated better with you?

- Is there anything I could do to improve my performance next month?

- Is there an upcoming project or a team member you can seek feedback from?

_____

_____

_____

_____

_____

Create a document online, a note on your phone or grab an empty journal and keep a record of the feedback you accrue. Just like the kids' stamp collection folders, but cooler (hehe).

Habit #9: See failure as your best teacher

Remember those terrifying teachers in high school? The ones who walked around the playground, inspiring fear in the hearts of every student. The ones you'd avoid making eye contact with, lest they uncover all the classes you'd skipped and lies you'd told to get out of your basketball class.

I had one of those teachers in my high school. I'd never been in her class, but I'd heard the stories. She was the super-strict, detention-loving deputy principal. Let's call her Mrs Moore.

When I got my class list in year 11, I freaked out. Somehow, I'd drawn the short straw and ended up in Mrs Moore's class. For the next two years, she'd be my teacher.

A few months into year 11, I was surprised to realise my worst fear was unfounded. Mrs Moore was unlike any other teacher I'd ever had. Yeah, she was strict. She didn't accept excuses, laziness or poor effort. But it was because she wanted us to succeed. She'd push her students to improve at every chance she got.

Out of all my classes, hers became my favourite. She helped me to learn in a way I hadn't before. She had high expectations of me, and she helped me to achieve them.

The terrifying teacher turned out to be the best teacher I ever had. The thing I was afraid of turned out to be an invaluable learning experience.

It's the same with failure in our careers. So often, people fear and avoid it. But failure can be your best teacher if you give yourself permission to learn from it. Each time you encounter a failure in your career (and there will be many), I want you to reflect on it in a healthy way. Ask yourself what the learning and growth opportunity is for you.

Over the years, I've had to adjust my view on failure. Instead of avoiding failure, I'm learning to embrace it. Instead of minimising failure, I see it as a growth catalyst. Instead of fearing failure, I now see it as my best teacher.

---

apply now

What failures can you reframe into learnings? Are there any themes that stand out? What can you do differently in future and how can you grow from it?

Failure	What can you learn from it?

Habit #10: Talk regularly with your manager about your career goals and desires

This is about building the habit of open discussion. If you want more opportunities at work, more often than not, your manager will be the one helping give you those opportunities. So be respectfully open about what it is you want!

When you notice that you're starting to get a bit bored, feeling like more of a challenge or want to try something new or different in your role, set up a meeting (informal or formal) to discuss it. You might come back to this discussion here and there throughout your time at work. Outline the things you're interested in being involved in throughout your career and see what opportunities exist near your current role.

Managers often have a lot going on in the background that you don't know about, so you might be able to tap into a new project that keeps you engaged and energised. You don't know if you don't ask.

We'll be working more on goals in the next chapter, to help you plan your long-term career goals so you can discuss them with your manager, so more on this soon.

---

apply now

What would you like to discuss with your manager? Write your thoughts here.

_____

_____

_____

_____

_____

Creating career opportunities in a new industry

Whether you're a student fresh out of uni, or someone looking to take their first steps into a new industry, you *are* able to create job opportunities. You aren't stuck.

Here are some useful tips to help you begin building career opportunities.

Identify transferable skills

Sometimes our previous experience can feel like a hindrance—maybe you've only worked in construction, been a sole trader selling your designs or worked at the drive thru at McDonald's. How can you flip that experience into a new job opportunity? Let's learn from Calum's story.

Calum (left), 32
Melbourne, VIC

I was fortunate enough to get a scholarship to a good school growing up, which allowed me a lot of choice when it came to choosing a university and a degree. My parents worked in healthcare so it was a safe and familiar career and my mum had always spoken well of physios so it seemed a good fit. Also, a lot of the kids at school had parents who were physios and it seemed to provide a comfortable lifestyle.

As I was studying physio, I had very little interest in it, but for the reasons mentioned I kept at it. I got a job as a new grad in the local hospital and worked for a private practice on the side, but neither job was particularly fulfilling, nor was the pay that impressive. One advantage though was the ability to work in London. I lived, worked, and travelled for a couple of years. But coming back to Australia I knew I couldn't continue with it. I hated it! I was in my late 20s and had a career crisis on my hands. But what could I do? I wanted to work in the corporate world. It seemed easier to progress, the pay was better and the city lifestyle was something I knew I loved after London.

Physio was such a niche degree and any jobs I applied for only saw me as a physio. I did have to start branching out. I started a Masters in Finance to show I had the skills and ability to do things other than physio and also started applying for any and every job in the city that matched the lifestyle I was after. I had heard of physios going into insurance and this is where the transition happened. I had to lower my salary expectations and take a few steps back. But to get ahead sometimes you need to do this. I managed to get a role with a life insurer that needed my physio skills to assess musculoskeletal insurance claims. I worked hard and showed I could do more than my physio degree pigeonholed me into. I then started working on the operations side of the business using the reasoning and problem-solving skills I'd learned as a physio. I'm using skills from my past in a new way! I'm making the most of my opportunities by working my way up. I'm now working as a business analyst in general insurance. I'm moving forward on my terms in an industry I enjoy with skills I'd worked hard to build during my degree.

Calum's training in physio was specific and seemingly didn't have the breadth required to move anywhere else. But Calum used it as a transferable strength—a background of training and knowledge that could be applied differently in a new industry.

This is what we want to find for you.

We spent a whole chapter talking about strengths and skills—what are yours? Think on this, and write them down in the following 'Apply now' section.

Get your foot in the door

You may not have the luxury of choice when first stepping out into a new industry. Don't underestimate the power of things like internships, volunteer roles and entry-level positions, particularly if you were higher up the ranks in your previous role. Your focus is to gain experience in this industry, so go get it! Look for any and all opportunities to get into the room where it happens!

---

apply now

What overarching strengths and skills have you gained from previous jobs? Strengths that can be applied in any role, anywhere.

_____

_____

_____

_____

How can you get in the room? Remember, you can move in all directions.

_____

_____

_____

_____

A final word

These 10 habits act as an opportunity magnet. As you consistently practise these habits, they bring exciting opportunities your way. It's the essence of owning your career. As your career options grow, it gives you a sense of confidence, control and the power of choice. It means if you end up in an unexpected situation, you're not trapped or thrown for six. You use the career equity you've built to find new opportunities.

resources **Scan the QR code for these resources and more.**

- Download the 'plan for the best, prepare for the worst' template.

- Download the personal brand builder.

- Check out the episodes on *my millennial career* around building your personal brand and how to market yourself to get the jobs you want.

success

and goals
on your terms

7

tl;dr

- Define what success looks like to you before you set your career goals.

- Your career goals don't have to be linear; you can move in all directions.

- Don't let external pressure influence your career goals. Instead, your goals need to align with your version of success.

- You'll reassess your goals regularly across the course of your working life.

Rethinking career goal-setting

I want you to do something for me. Google 'career goal-setting'.

Now click on images and go for a little scroll.

Cue stock image overload

You'll see some people in suits climbing up a ladder. You'll see a person next to a line graph that's pointing upwards. Or, my personal favourite, a stick figure skipping up a staircase full of goals.

Here's my rendition, in case you want to frame this quality piece of art.

If only achieving your career goals was as simple as skipping your way up the staircase of your dreams. Reality is a very different story. Most people's careers don't look like a nice line graph that steadily goes up and up.

For most of us, it feels more like a dodgy rollercoaster. One where you jump in, buckle up and hold on for dear life.

Typically, career goal-setting has been built around a linear career path, without recognising that the modern world of work is anything but clear cut. It has also failed to take into account people's overarching life goals, personal priorities and definition of success. When you establish career goals in isolation from the other parts of your life, you can end up at the final destination only to realise it's not where you wanted to be. You successfully hit the goal, but it doesn't feel like success.

Before you start setting career goals, you need to step back. Take an all-encompassing view of what you want your life to look like, with your career being one part of it. This involves considering what success means to you personally based on your priorities and life goals. Once you've clarified that, you can set career goals that align with the bigger picture of your life.

In this chapter you'll learn how to define success on your terms, and create career goals that get you there.

'Success' as defined by anyone but me

From an early age, we learn to measure success based on other people's standards. We look at what our parents, our mates, our sister Millie or second cousin Flynn think matters. And, let's be honest, I've even gone as far as allowing total randoms to influence what I think a successful life and career looks like (a bad move by all accounts).

The point is that we regularly allow people and external factors to influence our career goals and our definition of success.

If you don't define what success means to you personally, something else will do it for you. And when that happens, you end up with a poor substitute for the real thing.

One of my friends fell into this trap. She was the person who did really well in high school. You know the one: the overachiever, star student and dux of the school. She was also one of the nicest people you'd ever meet and super funny and creative too. So yep, she basically ticked every box.

At 18 years of age, she did what we all expected. She went straight to university and studied medicine. After years of studying and hundreds of thousands of dollars in university fees, she started work as a doctor in a major hospital in Melbourne. Her career goal was to specialise in paediatrics.

But the dream of becoming a doctor was less than dreamy. After 2 years, she wanted out. But how could she possibly make the change? What would people think of her? She'd sunk so much time and money into getting here. She'd forged this path based on what people thought of her, based on the status associated with a career in medicine. A shaky foundation on which to build your working life. She'd never taken the time to consider what she wanted for herself—to define what success looked like for her.

The people around her had become the backseat drivers in her career. She had to disentangle her goals from other people's opinions. She had to block out the voices telling her what to do. Instead, she imagined her future. Her long-term goals and life plans. She used this to craft her own version of success and made big career changes accordingly.

When you let go of the expectations of others and start to define what you want for yourself, it can feel like you're letting people down. But ultimately, you're the one in the driver's seat; you're the one responsible for getting where you want to go, so kick out the backseat drivers.

Success is bigger than your career. It's about what you want your life to look like.

We don't just work.

We live. We laugh. We love.

Sorry (but not really).

We're way more than what we do for work. We travel, have kids, eat food, paint, paintball, read books, fall in love, make homemade pizzas, keep bees, ride bikes, scuba dive, meditate, renovate, make friends, learn guitar, play board games, have pets, go to our place of worship, visit grandma, sing songs, ride in hot air balloons.

Your career is just one aspect of your life. If you give it too much weight and don't line it up with the other puzzle pieces of what matters to you, you'll end up hitting the goals only to find they aren't fulfilling. It's far too easy to end up living for work and having no other sense of success in your life.

Often, we look at others who have found a great work–life blend (and FWIW, 'blend' is a far better term than 'balance') and think, 'I could never have that. They love their job, *and* they get to do the things they love outside of work. There's no way I can make that happen for me.'

This is an all-or-nothing mindset. An excuse for why you're not happy where you are right now.

Finding the right blend of work and life is possible if you clarify what success looks like to you, and build goals that align with that vision. See the difference.

In this approach, we start by defining your version of success. It's not purely career focused; it's about what a successful life looks like to you based on your unique priorities and interests. From there, you design goals to support that vision. Instead of what people generally do, which is set career goals in isolation and hope they will feel 'successful' when they reach them.

Success on your own terms

There's a gravitational pull to compare your career to others. To try to measure your own success based on what other people think of you. But defining success based on comparison is a flawed strategy—it's not your strategy, it's someone else's.

Here are some external pressures that influence how we see success:

- I have to work my way up the corporate ladder.

- I can't stay in a small business long term as it will damage my future options.

- I can only move upwards; never sideways or downwards.

- Taking a career break will set me back in my goals.

- I need to earn over $150000 to be successful.

- I won't be taken seriously unless I manage a team.

- If I leave this job too soon, it will look bad on my resume.

- It will set me back if I take time off now to start a family.

- I won't get promoted unless I do all of these hours.

Take a look at the common themes in these statements:

- *I have to*

- *I can't*

- *I can only*

- *I won't be*

- *will set me back*

- *will look bad*

Each of these assertions is a) negatively geared, b) an absolute statement and c) based on external pressure. There's a lot of black-and-white, all-or-nothing thinking going on here.

If you've been making career decisions based on outer influences like these, it's time to redefine success.

In this section, you'll craft your version of success. You'll quickly see how your idea of success connects with your values and strengths. That's a good thing! We want to align your values, strengths and definition of success. They are the puzzle pieces. Once we've clarified these three areas, you're on your way to building a career you love.

Your personal priorities and life goals shape and guide what success looks like for you. It's crucial to identify these before you set career goals. Here are some of my personal priorities:

- I want to have nights and weekends off with my family and be more present and engaged.

- I want to go on two decent family holidays each year.

- I want to exercise four times a week.

- I want to grow my business.

- I want to work a maximum of 40 hours per week.

Your priorities influence your career decisions. They also reveal any trade-off decisions you have to make, becoming the guard rails of a strong career plan.

For example, one of my priorities is to grow my business, but another priority is that I only want to work 40 hours a week. It means that my desire to grow my business is constrained by the hours I am willing to invest. A trade-off choice, but one that ultimately serves my bigger life goals of being present and engaged with my family.

It's critical to identify the trade-off decisions you are making in service of a greater priority. Own these choices and don't succumb to external pressure.

---

apply now

My personal priorities or big-picture life goals:

- _____

- _____

- _____

- _____

- _____

- _____

Your definition of success

In the *my millennial career* community we hear a lot of people say:

- 'Tell me what job I should do.'

- 'I don't like my job and want to make a change—anyone got any career ideas?'

- 'I don't know how to make career goals.'

- 'I have no idea what I want to do with my career. *Help!*'

I hear you. Let's use this time to figure out what it is you actually want from your career by eliminating deal breakers first.

Before you jump in and start mind mapping your success story (yep, we love a good mind map), I want you to do the opposite. Success your way is best understood when you clarify what it doesn't look like.

We asked our *my millennial career* community for some examples of what they feel success may *not* look like:

- Working so many hours that I can't be present with my friends and family

- Feeling like I can't go on holidays or take leave because the work will pile up

- Getting stuck in a team that is not progressive or innovative

- Working in a transactional culture that values results more than people

- Working in a role where I'm not learning or growing

- Working in a company where there is no room for career progression

- Working in a toxic and cut-throat environment

- Working for a boss who blocks my future opportunities

- Working on projects that aren't energising and are boring

- When I have no flexibility and autonomy in how I get my work done

- When I'm stressed about money

- Not being paid what I'm worth

- Feeling undervalued and not recognised or rewarded for good work

- Working in a business where employees don't have flexibility to choose their hours

- Working shift work, rotating roster and night shifts

- Working in a self-managed team

- Working indoors on a computer all day

- Presenting and public speaking

- A long commute to work

- Being on the phone all day

- Frequent travel

- Working in a physically draining role.

What one person considers a drawback in a job (like frequent travel), another might see as benefit. So, it's important to create your own list. By articulating your dislikes, it will clarify the things you really want by pointing to the things you either love or hate in a job.

apply now

Now it's your turn. I want you to write as many points as possible about things you don't want from your career.

Success doesn't look like:

- _____

- _____

- _____

- _____

- _____

- _____

- _____

- _____

- _____

Now that you've articulated what you don't like in a job or career, you get to clarify what you *do* love. This is where we define success on your terms.

Remember this is unique to you. It's like your fingerprints—one of a kind. Be mindful of any ideas that sound like someone else's. If it doesn't sound like you, it's probably an expectation someone else has placed on you. Ask yourself if it's something you want, or is it something someone else wants from you. Keep in mind, defining success on your own terms is crucial in the next few chapters when we dig deeper into practical aspects of career building.

apply now

Success looks like:

- _____

- _____

- _____

- _____

- _____

- _____

- _____

- _____

- _____

Wait. I still don't know what I want!

Let's come at this from another angle. Think of the end of your life. You're 85, with grey hair and/or a beard, sitting in a rocking chair on the porch, smoking a pipe, looking into the distance and telling a young person, 'Y'know, I'm proud of what I've done in my life.'

How do you measure that 'success'? What are you proud of:

- the depth of your relationships

- work having meaning

- being able to have new experiences

- challenging yourself

- serving others / helping people

- being generous

- growing as a person

- building wealth for your family

- enjoying the lifestyle you wanted

- travelling to where you wanted

- people remembering me

- leaving behind _____

- encouraging/mentoring _____

- creating _____?

---

apply now

What do you want to be able to say about your life and career once you've retired? What statements come to mind for what success means to you?

_____

_____

_____

_____

_____

If you've gotten this far, it means you've defined success on your terms (which is a success in and of itself).

I want you to assess your version of success against your current work situation. How well do they line up? What parts are being met and what parts are not? Are the things that aren't being met non-negotiable for you? Or are you happy to compromise for a while?

If your success on your terms looks like having opportunities for career progression or role changes, does your workplace provide opportunities for you? If not, it may be worth having a discussion with your manager to see if opportunities could come up in the future. Otherwise, you may need to look for something new.

Combining life goals and career goals

What are your big life goals? Maybe you want to start a family. Or you want to travel around Europe for 12 months. Or your dream is to start your own business one day. Your life goals inform your career goals. They go hand in hand.

Let's look at a couple of examples.

- Your life goal is to save up and buy your first home as quickly as possible. This means your career goal around pay and salary becomes more important to achieve your big life goal.

- Your dream is to relocate to a small coastal beachside town 500 kilometres from the nearest city. This means your career goal is to find a workplace that's happy for you to work remotely full time.

The point is, your life and career goals don't operate in isolation. We want them to align and work in tandem.

Jess, 34
Newcastle, NSW

I knew that having kids was something I wanted in my life. My husband and I also wanted to buy a home for our family. When I had our eldest son, I had just finished working afternoons and nights. I was good at it and enjoyed it, but the hours didn't suit a family. The money also wasn't up to scratch for our goal of buying a house. Likewise, my husband works in a much less flexible industry, so my work needed to have a flexible arrangement.

Once our son was born I took some time out to figure out how to be a mum. I used this time to do some reflection and think through where I wanted to go next. I wanted to be home as much as I could, but still have the opportunity to use my mind and skills in a workplace because I love love love working.

I was sorting out my own money by listening to the *my millennial money* podcast as I walked our son in the pram around the block each day. We needed to get our money in shape to meet our expenses and buy a house. Glen mentioned on the show he was looking for a team member and my skills and experience lined up! After spending a few months working through my options, this role would be performed from home, and the income was steady enough to get pre-approval for a house. I'd also recently provided an audio sample for the show, so it was a helpful way to make a connection and show my involvement with the show prior.

I paired that with a side hustle of playing music gigs. I had worked out that in a time vs money assessment, gigging was one of the best ways for me to generate maximum income, doing something I loved, and spending the least amount of time away from my family. I'm stoked to say we bought

(continued)

a house just in time for our second baby! It was a serious hustle, but we worked as a family to achieve it.

These are my top five tips for working out how parental leave, for either parent, can be woven in with your career choices:

1. *Work closely with your workplace/boss.* It's important to take stock of the frameworks in place in your workplace around parental needs, pay and leave. Read through your contract, chat with your manager or boss and get familiar with the legal requirements that all workplaces must adhere to in supporting your career and family blend. Consider things like parental leave pay, superannuation, number of days you'd prefer to work, annual or personal leave (for the day that bub has the sniffles), and ask to meet with your manager or boss to ensure you're meeting the requirements, and that they're involved in the planning and decision making.

2. *Determine your life goals and use your career as a means to get there.* Do you also want to buy a house? Do you want to be waiting at the school gate at 3 pm each day? Do you want to be around for Saturday sports? Before thinking just about your career, think through how you want your family to work around it. What do you need to line up for it to look the way you want it to? What hours, pay, location and flexibility do you need to make it happen? Would you or your partner like to be with the family more, or both of you equally? Think through how everyone is impacted.

3. *It's a family discussion—it's not just about the mum/dad.* Having kids is a family decision and plan. Work with your partner, your kids and your supporting family members to figure out how both of your careers work together in your family puzzle. Having kids affects your money, time and career—have open discussions about how everyone feels and craft a plan to make it happen.

4. *Value your time as money.* Once you're a parent you never have enough time in the day. You want to spend as much time as possible

with your kids, but you also want to do your job well and earn the best money you can to support your family. Look at career options that enable you to be around for your family as much as you'd like while being paid as much as possible for that time.

5. *Use your strengths*. Your time and energy resources are really put to the test with a family—so pick a career that utilises your strengths. You'll find shifting into work mode so much easier if your job aligns with what you're good at. Nothing worse than being up all night with the baby, then rocking up to a job that you don't feel strong in. Work in your strengths.

Jess took the time to reflect on the things in her broader life that were valuable—things she wanted to make time for and invest in. Her family was important, but so was her career. She worked with her family to craft a life that included both goals: life and career equally.

Will, 26
Favourite place: the Canadian Rockies
Sydney, NSW

Travelling has always been high on my list of goals. So I've built a large set of skills and experience that gives me flexibility in finding work all over the world as a regular traveller.

Once I've decided on a location to travel to I use the 100:10:1 rule (contact 100 businesses, aim to have roughly 10 who might be interested, choose one role that suits) and fire off messages to get job opportunities rolling. I also advertise through local pages and social media. This tends to result in having the pick of jobs and often allows me to negotiate a price and perks. Failing that, I'm not afraid to branch

(continued)

out into types of work I've not previously been exposed to and I apply my previous experience to help me do this.

If I'm travelling in a location that I don't have a working permit for there are many incredible services online that link you with a host where you can volunteer part-time in return for free food/board and local knowledge and experiences.

Having good relationships with employers has often resulted in a referral for my next job/location. I also have an amazing contact who has always had a position for me within his company as a carpenter whenever I am back in Australia.

I have just enrolled in an online degree that will hopefully be an important step in my career progression and open up even more opportunities to maintain an income while travelling (doing remote work).

I purchased a property when I was 21 and am now navigating how to go about property #2 as a form of wealth creation due to my limited permanent income.

A quick comprehensive list of types of jobs I've had and continue to find myself working or volunteering in are:

- retail management
- carpenter/foreman
- barman/server
- tree planting and fruit picking
- hotel maintenance, front desk and cleaning.

Throughout the process, I have developed and refined my skills and knowledge, and through experience I've learned I'm not afraid of rejection. Rejection has been a chance to grow, build skills and improve the work I do afterwards.

Will lives for adventure. The chance to travel. It's a personal priority and life goal, so his career is crafted around achieving those personal goals. He's skilled and experienced enough to be flexible, and willing to learn whatever necessary to apply himself to a number of roles. Remember we said your career doesn't always have to go upwards—you can go in all directions, and Will is living proof of that.

Create your career goals

Now that you've defined success on your own terms, you can start to create career goals that will support your success. In this section, we'll walk through our step-by-step guide to setting career goals. And when we say 'step-by-step' we mean that metaphorically. It's a framework. No step ladders of any kind.

Here lies the career ladder, may it rest in peace and/or pieces

Ben Crothers, a strategist, designer and all-round creative, joined us on the *my millennial career* podcast to teach us how to use what's called 'design thinking' to solve career problems.

In classic Ben style, he transformed how I look at my career.

'It's not a career ladder,' Ben declared with all the enthusiasm of a kid in the playground on their lunch break. 'It's a jungle gym!'

The career ladder is long gone.

'You can go left and right in the jungle gym,' Ben tells us. 'You can swing across to a whole other part of this crazy world of work if you want to! It's not a straight up and down line.'

The traditional career ladder has been messing with our career expectations for a long time. It tells us there's only one way up and one way down. It tells us to hold onto the ladder with everything we have. And it tells us that we have to keep on climbing up, rung by rung.

The world of work has changed so much over the past decade. Yet the traditional ladder has stuck with us. It continues to have a profound influence on how people set their career goals. It's forced us to adopt unrealistic and outdated expectations of what our career progression should look like.

You have permission to move in any direction you want. It doesn't have to be linear.

It doesn't have to be about upward progression (unless that's what you really want). Your goals can involve sideways moves. They can be unconventional. You can set a goal to take a career break and go hiking with your family. You can set a goal to start your own business or to complete your Masters degree. To move overseas and work wherever you can while travelling.

Your goals are about achieving your version of success.

Let go of the ladder. Climb onto the jungle gym.

---

apply now

The five-step guide to setting your career goals

Give yourself some time for this section. Mark this spot in your book and keep it close by to jot down notes as we dig into research.

Step 1: Define your version of success

So you're gonna love step 1 because, hey, you've already done this! You've mapped out your personal priorities and defined success on your terms earlier in this chapter. You've got the foundation for crafting effective career goals sorted. Keep your personal priorities, life goals and definition of success in mind as you move through the next steps.

Step 2: Revisit your values and mindset established in part I of this book

Your career goals need to align with your values and mindset. Refresh yourself on them to make sure your goals line up.

My values:

_____

_____

_____

_____

_____

My mindset:

My mindset traps:

_____

_____

_____

_____

My *chosen* mindset:

_____

_____

(continued)

_____

_____

_____

Step 3: Do a career opportunities check-in

We unpacked the value of career opportunities in the last chapter. Tick any of the habits you want to start developing to create opportunities in the industries or roles you've selected.

- Find a coach or mentor.

- Diversify your career portfolio.

- Plan for the best, prepare for the worst.

- Build your personal brand.

- Build up and encourage others.

- Develop your relationships.

- Don't just build your resilience, work on your 'antifragility'.

- Be a feedback collector.

- Reflect, don't ruminate.

- Talk regularly with your manager about your career goals and desires.

- Stay educated—both formally and informally.

Step 4: Create a long-term career vision

Fast forward to 5 or 10 years' time. Where do you see yourself? What does your career look like?

This is probably the hardest step. We don't often think so far in advance, and we know the future is difficult to predict. As such, your long-term career vision isn't set in stone. Think of it as your north star: a gentle guide to inform your tangible short-term goals (coming up in the next step).

Consider these questions:

- What do you want to have achieved at work?

- What jobs would you have loved to have tried in that time?

- Are you running your own business?

- Have you completed more study?

- Are you leading a team, or specialising in a new area?

- What do you want to be earning?

Paint a vision of the future. Make it aspirational. You want it to feel like a stretch. Be sure to tune out any negative self-talk or limiting beliefs during this step.

My long-term career vision looks like this:

_____

_____

_____

_____

_____

(*continued*)

Step 5: Establish focused short-term goals to support the long-term vision

Now that you know the long-term view, you can set your career goals to get you there. Unlike your vision, these are tangible short-term goals. We can measure them easily.

I want you to have a range of goals across multiple domains. It's not enough to simply say, 'My goal is to become the head of marketing by X date'. We want to create a range of goals that help you get to that future vision sooner.

This means you will have the following goals:

- Role-specific goals (main goal):

  Set goals for jobs that you want to land in the future. It might be a promotion or a change from where you are currently or several job changes over an extended period of time. Remember it doesn't have to be linear. Your sideways move might just be your best move.

- Strengths and skills goals (supporting goal):

  What skills do you need to develop in order to land your desired roles? This could be about bridging the skills gap between where you are now and where you want to be.

Are there activities you can be doing to grow your strengths further?

- Risk goals (supporting goal):

  What risks do you need to take in order to obtain the main goal you're aiming for?

Example

Reva is working as a marketing specialist. Her ultimate goal is to become the head of marketing one day. Here's how she created her goals:

1   Land a head of marketing role by X date.

2   Strengths and skills goals:

- o   Build skills in people management by completing X training by X date.

- o   Engage a mentor who can help me develop marketing and leadership skills.

- o   Build depth of technical knowledge in X areas by X date.

- o   Share my career goal with my manager by X date and ask them to give me ongoing feedback to support my development and growth.

3   Risk goals:

- o   Ask my manager if I can perform higher duties and an acting head of marketing role while they are on annual leave by X date.

- o   Ask my workplace to invest in my career development by providing study assistance by X date.

Your turn

Note: You want your goals to be specific, measurable and time bound.

- ●   Role-specific goals (main goal)

My role-specific goals include:

_____

_____

_____

_____

_____

(*continued*)

- Strengths and skills goals (supporting goal)

The strengths and skills I need in order to achieve my main goal are:

_____

_____

_____

_____

- Risk goals (supporting goal)

The risks I need to take in order to reach my main goal are:

_____

_____

_____

_____

So, what's your goal?

Where are we at? You might have shaken this Magic 8 Ball and gone 'Nope'.

So shake it again. Revisit your answers. This is where your career ownership kicks in.

Also, you're not necessarily looking for a unicorn answer either. You might have a couple of big goals to choose from at this point. That's perfect!

Remember, neither I, nor anyone else, can tell you what job you should do. You need to draw out your options based on what energises you and where your strengths lie.

If it helps, move to a new location to think these things through—go to a cafe, go for a walk, go for a drive, look at the ocean. Think strategically. Think differently than you have before.

This process of goal setting may be something you do every 2, 5, 10+ years! Your life will change, and so will your goals on all fronts. Keep this book on hand for when that time comes and shake that Magic 8 Ball again.

A final word

The goals you design for yourself will always be more authentic to you than those given to you by someone else. By choosing goals yourself you'll not only perform better in whatever role you work in, but you'll also be happier overall.

Remember, this is about defining success on your own terms: defining goals that align with who you are and what you value.

resources   Scan the QR code for these resources and more.

- To hear Jess's story around family growing and parental leave, check out episode 528b on *my millennial money*.

- Download the five-step guide to setting your career goals.

how to nail your resume, interview and networking drinks

8

tl;dr

- Your resume should not be the first thing you update when you're looking to fix career problems.

- Your cover letter should not be more than one page and your resume not more than three pages.

- There are multiple job interview approaches and there's plenty of preparation you can do to successfully nail your interview.

- Networking and LinkedIn are essential ways to establish key career connections and relationships, and it can be done in a 100 per cent cringe-worthy-free way.

- Scoring a promotion at work is not about simply having worked there long enough. It's about demonstrating the value you have added by being there. Your business case should include key measurables you have delivered.

Okay, this is probably the first chapter you were expecting to read in this book.

But hopefully now you understand why it's chapter 8 and not chapter 1!

Too many people think an updated resume will solve their career problems. They spend hours redesigning their resume without doing the deep work first. No font change on *earth* has this much life-changing power (sorry).

The good news is that you're not this person. If you've got this far, you've already done the hard yards.

Our focus now is to get you into the room where it happens (*Hamilton* fans, anyone?) and to show your future employer you've got the goods.

I also want to focus more heavily on the topic of networking (yeah, not my favourite word, but it's important) and how this helps you get into the right rooms.

Cover letter and resume

Stop googling resume templates for a minute. We'll provide you with a downloadable template at the end of this chapter. First, we need to talk.

Your resume, or CV (curriculum vitae), is the very first contact point potential employers have with you so it's your first opportunity to make an impression. Your goal is to make it easy to see how you fit the role they're looking to fill. Remove all barriers to entry.

But as much as curriculum vitae is Latin for 'course of life', recruiters do not (repeat: *do not*) want to read your life story. They are scanning through hundreds of resumes so it's important to be succinct. You want to make reading your resume as easy as possible.

Your goal is to get your resume into the 'Yes' pile. So let's help you get there fast.

Cover letter

Want to make your application stand out? The cover letter is your secret weapon. It's your personal introduction, your handshake in the room without you being there. A cover letter is provided alongside your resume. It's typically the first page the recruiter or hiring manager will read, which is why it's essential to nail it.

Your cover letter is written in letter style (no surprises there), with a few simple paragraphs about the role, who you are, where you are currently working/studying and how you can fulfil the job requirements.

But here's the most important thing to remember about cover letters: you need to tailor your cover letter to the role and the business.

This is crucial, so I'll say it again: tailor your cover letter to the role and business.

Imagine being asked out on a date like this:

To whom it may concern,

I consider us to be a suitable match. I enjoy drinking coffee, binge-watching bad reality TV and going for brisk early morning walks. I look forward to hearing from you at your earliest convenience.

Kind regards

Yeah. It's no for me.

Asking someone out on a date isn't a copy-and-paste exercise. It's an opportunity to connect with another human. You make it about them, not about you. And, you want to throw in a bit of personality to build some chemistry too.

The same is true for your cover letter. It's a chance to show you've done your research. You focus on them. You know what's important to that business, and you can show how you will help them achieve their goals and objectives.

Before you start writing your cover letter, you need to do your research on the business you're applying for. Look for:

- their business strategy or long-term goals / plan

- their mission, purpose or core values

- their brand identity

- an annual report, if they have one

- their social media accounts to get a sense of their brand tone

- everything on their careers page, if they have one.

From here you can craft a cover letter that connects with the business you're applying for.

Top tips for crafting your cover letter:

1. *Aim for one page in length* (unless they have a requirement for you to respond to key selection criteria, which may require additional pages).

2. *Make it personal.* That means no 'To whom it may concern'. If you can, find out the name of the hiring manager, recruiter or HR team

member. If you don't have access to that information, address it as 'To the hiring manager'.

3. *Capture their attention early*. You want the opening paragraph to demand attention. The best way to do that is to talk about them. Most people's cover letter is a sales pitch of all the things they are great at, but they forget who the audience is. You'll stand out by focusing on the business you're applying for. Explain why the role and the business excite you before you talk about your skills.

   Demonstrate that you've done your research by adding in a couple of sentences about the business strategy, mission or values and how you align with those.

4. *Incorporate their language from the job advertisement*. For example, if they used the words 'dynamic', 'excellence' and 'adaptability' to describe their culture or the desired candidate in the job ad, incorporate that language subtly into your cover letter. By using the terms they use, you'll create a sense of familiarity and connection—feelings that go a long way to getting you shortlisted.

5. *Avoid including personal information that could lead to discrimination* (things like age, gender, sexual orientation, marital status or whether you have children). In Australia, it is illegal for an employer to discriminate against a person based on these factors. Sadly, there are still many employers out there who may hold unconscious or blatant biases towards information like this. Focus on your skills, experience, what you value and how you want to contribute to their business.

6. *Refrain from sharing that you have two Persian cats and are hoping to scuba dive one day*. Focus only on the essentials and show the recruiter how this could slot right into what the business needs are.

Resume

Now for your resume, the part where you outline your skills and experience in detail.

1. Aim for a maximum of three pages (but two pages is ideal as less is more IMO).

2. If you're a recent graduate, fresh out of school or university, and your experience is slim, don't stress: include your most recent study and work experience regardless. Pad out your resume by including your top five strengths (Gallup/Clifton Strengths) if you have taken the assessment. This works really well for those in their early career who haven't yet got much on-the-job experience.

   Further, if you don't have years of experience in the role you're applying for, talk about your ability to learn and grow. Why? Because employers want their business to grow, and to do that, they need employees who can grow with them. They want people with a growth mindset. The kind of people who stay curious, learn from failure and see challenges as a chance to grow.

3. Use your resume to demonstrate how you've continually grown and developed new skills throughout your career. If you're thinking, 'Hang on, aren't I meant to show them how I tick all the boxes?' Nope. You don't need to tick every box. Recruiters don't expect you to meet every item on the selection criteria. Many applicants only hit between 60 and 70 per cent of the criteria. So show your commitment to growth. Workplaces, teams and jobs are changing rapidly. The most valuable skill is your ability to learn.

   Your resume and cover letter can tell your story of your personal growth. Share how you've pursued learning opportunities and built new capabilities.

4. If you're more experienced, you don't need to include everything you've done since your very first job. We recommend you only

go back 10 years (e.g. your job at the video store in the early 2000s — cool gig back then, but not relevant now) and choose roles that align perfectly with their job description and criteria. Show them how you fit the role that needs filling.

5. Remember your focus here: stick to the job advertisement criteria and relate what they're asking for to times where you have demonstrated that quality or skill in your training or a previous workplace.

6. Line up your referees in the background and ensure they are ready to answer a phone call if you're successful in gaining an interview. *But!* We recommend you do not include them on your resume. Tell your referees about the role you've applied for so they have some guidance as to the kinds of questions they could be asked. Ask them to outline any time constraints they may have around answering recruiter phone calls and express these details in your interview. Make it easy for everyone involved to recommend you!

General formatting

Don't crowd the page, and stick to A4 pages. Reduce the number of words you include and balance them with white space. You want to have decent white space around the edge of the page, and between each paragraph. If something can be said in 10 words, don't say it in 20. Cut your words down, choose a plain font (that means no comic sans) and don't use bold colours. Use dot points over big, juicy paragraphs. Allocate one page for your cover letter and three pages maximum for your resume. Help the recruiter understand your point as quickly as possible!

Make sure your resume is submitted as a PDF (portable document format) if submitting online (this is the best format for a large variety of devices) and ensure your printing is legible and organised ahead of submission day if being submitted in person.

The finer details

Let's get into the nitty gritty of a resume:

- Ensure one personal mobile number is listed (definitely not your current workplace number).

- Please, for the love of all that is good in this world, do not use your current work email address (not a great look). And okay, misssparkles@email.com was cool in year 9, but not so much on your resume!

- Check that the company information, and your personal details, are all correct.

- Ensure your LinkedIn profile is up to date (more on this shortly).

- If you're going to include photography of yourself, ensure it is professionally photographed and captures you in a professional light.

- Leave your referees off your resume, but have them lined up and prepared in advance.

At the end of this chapter is a QR code that links to templates for both your cover letter and resume.

How do I include jobs where the workplace, managers or colleagues were toxic and I just had to get out of there?

First note: you don't need to mention on your resume why you left. Recruiters know that the chances of people coming up against a difficult previous workplace is high.

It's a common occurrence and you don't need to attempt to cover it up (please don't!). And you don't need to overly highlight it.

Should you include that job on your resume? Yes.

If asked about it in your job interview, should you be honest? Yes, but not brutally. Don't bad-mouth your previous employer—it's a big red flag to a prospective employer.

Identify what about that experience didn't work for you.

Example 1: You left due to micromanagement

Recruiter: Why did you leave your last role after such a short time?

You: I perform best in an environment where I'm trusted and I have autonomy to do the best work I can. Unfortunately, the culture of the workplace didn't allow for that working style, so I left that role to find an environment that provided that.

Example 2: You left because the role was boring and you weren't engaged

Recruiter: Why did you leave your last role after such a short time?

You: The organisation and leadership was amazing; however, the role wasn't the right position for me. It focused on areas that were outside of my strengths, so I decided to look for other opportunities better suited to my strengths. While it didn't go how I had hoped, I learned a lot through that experience about my work style and preference.

Final steps and submission

Have a few turns at writing both your cover letter and resume. Ask a trusted friend or family member to review them. Once you're happy with the final version, do one final proof: look for grammatical errors, missing information, and misspelt words. There are plenty of online tools available for this, or you could ask a friend who's brilliant with words. Proofing is a very important step!

Ensure you're submitting your documents as the recruiter or employer has requested—that is, through the correct channels. Do not try to bypass their submission site and email it to their receptionist. This doesn't make you look impressive, it places your resume outside of their recruitment processes and you run the risk of your application being lost.

If you're providing your cover letter and resume in printed form, ensure you leave enough time to have it printed—ensure it's legible and do not print on obnoxiously bright yellow paper (like this book cover for example)! If you're submitting your document digitally, exporting it as a PDF is typically the best format.

Cover letter and resume checklist

I have:

- ☐ read the job ad thoroughly and aligned my experience/training with the stated criteria

- ☐ familiarised myself with the business's activity

- ☐ included specific evidence of meeting the job ad criteria

- ☐ included only my most recent activity (maximum 10 years backwards)

- ☐ ensured my personal information is up to date (name, address, professional-sounding email, one personal phone number)

- ☐ ensured I have two referees lined up (not included on resume)

- ☐ submitted my resume through the requested channel (Seek, business website or other)

- ☐ included the correct business/recruiter details

- ☐ updated my LinkedIn profile to align with my resume

- ☐ included a professional photograph (if choosing to include a photo)

- ☐ provided my cover letter and resume in PDF format or printed them appropriately

- ☐ made my cover letter one page maximum customised it to the job and business

- ☐ made my resume three pages maximum and customised it to the job and business.

The interview

So you've been invited for an interview: congratulations! It's significant to have made it this far. Your cover letter and resume have made an impression—let's build on that impression and get you over the line.

Or perhaps you're reading this because interviews are where you feel you have let yourself down in the employment process previously. Good on you for being here! Let's workshop your interview approach and see where we can improve things.

Now we need to think visually, audibly and tangibly about your impression. You're not just a piece of paper anymore, and it's more than just your desired skills to be assessed: the recruiter is looking for the 'right person' to fill the advertised role.

But what does 'the right person' even mean?

To work this through, think about the job advertised and the following details:

- What is the level of the role I'm applying for? (entry, mid-level, executive)

- Is the organisation a corporate business, or is this industry technical or trade based?

- What is the tone or culture of the business? What are its values?

- What kind of energy do I want to bring to this interview to authentically represent me?

- What questions do I have for them during the interview?

- How did I represent myself on my resume?

Remember, if you're unsuccessful in gaining a role it's not a personal attack on you. It's typically because you haven't found the right organisation where their values and your values align perfectly. You'll enjoy your job way more when you find the organisation that 'clicks' with you. Don't linger on a job you didn't score; stay focused on the one you're out to get.

Types of job interviews

There are quite a few ways you could be screened or interviewed for a job role, and it's not uncommon (depending on the role) to be put through several interviews before receiving confirmation of 'yay' or 'nay' to your desired role.

If you receive a phone call to say you've landed a job interview, don't be afraid to ask what kind of interview it will be and what dress style would be appropriate on the day (if in person). This will help you prepare. It's not a bad thing to ask them questions! It shows an interest in meeting (and exceeding!) their expectations.

At the end of this chapter you can download a list of the different ways businesses run interviews—recruiters can use one or multiple stages of interview, and the way these look can vary, so download the list and have a read.

Preparation is power

Let's get into what you can do right now to prepare for the job interview. You may think it all comes down to that single moment when you're in the room, but there is a tonne of preparation you can do beforehand to crush your next interview. Be your best support crew and train yourself up for the interview!

1. Revise your resume documents

Revise the job advertisement and the criteria stated for a successful candidate. Remind yourself of the key skills, education and training you want to highlight. Revisit what you communicated in your cover letter and resume about what you want to bring to the business.

2. Research the business

The business has done its research on you. But have you done the same? It's a big turn-off when a candidate shows up for an interview and they haven't done their research on the company they are applying to work for.

Think of it this way: the hiring manager has read your resume and cover letter. They've probably checked out your LinkedIn and they may have looked you up on Instagram, Facebook and TikTok. Why? Because they want a snapshot of who you are before the interview. They've done their research, so it's crucial you do the same.

Check out their website, LinkedIn and socials if they have them. Download their annual report if they have one and read it. Find their company values or strategic goals. And use these insights during the interview to show you've done your research and you know what the business stands for.

3. Be prepared for the ice breakers

Recruiter: Tell me a bit about yourself and your career so far.

Me: My career is like a true-crime podcast. It's equal parts horrifying, addictive and unresolved.

Ahhhh, the dreaded 'tell me about yourself' question. It's one of the most overlooked parts of an interview process.

People prepare for all kinds of complex technical questions. But we forget the simple ones. The ones that build rapport and connection. A warm-up before the main event.

Instead, we need to think of interviews like public speaking. The opening few minutes can be make or break. The response to the 'tell me about yourself' question is just as important as the responses to technical questions.

Here are some examples of ice-breaker questions that you could practise answers to. I've also included tips for how to respond to commonly asked questions.

Ice-breaker questions include:

- Can you tell us a bit about yourself?

- What motivated you to apply for this position?

- Have you ever been a customer of our business?

- How did you learn about this position?

- What interests you about this organisation?

- What are you looking to achieve in your career?

How to answer ice-breaker questions

Okay, the moment of truth: to ace these questions, you need to practise! I know you're nervous, but that's why we're here—to help you prepare and walk into that interview with as much confidence as possible.

Let's start by working our way through an example of an ice breaker that kickstarts a job interview.

Recruiter: Tell me a bit about yourself and your career so far.

Here are three ways to prepare for this question:

- *Keep it simple.* You don't need to share your full career story. Give a snapshot of why you love what you do.

- *Give it personality!* It is not all business. Do you love reading sci-fi novels in your spare time? Are you into baking? (trust me, hiring managers love this one!) Share about who you are, not just what you do for work.

- *Share one of your big career goals.* It could be something like, 'I'm hoping to move into X one day'. Show them you've been active in planning your career moves—they love to see people looking for opportunity.

---

apply now

Grab a pen and paper and jot down all the possible ways you could answer the ice-breaker question above. Or practise solo in the car. Or grab a friend and act it out. Not dorky, empowering.

_____

_____

_____

_____

_____

---

4. Prepare for the technical questions with examples

After the ice-breaker intro, your interviewer will ask more technical questions relating to your technical training and experience. They will typically want you to provide specific examples of when you've used your skills to the benefit of the customer, team or business.

The best way to prepare for this part of the interview is to make a list of your biggest wins, learnings and achievements in your work and study. Before the interview, think of how you can link your examples and stories with the job requirements.

You can use these examples in response to a range of questions. This gives you an edge and stops you from going blank in the interview.

Imagine you were going for a role as a project manager. To prepare for the interview, you could write down detailed examples of:

- a challenging project you've led or been part of

- the most successful project you've been part of

- what you've learned from these projects.

In the interview, if the recruiter asks you to share about a project you led that failed, you're ready to go! You could quickly draw on your challenging project experience and then outline what you learned from it.

By using this approach, you can tailor and combine your examples to the questions. This enables you to showcase your strongest experiences, while reducing the chance of your nerves getting the better of you. No awkward silence, crickets or tumbleweeds.

Now that you've prepared your examples, you can start to practise how you would communicate them.

How to communicate your answers clearly and succinctly

We like to use the following formula for interviews. It helps you to be clear and succinct in your responses. Here's how it works:

- Spend 20 per cent of what you say *explaining the situation*: 'I was the lead account manager on the X campaign, where we hoped to achieve a 20 per cent growth per quarter in the client's product sales'.

- Spend 60 per cent of your time *explaining the action taken*: 'This involved leading a team to come together and analyse sales performance, determine the most profitable product line, draft a presentation outlining this information and present it to the client'.

- Spend 20 per cent *explaining the result*: 'The client took our information, actioned it and saw a sales growth of 23 per cent the following quarter'.

Highlight what you did in the situation to move it forward. Highlight *your* role in the moment. Don't use too much 'we' language. Focus on your part in it.

You have your list of job criteria and your skills from previous pages—let's pull together specific examples of when you demonstrated these skills to bring out in the interview. Some people like to prepare a few key work scenarios that can be applied to a number of different skills so in the moment they can adapt examples to the questions asked. It's up to you as to what is easier for you.

apply now

1 Think through the examples you could bring forward in an upcoming interview. List them here.

Key skill	Example of when you demonstrated this skill
e.g. leadership	I was the lead account manager on the X campaign, where we hoped to achieve a 20 per cent growth in the client's product sales. This involved leading a team to come together and analyse sales performance, determine the most profitable product line, draft a presentation outlining this information and present it to the client. The client took our information, actioned it and saw a sales growth of 23 per cent.

2 Practise speaking about these examples out loud as you've written them here. Speaking out loud is a great way to prepare for a smooth vocal delivery and shake off the nerves.

Here are some examples of technical job interview questions:

- Can you tell me about a significant project you have led?

- What do you think you could bring to this role?

- What would you say is your greatest strength? And likewise, your greatest weakness? (Don't say you 'work too hard'! Be real with your answer.)

- What unique experience do you think you could bring to this role?

- Tell me about how you've handled competing priorities?

- What would you do in the first 90 days in this role?

- How have you handled team conflict in the past?

3   Look back at the examples you prepared from your own training and work experience. How could you connect them to these questions?

Jesse, 35
Perth, WA

When I first applied for the police force, I got to the interview stage but did not progress. Upon reflection, I knew all my written application and testing was good, but I was weaker in interviews. I felt fairly dejected, I guess, and left my next police force application until four years later.

I did an unreasonable amount of interview question practice. I knew roughly all the questions/themes of interview questions now from study and my previous two job applications. I spent hour upon hour talking out loud, interviewing, while watching myself on the computer (as it was going to be an online panel interview).

I did a fantastic interview, was super calm and had great answers. Unfortunately I messed something up regarding an integrity issue (due to my prior application). I knew the second it happened (at the end of the

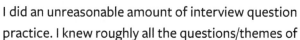

(continued)

interview) that I was unsuccessful; however, I walked away very confident with my interview skills.

I lasted a while in my current role before I completely burned out, and decided that job security isn't worth it if you're not happy. So I applied for a few mining jobs, the same detainee officer job I had already applied for, and jobs as a youth correctional officer and a trainee locomotive driver. I knew I would be successful in something—I just wasn't sure what.

I followed the same interview prep for every job. Each one was successively easier, more flowing and more confident, with answers targeted a bit more for each varying role. I had fantastic answers for the safety questions, teamwork, conflict with various people, empathy, integrity and so on. I was offered four different jobs, and now I'm a trainee locomotive driver, after a whole lot of decision making!

On reflection, confidence is what I lacked more than anything. I never really thought of it as a muscle you can train, but it most certainly is. Going through that whole process I feel like I've evolved quite a bit.

Jesse highlights a key thing in his story: practice! Answering interview questions is a practice: a muscle you have to work consistently to have it warmed up and ready on performance day. Sometimes this practice is the way to work through your confidence issues and nerves—if you've practised and practised, you've given yourself the *best* chance to perform well on the day. So talk to the bathroom mirror, and talk while you walk the dog and sit at the traffic lights!

5. The way you look tonight

When you are offered the chance to be interviewed, remember to ask what style of interview it will be and what kind of dress style is most appropriate. If the workplace is typically one where staff are wearing high-vis and steel cap boots, arriving in full-size stilettos may not be suitable!

Likewise, you wouldn't wear a hard hat to an admin office job interview. Some environments will be more formal, and others more relaxed—you really need to do the homework on your desired work environment and work through what would be most appropriate. As a general rule of thumb, it's always better to be overdressed than underdressed, and ensure you feel comfortable in the clothes you've chosen: you don't want to stand there adjusting your shirt and shoes throughout the interview. Try on your desired outfit ahead of time: look in the mirror and ask someone to review what you're wearing. Does it represent you? Is it neat and professional? Can you walk in the shoes confidently? Does it fit you properly? If the answer is yes to all of the above, you're good to go.

6. How to seal the deal

At the end of the interview, the hiring manager will ask, 'Do you have any questions for us?'

This moment is like the final seconds of a game of basketball. The scoreboard reads 52–51. It's tight. You're down by two points. There are 10 seconds left. Enough time for one final shot *cue slow motion cinematography and inspirational music*. You've got one final chance to take the shot and win the game.

The candidate pauses for a moment. And then they respond with: 'Umm, no I think you've answered most of my questions.'

Time's up. Shot missed. Game over.

The 'Do you have any questions for us?' point in the interview is crucial. It's your chance to stand out from the crowd. Have you ever gone on a date with someone who talks endlessly about themselves, but fails to ask a single question about you? Yeah, not ideal partner material! There's only a small chance they'll land a second date.

Like the opening few minutes, the closing moments of the interview are critical. This is your chance to bring it home. Show curiosity and interest in the business and the hiring manager. You'll score big points by asking great questions.

But more than that, an interview is as much about you asking the interviewer questions as it is about you answering their questions.

It's not just about them working out if you're the right person for the job. It's your opportunity to work out if the business is the right option for you and your career goals.

Here are some examples of questions that you could ask the recruiter during the interview. You can have these questions written down and bring them in with you to the interview:

- What is the vision for the organisation?

- What do you see as the greatest challenges and opportunities for this business in the X industry?

- How would you describe the culture of the organisation and why do you like working here?

- Can you describe the team to me, and particularly who I'd be working with?

- What kind of people are really successful in this business?

- What kind of working styles don't suit this work environment?

- What does success in the role look like?

- What do you want this role to focus on in the first 90 days?

Mark in your mind which of these might be relevant for jobs you're considering.

Emily, 32
Sydney, NSW

I think researching or getting to know a business before the interview is really key. I start off on their website and go straight to the 'About us' page and then the 'Meet the team' page. I then read client reviews and might even hit up ex-employees on LinkedIn for an honest review and their experience.

From the research I can already get a good understanding of the type of clients they service (businesses or individuals) and if I get a review from an ex-employee, I always ask if there were issues (often these are poor management, no room for growth or unrealistic workload expectations). Then, at the interview, I would ask subtly re: the issue and ask really specific questions, such as:

- Please describe an average day in the role.

- How are employees recognised, valued and rewarded?

- What does career progression look like and would the business be willing to tie reward with output?

Of course, I also ensure I highlight all my previous key achievements and strengths. When asked about my weakness, I would turn it into a strength. For example, a weakness of mine is at times I tend to talk more than I listen as I am an efficient communicator. I am conscious of this and often match the pace of the person I am speaking with (colleague, manager or client) and I tailor my approach, word choices and speed as it is most important in my role to communicate clearly (as immigration law can be complex and getting permanent residency in Australia can be life changing for a client)!

Emily has found some really direct ways to know as much about a business as possible before getting into the room with them. She's mastered the art of doing research to ensure the business suits her needs as well, which is a key element to career success on your own terms. She's also found a way to talk about her strengths, which is something we love hearing!

• • •

Here are some final points to consider in relation to interviews:

- Interviewers could be doing eight interviews a day (yikes, that's a lot of listening). Be brief and to the point. This will ensure you can answer all questions and that you keep the interviewer engaged. They can and will cut you short if you ramble for too long. Don't risk missing out on the role.

- How far away from your house is the interview going to be? It doesn't hurt to do a transport practice run to ensure you give yourself enough travel time.

- Remember, you're also interviewing the business. So, if a hiring manager or interviewer asks you a question that is biased or could lead to discrimination, it's a big red flag and an indicator of the business culture. Use the interview to assess whether you want to be part of that kind of environment. If it's not a healthy environment, don't settle.

Networking and LinkedIn

Yes, we've established the term 'networking' makes most people (including us) shudder. Yeah, we like happy hour on a Friday, but do we have to mingle with all that awkward small talk?

So, if you're struggling to adjust to the 'networking' term, remember, it's all about building relationships. No more cringing.

Like we talked about in chapter 6, what's the point of networking and building relationships? The top benefits of professional networking include:

- meeting potential business partners, some of whom could become long-lasting contacts who you draw on throughout your career

- getting fresh ideas to revive your business or career—get out of that rut!

- building your professional profile in the industry so people know who you are and they come to you for guidance (hello confidence)

- gaining useful industry knowledge that is only shared 'in the room'

- opening up potential job opportunities—it's all about who you know

- finding mentors who can answer your questions and offer guidance when you're stuck

- meeting high-profile individuals in the industry—learn from their journeys and apply what you learn to your own.

Have we convinced you to start building your own network? Good. Let's go!

The networking guide for a newbie

Imagine you walk into a room full of people from your industry. Nervous? You wouldn't be alone. Networking can feel so daunting. How do you even do it without shaking at the knees?

We have some tips to help change the way you feel about it and give you some actionable skills in network building both in person and online (particularly with LinkedIn).

Networking internally

Networking starts from within—within your organisation, that is. Before you jump to external connection building, start closer to home by getting to know those within your team and organisation as a whole. You work alongside these people every day and building stronger connections can only benefit the work you all do together. This is also a great way to practise your networking skills before heading out to meet new people.

Try these simple tips when networking at work:

- Simply smile and say hi to people as you walk into work each day

- Join in on communal conversations in the office or online—whether over coffee or lunch breaks. Have a laugh and get to know each other outside of your position description

- Get involved in work social events, or see if you're able to start them yourself

- Go to regular work events like Friday drinks or conferences—make the most of those opportunities

- Be encouraging with those you work alongside—highlight the great work they've done on a project and demonstrate that you enjoy working with them

- Add people from your workplace on LinkedIn.

Networking externally

At external networking events, try following these steps:

1. *Find a networking event*

   Don't just go adding people on LinkedIn cold—you don't know them and, frankly, it's a bit weird to try and add someone you haven't met! You need a professional and social event to begin networking. Search online and across social media platforms for professional, business and industry networking groups—groups that run monthly breakfasts or drinks events in your city or town. Sign up and put your name down for their next event.

2. *Attend the event with these tips in mind*

Start by taking a friend or colleague you are comfortable with. As you walk in, remember that everyone is there for the same reason so you have nothing to lose! You won't get along with everyone, but there will be someone or a group of people you will connect with. Go early and stay later to maximise the opportunity to connect. Don't be afraid to say you've never been to the event before! If you have a business card, take it—you might get the chance to exchange with those you meet.

Look to connect with the person first, not the position they hold.

Walk up to someone you don't know and introduce yourself. Start with questions like:

o   Have you been to one of these events before?

o   Where are you from?

o   What business do you work for?

o   What role do you work in?

o   Let me introduce my friend/colleague to you!

Then let the conversation unfold. Work alongside your friend or colleague to start getting to know the people there.

3. *Connect with your new contacts online*

If you met someone for the first time, now is a great time to touch base by either adding them as a professional contact on LinkedIn or shooting them a message or email and saying, 'Hey! Was great to meet you! Looking forward to connecting again at another event.'

First event down! Well done. You've just opened the first door to opportunity.

Plan to go to that event a few times or to a few different events. You'll start to connect with people you see regularly and people will notice. They'll start investing back into you as well.

Using LinkedIn to your advantage

LinkedIn is probably not your go-to social media platform (in fact, you may avoid going on LinkedIn at all costs). But, it's a super helpful tool for your career.

Think of LinkedIn as a digital version of your resume, with the opportunity to 'speak' in real time (like, post, comment, share) and connect with and learn from people from across your industry.

How to make the most of LinkedIn

Get some great photography! Don't crop an old picture: capture yourself the way you want potential employers and colleagues to see you professionally.

Connect with people on the platform who you work with, or have met at industry networking events. The only time you would add someone cold on LinkedIn is where there is what we call a 'value proposition': you're hoping to work together to benefit both your business and theirs. That might be a partnership opportunity like having someone as a guest speaker or a chance to work together on a project.

Be active on the platform: take a picture with your amazing team and thank them for their skills. Post about encouraging results in the business (obviously not private business information) and share the new things people can expect to see from your business!

Like and comment on other people's posts. Congratulate them on their new role, support the positive things they share and champion their success. This will come back around to you when it's your time to celebrate on the platform.

Remember, you're a brand ambassador for your business. Remain professional in your approach, language and attitude.

Recruiters use LinkedIn to verify information provided on resumes, and as general research on you as a person, so it does matter. Using the excuse of 'I'm not tech savvy enough' is not justifiable anymore. Make sure your profile is up to date and reflects your most recent experience. You never know, you might just get a direct message with your next job offer.

Once you're happy with how your profile looks, ask a trusted colleague to review it. How do you come across to them? Listen to any suggestions and do what feels right to you and for the way you want to be perceived professionally online.

The LinkedIn essentials checklist

I have:

☐ included all relevant education and training (refer to your resume)

☐ included all relevant work in your desired industry (refer to your resume)

☐ included professional photography

☐ connected with my colleagues

☐ connected with others I have met in person or online (at those networking events) (*wink*)

☐ shared a post, article I read, photo or workplace success (even just once a month)

☐ liked, commented or shared the posts of my connections (champion their success!).

Landing that promotion

If you're aiming for a promotion within the business you already work for treat your application as you would a new position outside of the current business. Don't assume that just because you already work there, you're a shoo-in for that management role. View your hiring manager or recruiter as a person who has never met you before and do the preparation detailed in this chapter.

Prepare your business case

You'll want to prepare your case, focusing heavily on things you have achieved during your time at the business that has advanced the business. What have you done in this role that has:

- improved internal processes?

- increased sales?

- reduced costs?

- grown the audience or customer base?

As with pay rises, the length of time you've been at a business is not a factor for guaranteeing a promotion. You need to show tangibly where you have benefited the business towards its goals or vision.

Prepare your resume

If the advertised role is treated as a formal in-house process, prepare your resume like you would for any external position. Don't assume the recruiter or hiring manager knows who you are: your business could have thousands of staff members! Follow our guidance in this chapter around preparing your resume.

Prepare for a meeting or interview

If the recruitment process is more traditional and they're going to use an interview style, follow the instructions in this chapter for interview preparation.

If the opportunity to discuss suitability for the role is something that could be more casual, start by asking the hiring manager or recruiter how you could be considered for the role. Would you be able to present your experience in a meeting? If so, ask when they are available to meet, set up a meeting and bring along your resume with a solid list of tasks you've performed within the business that meet the position criteria.

A final word

You're well and truly cruising now. Keep your cover letter and resume relevant and real. Practise your interview skills now—don't wait until you're in the room. Start networking in person and on LinkedIn today to build your relationships and open up a bunch of opportunities. Go get it.

resources   **Scan the QR code for these resources and more.**

- We've provided the following as downloads:

    o   a cover letter template

    o   a resume template

    o   a list of types of job interviews

    o   an interview example preparation table.

- Check out the episodes on *my millennial career* about crushing your next job interview, writing a killer resume and cover letter, and mastering your networking skills in person and on LinkedIn.

make
more money
(your new
favourite hobby)

9

tl;dr

- If you hate your job, no amount of extra money will make you happy or satisfied.

- There are four main ways you can increase your income significantly, move to an uncapped salary or not be captured by normal market forces. They are: be a specialist, manage people and/or processes, be in sales or be a business owner.

- Confidence is a key part to seeing your cash increase.

- Negotiation is an art, and it's one you want to do with class. Don't be greedy. Look for win-wins.

- Side hustles are a great option to increase your cash, but we'd only suggest doing so if a) you're paying off consumer debt, b) you're aiming for a certain goal, c) you're transitioning to running your own business or d) you just love a task/job/hobby.

- When negotiating pay for a new job, aim to have the discussion in the interview stage.

- The best steps to getting a pay rise involve preparing your business case based on amazing performance. Go in for 'the ask' and accept the response with grace (whether it's yes or no).

Glen in the driver's seat

Your career is single-handedly one of the most effective ways for you to build wealth.

That's why investing in yourself—your work-related training and career—is so important.

It's not just about being rewarded for the work you've done, although that is significant. It is also about creating the opportunity to invest in your future wealth.

And we aren't just talking about being greedy (hello high life!). The more wealth you create, the more opportunities you have, but you also have a greater opportunity to be generous with others, which is something we both really value.

That's why investing in your career is so important: the more skilled and proficient you are at work, the greater your opportunity to make more money for yourself, but also to open up possibilities to invest in others.

Remember, however, if you hate your job, no amount of extra money will change your job satisfaction. That's why addressing your values, mindset and tolerance for risk (as we did earlier in this book) is so critical before talking about how much you earn.

So: if you're here having taken the necessary steps to pulse check your career, and it's time to see your pay increase, let's talk about the various ways that can happen.

Spoiler alert: there's more than one way to increase your income.

Is your income a result of market forces?

Getting a pay rise isn't your only income-increasing option (Shell will walk you through how this works later in this chapter).

Let's pretend you're an employee working as a landscaper. You're 28 years old, paid at level 5 of the award (Gardening and Landscaping Services Award 2020 in Australia) and that's $25.54 per hour plus superannuation at the time of print. You start early but finish early, which is great—particularly over summer. You love what you do, but you have specific career and financial goals. You hang on for that annual salary increase. It's not an increase your employer gives you because they are kind; they're just following the award.

So what do you do?

Sure, you can ask for a pay rise and your employer may increase your hourly rate as you've worked hard, taken on extra responsibilities, completed some additional education or training associated with your role or there's a market squeeze and to keep you from moving to another company who has offered you more, your employer has matched the offer. You may need to change something up long term if increasing your income significantly in your desired line of work is a goal of yours!

Understanding market forces

This is effectively supply and demand, but I'm talking about this in relation to the labour market and the service industry. When a natural disaster rips through an area where produce is grown, there is usually a spike in the price of the produce affected.

(continued)

I can remember many years ago bananas were over $11 per kilo for a time!

Can you think of any other supply-and-demand issues in the past few years (lettuce, second-hand cars ... the list goes on!)?

When prices increase, this is because the demand for consumption doesn't decrease all that much—therefore the price increases. For the banana example, the market has determined that to secure these temporarily reduced goods, they are worth $11 per kilo and has capped out at that. The market won't pay more for these goods based on the supply at the time.

Market forces come into play in almost every area of our life.

I heard stories during the early 2000s about the Australian mining boom where there was huge demand for iron ore from Western Australia to be sold to China. The rise of the FIFO (fly-in-fly-out) employee began. There was such a demand for iron ore (and other minerals) that the only way the market could deliver was to pay extraordinary wages to attract people to get the job done. I had a plumber client earning $80000 in 2011 who gave that up to operate a machine in the mines for $180000 per year. The crazy thing about this story that puts it into perspective is that a machine operator in civil excavation would unlikely be able to earn $180000 per year.

Back to the example of the landscape gardener: they couldn't turn around and tell their boss, 'I'd like $100 per hour or I'm leaving' because they would likely be told to enjoy the view on the way out!

Similarly, an example of a more permanent fixture of this in our economy would be my ankle surgeon. He is a specialist surgeon and only operates in the private system. My GP researched him and informed me I'd have to travel to my nearest capital city for this surgeon. I remember paying an out-of-pocket cost—on top of what he received from Medicare and my private health fund—of around $3000 for a one-hour procedure. I was paying for his expertise and experience—and I was happy to pay for that—but if there were more orthopaedic surgeons who specialise in feet and ankles with a sub-specialty for keyhole procedures, he would not be able to charge such big out-of-pocket costs. Market forces would dictate that it would need to be lower.

The point here is to understand market forces in general, and while you may be able to ride a wave created in labour markets due to market forces for the short or medium term, you need to remember that you didn't create the wave and have no control over how long the ride goes for. You can't rely on things out of your control as part of long-term planning. In fact, plan that there will be swings and roundabouts; however, you need to become your very own market force!

You can do just that by building highly competitive skills (as discussed in chapter 4) in areas that are in high demand.

High-growth industries and sectors

Science, technology, engineering and mathematics, or STEM, are areas of growth and those who focus on these types of sectors will enjoy a higher level of income. There is a labour shortage in the Australian market for many occupations that utilise STEM fields. STEM fields are a global market force.

Gustavo is a close family friend who recently migrated with his family to Australia from Argentina. He is an electrical engineer with many years of experience and he moved here with a student visa (subclass 500) as he will be continuing to work on his English with formal study. The issue with his visa is that he is limited to 40 hours of work per fortnight. However, at the time of print, due to the current labour shortage in Australia, this condition has been temporarily removed for all sectors of the economy, so individuals with this class of visa can work as many hours as they wish.

I asked a friend of mine who is a manager of electrical engineers at a large workplace if he knew of any jobs available and he said there are currently three electrical engineering positions vacant at his workplace, all with a starting salary of $180000. He also said, if Gus wasn't suited to the role, he knows of two other places with several vacancies.

Before I could give Gus' resume to my friend, he had already lined up an interview with another firm through someone else in our network. He got the job within two weeks of being in Australia. His tax file number hadn't even been issued so his first payslip had the maximum tax withheld!

His employer is supportive of him and Gus' boss is happy to assist with an application for a change in his class of visa to keep him long term. Funny that!

Do you think Gus will have a problem with his career and income in the medium term once he is up to speed with Australian engineering standards?

Gus picked a winner. He's working in a high-growth industry. There's high demand and low talent supply. It gives him bargaining power and ample opportunity to increase his income. Plus, the demand has given him the opportunity to travel across the world for his career. His story shows the power of understanding market forces and capitalising on them for your own future.

Contrast the FIFO for the mining boom in the early 2000s in Australia with what we're seeing in STEM today. There's a clear difference because STEM industries are booming in most advanced economies and are not specific to a small part of the world. STEM is also not constrained by a finite resource (coal) on a ticking timeline. Tick. Tock.

Sorry, the robots are already here

In the early 1900s, if you were in the business of manufacturing, you would have made a lot of money. This industry was taken over by machines and globalisation, so there is now a low demand (relatively speaking) for factory workers in most modern economies.

This may also soon be the case for careers like professional drivers over the next 10+ years (hire car, taxi/Uber, long-haul truck drivers and, dare I say, airline pilots! Yikes). Technology is disrupting market forces so you need to be part of the force, not a victim of it. But you can get ahead of the curve and adapt your career to future proof it as much as possible. This may mean a career change at some point, but leaning on a solid mindset, understanding your strengths and skills, values and goals and taking some risks will enable you to transition as easily as possible.

It's all not as bad as it seems. At the turn of the century, so-called experts said the internet was going to decimate the travel agency industry and make yoga instructors obsolete because you can book your flight online and watch a YouTube yoga session. Technology was going to put a lot of surgeons out of business, too. To date, this is far from true. Travel agents have still thrived, as have yoga instructors because humans need connection and accountability. Surgeons are now just using the technology as an aid to make the surgery more precise, less invasive and better for their patients.

On a personal note, when I worked as a financial adviser, many of my colleagues were worried about their careers long term. Technology can now produce advice with a series of inputs and a low cost point. The issue is a computer can't yet work out if there is a couple sitting at the computer and one person is squirming in their seat, uncomfortable with an output regarding risk or investments. This is the power of human-to-human connection and interaction.

(continued)

Technology and artificial Intelligence (AI) will play a big part in everyone's life both now and in the future and it should be embraced. Used the right way, it can enhance your career, job or business. It can automate the boring and routinised parts of your role and allow you to be more efficient and to ultimately make more money.

The key here is to build skills that cannot be automated. Focus on what it means to be human. Build your interpersonal skills, creativity, communication and critical thinking. These skills future proof your career.

What if you're not suited to STEM roles?

The problem is that many people are not wired for these types of jobs (I'm not, and Shell is definitely not—remember her maths results?). But, just because you're not a technically minded person doesn't mean you still can't jump into these industries because every industry is an ecosystem that has many parts.

Can you consider the following?

- Marketing for a company in science (think Bayer)

- Human resources for a medical laboratory (think CSL)

- Sales for a technology company (think Microsoft)

- Internal accounting in a company that specialises in sustainability (think AECOM)

Sure, you don't need a high level of deep technical understanding of the particular STEM industry that you're working in, but to be part of the ecosystem you can learn enough to be dangerous. I have met many amazing, talented and all-round great people in the financial services industry who are not strictly financial advisers, accountants or mortgage brokers but they are in this world and have thriving careers!

While I believe the STEM industries will have a very long and likely perpetual tail, can you look at some niche parts of this world and their ecosystems? For example:

- AI and robotics

- climate, sustainability and renewable energy

- medicine

- astronomy (the other one, not the star signs)

- something no-one has thought of yet.

When I left school, my current role as a podcaster wasn't even a career option, nor was it even invented. Keep learning, look for macro-level trends and catch a market force slipstream as part of the STEM ecosystem.

My advanced income quadrant

I believe there are four main ways you can *increase your income significantly*, move to an *uncapped salary* or *not be captured by normal market forces*. These will allow you to be the most beneficial financial asset in the marketplace to ultimately make more money from the time, energy and hard work that you have invested into your career.

The advanced income quadrant is founded on the premise that you know your stuff and you're suitably skilled and qualified.

To be clear, this quadrant is only to be entered into if you wish for a role or career that will likely lead to an un-capped or significantly higher income than an award-based employee role.

If you're looking to increase your income significantly, you'll need to step back and consider the four parts of the quadrant illustrated in figure 9.1. You'll also need to think through any other extra training and education for your current role, and whether your employer has set you a framework to increase your pay.

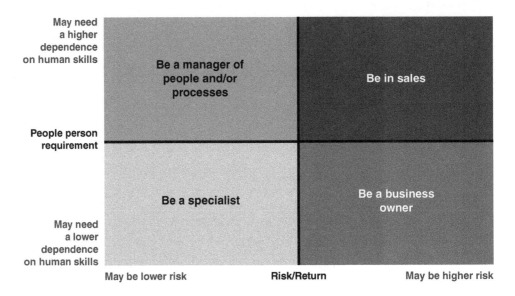

Figure 9.1: Glen's advanced income quadrant

Let's take a look at each of the four parts of the quadrant.

1. Be a specialist

A specialist is someone with unique skills, very targeted on a niche area. These professionals fall outside of award rates or conventional roles. The more specialised you become, the more capacity you have to name your price. It could be a very narrow field in engineering, psychology, construction, software development and so on.

Maybe you're the only surgeon who can perform a very rare surgery at high altitude while speaking French. Random example, but you get my point. In this situation, you might be one of a few or the only person who can perform a very unique role. If someone asks for your services, name your price because there is no-one else to call, and no-one else to compare the cost of your services to.

Risks
- Your specialty may become commoditised with technology over time.

- The market may not need you anymore.

People component
- You may not need to interact with lots of people day to day if you're an employee engineer in a small team.

- Some specialties will allow you to spend lots of time alone (think software developer, artist, etc.).

Other considerations
- Specialists who are self-employed can earn more money than an employee. There are risks to this because you'll have to put yourself out there to get work and be more dialled into the 'people side'. There may be periods between jobs. While we don't have permission to share the quote, remember the movie where someone kidnaps the daughter of an elite dude with a specific set of skills and then he gets on the phone with the kidnappers and...be like him.

(continued)

2. Be a manager of people and/or processes

Teams need to be managed and led by good people. Many businesses need a member of their team to ensure that people in the organisation perform at their best, and that processes are smooth and well oiled. This kind of role has the potential to increase quality and performance across the board so such a role pays well. It's all well and good to say, 'now we sell yo-yos!' but if there's no team or process to back that up, it might not be so successful. Effective leaders are essential to the long-term performance and success of any business, so they are worth their weight in income.

If you're keen to lead a team one day, here's a word of warning. Leadership is not a role for everyone. Before pursuing a role like this, genuinely consider if managing people is what you want to spend the majority of your time doing.

It's not enough to be technically good at your job, so voilà, the next step is a leadership position (BTW: this is why we see so many ineffective managers in the workplace). It's not something you do to move up to the next income bracket. A lot of people who become leaders simply to get more cash in the bank or because they think it's the only option for progression, only disrupt the people and processes they need to improve.

The motivation to lead a team needs to be equally about serving the people you lead and helping the business achieve its goals. The benefit is that the pay can be higher. But this is not the main driver for why you'd seek out a leadership role.

Risks
- The biggest risk of managing people is that you fall into the role without intention and you're not suited to it.

- Middle management at larger companies can sometimes be the first to go in corporate restructures.

People component

- You need to be able to work with people in the main if you are a direct team leader.

- If you're in a role that manages a process, this could be like a rostering manager for a large organisation or a production line manager—it may be less face to face.

Other considerations

- Think of leadership like any other skill. It's not something you're born with. It's something you learn. And the best way to learn about leadership is through practice. Gain exposure and experience by stepping into leadership roles temporarily at first (for example, take on higher duties while your boss is on leave) and assess whether the role is right for you.

3. Be in sales

Many sales roles can have an uncapped revenue potential because typically they involve a combination of ongoing salary plus a percentage of sales made. Your role creates revenue through the creation of products and services in exchange for money from your customers. This kind of role is directly linked to business revenue so your strong performance will demonstrate strong sales, and ultimately strong financial performance.

Risks

- If you're an employee, a lower base salary means a higher commission structure.

- The harder you work, the more you're likely to get financial results so you can't take on a role thinking you'll earn money without doing the hard work.

(continued)

- Sometimes there can be boom-and-bust type cycles, depending on your industry and sales pipeline. You need to set your life up based on your base salary.

People component

- Anything to do with sales is all about people. You need to love people. Sales is a people business.

- You have two ears and one mouth. Use that ratio when communicating: 2 × listening to 1 × talking.

Other considerations

- You need to genuinely be passionate about the products or services you're selling. If you sell a certain brand of mountain bike, you'll have the most success if you use the brand you're selling in your spare time.

4. Be a business owner

Building and running a business is the final part of the income quadrant. But there's risk involved. The costs lie with you. You employ others. You have to build and maintain a product or service moving forward. You need to attract customers and you wear a lot of hats in the beginning. And success is heavily dependent on you. But there is uncapped income-earning potential there—it's only limited by your focus and effort. When you have a business you'll generally employ people, so you tick the 'manager of people' box of the income quadrant, too.

I would put sole traders in this quadrant, if they have a specialist type of role. Specialists earn more money than those in 'commodity vocations' and essential trades and services (think hairdresser, beautician, plumber, electrician, motor mechanic, for example).

There is, however, a higher chance of income if you are a sole trader who works for themselves, as your income will not cap out as fast as being an employee—but the risk or trade-off for the higher chance of income is that your income is not guaranteed.

Risks

- You got lucky when you started your business, but the market moved and you didn't adapt. Don't try to take over the world selling fidget spinners, as these types of fads have a short business life cycle.

- Poor cash flow planning is the single most important thing for starting a business—no cash flow, no business!

- You will have employees and you need to ensure your team is paid every single week.

- You find out that you are not cut out for business and the level of risk and drama that it can carry.

People component

- Generally, you need to be good with people, but as your business gets to a decent size with employees you may hire a manager to take care of a lot of day-to-day people things. You are still responsible for setting and guiding the culture with the team though.

Other considerations

- You may need to start with just yourself, but being a sole trader is just owning your job (not a bad thing) and market forces will cause your income to cap out as there are only so many hours in the day you can put your energy to a task.

- You are able to have multiple income streams within the business.

- Your business may have value if you have a recurring income, a solid database and a proven track record. A good business is a financial asset. This is generally not the case for sole traders.

(continued)

A note for the self-employed/sole traders

If you have a job or career you love, you are far ahead of many other people, regardless of what that is. I have used the examples of traditional trades and services such as hairdresser, beautician, plumber, electrician, motor mechanic and so on because we all know of these much-needed people and services in our society. If you're working in these industries and want to take your income further and above normal market forces, you need to find the right pathway based on the income quadrant.

The first port of call is as a sole trader, which fits in the business corner of the quadrant. This can and does lead to having a business that employs people and can have huge growth over time. I started my business as a sole trader, then moved to an incorporated entity once I was employing a team of people.

This will allow you to earn more money as self-employed people are responsible for generating the work, but it enters the risk/reward spectrum. The self-employed are taking on more risk of not guaranteeing any work each day, but will be rewarded more than an employee. Over time, this risk decreases as you become more established because you become known and you receive repeat business. You just need to know that a sole trader will then cap out either by market forces or by the physical time they have each day to perform their trade.

My motor mechanic is self-employed and has been for some time. He is the only one in his business. He also has a very profitable business and is well known in the community. He services many cars, old and new. He can make more than an employee motor mechanic at a dealer or private business as he also makes a profit on car parts he replaces for each car service. The problem is, if he wants to earn more money, he may be captured by market forces. As good as he is, if he said to me next time I got my car serviced that it would now cost $500 per hour for labour, I'd likely go somewhere else. But because he is good, the only one who works on my car and he knows the history of my car (and I actually like the guy), if he said he is increasing his hourly rate by $40, I probably wouldn't care.

As a sole trader, to start to make money above normal market forces you would either need to specialise or grow the business and move into other parts of the income quadrant. The balance here is knowing your market. While my mechanic couldn't specialise in Aston Martin cars where his business is (no market), he may be able to become the 'go to' for all Audi owners or other European automakers and charge a premium for this specialty.

This broad example applies to all sole traders, regardless of the trade or service.

Figure 9.2 shows what stepping into the advanced income quadrant may look like over time, as opposed to a traditional award-based role.

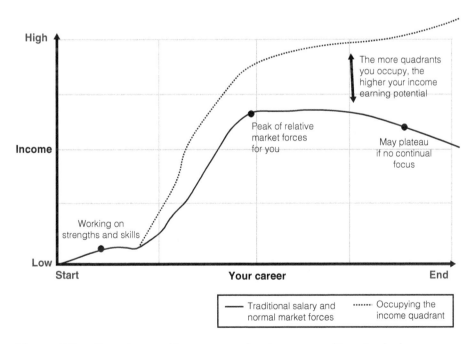

Figure 9.2: the advanced income quadrant compared to a typical award-based role

Blending parts of the advanced income quadrant

Like many things in life, it doesn't have to be all or nothing! What if you wanted to just focus on one part of the quadrant? That's totally fine. But often one will lead to another. What if you could layer two or more of the quadrants?

Here are some examples:

- *The change management specialist who is a self-employed contractor.*

  While this isn't strictly a 'business' until staff are hired and other change-management specialists are employed, there is a higher chance of income generation after taking into account the associated risks. They may consult to several businesses at one time.

- *The physiotherapist who owns their practice and has other physiotherapists working in their practice.*

  They are a business owner and also a manager of people and processes (even if they have a practice manager).

- *The specialist software developer who is responsible for a team of other developers.*

  This specialist is an employee of a large organisation. You can still be an employee and blend areas of the quadrant.

- *The state-based sales manager in charge of a team of business development managers for a national company.*

  They are responsible for people and processes and enjoy an uncapped income in the form of bonuses.

- *The business owner who sells homewares out of a physical location but also has a decent online presence.*

They employ a team of people both in the store and also have a packing area out the back for online orders. They also have scale online for their sales, which means this can be an uncapped income and they can sell products on Instagram 24/7.

Occupy all quadrants

I'm fortunate enough to have a foot in each camp of the advanced income quadrant. I can't stress enough that a lot of the quadrant speaks to the chapters on risk, and strengths and skills and can't be done overnight, if increasing your income above market norms is of value to you.

Here is what my world looks like at the moment.

Specialist

I've become a well-known personal finance commentator and an authority within this space in Australia. I'm often asked to speak at events and paid very well to do so. I am a go-to for many journalists for comments on topical money issues. Before my current career, when I was a financial adviser, I had a subspecialty of business succession advice because I loved working with small businesses, too. Being a specialist will always attract good money. Like any specialist, I do have a responsibility to be across most personal finance issues so it requires ongoing involvement in the space.

Manager of people and/or processes

At the time of print, I employ five people in the immediate team, engage eight hosts and we run at least seven weekly podcasts, with multiple episodes at any one time. I am only a host on two of these shows. So I have cultivated other quality professionals in their respective fields to bring their expertise to the podcast table. I have created systems and processes in concert with my team to allow these shows to run week-on-week without my input. These shows often produce income without my weekly touch. The buck does stop with me to be a driver of team culture and vision, but I empower my team to own their specific roles.

Sales

My business is 100 per cent online and this means we have scale, which means as our podcast listeners grow, we don't need to employ more staff. An extra 100000 monthly listeners can enable me to sell more sponsorship packages and not have to increase my expenses. I also sell online courses (and I have some free ones to genuinely help people—for example, those you need to get out of debt). I have books in most stores and do webinars for corporates. The business has about 10 different income sources and many do not need a direct trade of my time for money.

Business owner

I'm the sole owner of my business, which employs people, produces content and effectively owns all the profit that is generated. My income is truly uncapped; however, I carry a lot of risk. It hasn't happened overnight, but I have been intentional with this part of the quadrant. While my business isn't perfect and 100 per cent free of me (as I'm part of the product we sell), it's my goal to continue to build it so if I was no longer around, it could continue and still employ staff and produce quality content.

There's no cause for alarm

These four areas take planning, focus and a little drop of courage to achieve, but they are by no means unachievable. If increasing your income is your goal, you'll be fairly driven, so use that momentum to get a good thing going in one of these areas.

I can't stress enough that I have met and know many people who are very happy and content with their current role and career and wouldn't ever want to or need to even think about stepping into the income quadrant.

It's so important to remember that like risk, you should only walk down a road if opportunities align with your personal values and career goals.

Which of the four items listed in Glen's quadrant are right for you?

_____

_____

_____

_____

_____

Confidence

Your confidence is like a muscle and you need to work on it as early in your career as possible. But if you are well into your career and feel you lack confidence, that's totally fine. You are here now and can start to exercise.

I alluded to confidence in the risk chapter, and it goes hand in hand with producing an income. The only person in your life looking out for your career is you. You can still be an introvert—meek, quiet and shy—but you need to know that sometimes it's the confidence that will get you the extra income (that is, you only had to ask your boss!).

The cool thing about confidence is that like muscles in your body, the things you first thought were heavy to lift are now easy. You just had to start.

What can you do today to start to lift your confidence?

Remember, confidence is contagious. When you walk into that meeting with your boss, and you ask for a raise with confidence, it transfers. Don't be apologetic about knowing what you're worth. Be confident in it.

Learning and being inspired from the following negotiation tips will help you go with your confidence. How can you add to them in your own life?

Negotiation

Most things in life are a negotiation. From trying to get your three-year-old child to eat their veggies or arranging a trade-off with your spouse for a weekend away with friends, to buying or selling items on Facebook marketplace or trying to get the best deal on a driver while on your holiday, you have likely developed your own skills that you fall back on.

But what about your workplace, job and career? There are times you'll need to have robust talks with people at work, which can be a challenge. You may need to negotiate flexible working arrangements, working conditions, training opportunities and salary among a variety of things in your career. The point here is to expect negotiation to be part of your career at different times.

Negotiation can be a scary word but it's a day-to-day part of life. I don't believe healthy and true negotiation needs to be aggressive or confrontational. It's about two parties coming together for the best outcome for both.

As I talked about in the risk chapter, negotiation is the execution of your research, preparedness and the start of a process and conversation.

Shell will talk about some tactical things relating specifically to pay later in this chapter, but I want to step back and give you some of my tips for success in any negotiation. I will use examples of an employee speaking to their boss, team leader or manager.

A negotiation mindset

I have a bit of a confession to make. I love negotiating. It's like a sport for me. Each time I negotiate with a person or business, I'm always looking for the value exchange, for the win-win and for the deal to be struck and all parties happy with the outcome. They do say though, if no-one got everything they wanted, it was a successful negotiation. Following are the intangibles that I've learned from my own negotiation over the years.

Make sure you're aligned

Alignment is important because if you want to negotiate a pay rise with an employer whose business values and mission don't align with yours, your energy may be better spent finding another place to work. Perhaps your employer is passive aggressive and after many years you note they are not changing. Are you really happy to continue to be aligned with this team? Make sure you have your values and goals front of mind before any negotiation.

Make sure you're all good before you pull that thread

It may be a big thing to step up to the plate and begin a negotiation. I would suggest you have peace in your personal life before you start adding any undue stressors to your life. This also goes for your own mental health. If you're unwell, you may not have the capacity to deal with the extra stressors that may come from the negotiation. My point here is to ensure you are in a good headspace and have a relatively settled life going on, to avoid distractions while you prepare and execute your negotiation. If it can wait, it will likely be worth waiting until you're as stable as possible.

Read the room

If your workplace has just been through some financial troubles, now might not be the time to ask about pay. Similarly, if you're in a government role, there may be set bands of pay that your immediate boss can't do anything about—so you may need to ask about other learning and development benefits available to you as part of their budget. Also, if last time you caught up with your employer they stated a few things they wanted you to work on, you'd better make sure those issues are well resolved!

Seek first to understand

Get to know the perspective of the person you're negotiating with as soon as possible so you're not negotiating in vain for a deal that isn't going to happen. You may ask your employer a question like, 'Are you happy with my performance at the moment?' This might bring up an issue that would have been known if you had 'read the room'. What if your boss said, 'Well, I'm glad you wanted to catch up because I wanted to talk to you about being late most days and when I look over at you, you're always on your phone.' *Bingo!* You have just learned that there is no way on the planet you could proceed to ask for a salary increase. In this instance you may reply with, 'Thanks for letting me know. I wanted to approach you outside of our scheduled reviews because long term I want to do better and be better so that I can one day sit here and talk to you about my salary and future opportunities.'

Do deals with people, not positions

You are talking to a person. This person may carry a lot of responsibility. You need to learn to respect not only the position, but the person. Even if you are in a workplace that you don't love and/or have a manager you don't gel with, it is important to respect the position. Always try to connect with the person.

If appropriate and you know that they need to take your proposal up the chain, you may ask, 'What do I need to do to make this easier for you to get over the line?' Connecting with the person will also ensure there is a higher chance of them going in to bat for you if they are not the direct decision maker. Did you know that as humans we have more in common than what we don't? Can you find something you have in common with your counterpart on a human level? Perhaps you both enjoy watching tennis or are from the same hometown?

Only look for genuine win-wins

Know that each side of the negotiation wants a good outcome. I have a rule in my life that I do not do any negotiations or business partnerships if it isn't a genuine win-win. I don't want to go so hard on the deal to get it over the line, that the person on the other side feels like they got nothing out of it. This also plays into doing deals with people, not positions. Sure, your manager may not own the company, but allowing them to also win from the outcome will ensure they have buy-in to the deal.

Make sure you know your best- and worst-case scenarios

Like anything in life, you need to know your target. As part of your preparation, you need to know what you want as a best case and also what you'd be happy with as an alternative. This is about hoping for the best-case scenario but also covering off any trade-offs or setting reasonable expectations. You might be asking for a pay rise, but if money is tight, would you value an education course paid for by your employer from the learning and development budget or one day off extra per month. Shell will talk more about this on the following pages.

Know your worth

Perhaps the most important part of any negotiation or deal is about you as the asset. You are valuable, you are creative, you are unique and everyone is good at something. If you get a sense that you are being treated with any type of disdain, prejudice, sexism, racism, ageism or any other disparagement, it might not be the right place or deal for you long term — even if the salary component is amazing. You are worth more than putting up with that. On the other hand, if it's the most welcoming place on the planet and they are not willing to pay you what the market would otherwise, it may be time to look elsewhere. But go back to the cost-benefit analysis in chapter 3 as there may need to be some trade-offs at some point.

Negotiation practicalities

Following are some practical learnings that you might want to consider when you're next negotiating in the workplace.

No ambushing

If you want to talk to someone about an issue, make time for this in advance. Give the other party notice about what you'd like to discuss. Otherwise you will only make things awkward: when people are caught off guard they can say things they don't really mean and will not be in the headspace to chat about the issues you want to discuss. You may send an email to your boss saying, 'Would you be open to catching up in the coming weeks to have an informal chat about my role? It's not urgent.' If they reply with a yes, you could then ask what date and time would work and then lock that in.

Be prepared

Make sure you don't go to your employer asking for more pay not knowing that you're already paid very well based on equivalent workers in the market. This is about understanding market forces and not sounding entitled. The less prepared you are, the more chance your negotiation will end poorly. What do you need to prepare for? Can you put together a summary on paper or email before or after the meeting? Can you write down some questions you wish to ask before the meeting so you can read them out?

No ultimatums or shake-downs

Most people do not react well to threats (let's face it, you don't!) and there is absolutely no reason why this would be any different in the workplace. 'If you don't do this, I will ...' or 'I need you to decide by the end of the week or ...'. This is a sign of immaturity or poor judgement. It's also not valuing the other side of the equation—the person you're trying to strike a deal with.

There are times in the commercial world where there may need to be a deadline for a party to get back to you with a decision as a broader negotiation strategy or in a genuine case of you being headhunted for a similar role. You then let your employer know about this and see what they can do to meet your request if they wish to keep you (because you like the role and team).

After all, you need to put yourself first. Just make sure you're communicating it honestly, without it feeling like an ultimatum.

No immediate deadlines

'Okay, so is that a yes to the salary increase?'

'Can you let me know by COB tomorrow please?'

'I'm applying for a loan for my new plunge pool, so I'd love to know as soon as possible.'

Impractical deadlines like this don't go down well. The person you're negotiating with may have other stakeholders who they need to discuss the matter with that you are not aware of. They might not be able to see that person for another week. Instead, you can say, 'I know you'll need time to consider this request. Perhaps we can catch up again to discuss more. When works for you?' Then, schedule in the meeting, which serves as an easy follow up and means you don't have to awkwardly ask, 'Where is this up to?'

Ask open-ended and calibrated questions

This will allow you to extract the gold. These questions have 'what' and 'how' in them.

What would work better:

'Are you happy with my role to date?'

or

> *'How do you think I am going in my role to date. Do you have any feedback?'*
> and *'What things do you see that you are happy with?'*

This may also get your counterpart talking more and they may reveal things that are not planned. This is one you should always prepare beforehand.

When I negotiate brand deals, I always ask, 'What does success look like to you as part of this campaign?' This always helps with understanding where they are coming from and what their expectations are. It also helps you to understand if what is in their mind is in line with what you can deliver.

Embrace silence and those 'awkward pauses'

You don't always have to fill the void with your annoying voice! As much as you think it's about you, it's also about the other side getting what they want out of the discussion. So it's totally normal to allow for silence for thought to be baked into the cadence of the conversation.

You're also allowed to ask if you can have a moment to think about your answer if you're really put on the spot. This will show confidence and keep the conversation at a reasonable pace.

The last thing you want to do is get swept up in a conversation that is moving so fast that you have not been able to consider the offer that's put in front of you on the spot. It might be hard to unscramble that egg if you commit. While it might feel normal for your counterpart, it could be hasty for you. It's totally fine to ask if you can have some time to think about what they've expressed and regroup in a few days.

Try to be on neutral territory

When organising a meeting with your boss or team leader, can you do it on neutral territory? Like meeting at a café, or going for a walk, or in a common meeting room instead of their office? It's not doable in every workplace (or if you work remotely) but I've seen this approach work well when people get out of the normal work environment. Offering to buy them a coffee or lunch will not only humanise the encounter, but also, food and drinks relax people. It will slightly shift their mindset of being in 'boss mode' at their desk. Offering to buy them a coffee or lunch will also show you're not stingy and is the international sign of goodwill.

> Just make sure the environment is somewhat controlled. You need to be as relaxed as possible. A busy, popular place may be a distraction if people are stopping to say hi or a loud motorbike is driving past just as you're trying to put your case forward. Being on neutral territory will also help remove any awkwardness as opposed to just sitting down at a desk—and you can chat on the way to the cafe or while waiting for coffee to be served. Don't be afraid to plan your 'small talk questions' so they don't appear to be small talk. For example, 'What is your current take on the recent news about XYZ in the industry?'

See it as a healthy chat

Negotiations should be healthy, robust chats. They need not be aggressive or contain any type of malice. If you encounter this type of activity it's important to not respond in the same way. Stay cool, calm and collected. Try to act in good faith, and remember you can only control how *you* react. It is really hard to have an ongoing relationship with someone who isn't showing good faith as there is likely no alignment. I believe negotiations are also a good way to see how the counterparty behaves and whether you'd want to actually do business or engage with them long term if they are, simply put, not nice people.

Use labels as opposed to making accusations

Do you like being accused of something, rightly or wrongly? Didn't think so. So if you need to broach a topic or issue as part of your negotiation you can label the issue, making it stand alone next to the table as opposed to your counterpart thinking that 'you' are telling them something that might be awkward. This could throw off the negotiation and essentially turn the other person hostile or make them feel that they are not in control. It's about making neutral statements.

Part of this process is not using the word 'I' or 'I'm'. So once you spot something that is said or you want to bring up, label it. When we hear someone else say 'I think you', or 'I'm hearing that …', our guard gets up.

Instead of saying, 'I'm hearing that you're not willing to …', try, 'It sounds like at this time there is no …'

It will soften the room and will also make it less awkward for the person you're talking with.

I learned about labelling from the book *Never Split the Difference* by Chris Voss.

Have a pen and paper with you

This will always help you. Particularly when you are writing down their key thoughts, and particularly if you write down 'what success means to them' as part of the deal. You can even pause and say, 'Just let me write this down, as I now know it's important to you.' Not only will you be able to have pre-written questions in front of you, you'll also come across as attentive, prepared and dialled in.

Over deliver

Once you have finalised the win-win negotiation, don't just deliver the bare minimum on what was agreed. Sure, there are times in the commercial world where you only have to deliver what was contracted, but when it comes to your role at your workplace, I believe you need to continue to work hard, add value and not have a 'bare minimum' mindset. This will help you when you are back at the negotiating table and, when all else fails, you can go home knowing that you added value and did great work.

What if the negotiation fails?

Not all negotiations are fruitful. Not all of them end with a genuine win-win arrangement. I would encourage you to stick with an employer, team or workplace that has a good long-term upside if they are genuine when they say, 'We can talk about your salary, but it needs to be in 6 months.'

The main issue I see with failed negotiations is that one party is not serious about having a good outcome and likes to 'kick the can' down the road and hope the problem goes away. If you are in a workplace where you can't lock them in for some serious talks about your role, flexibility, improved conditions or pay, it could be a greater sign of the culture of the place not valuing good people or something else that isn't right long term.

Stick with it and give it time if you believe there is good faith. The more we are addicted to our phones and instant responses and gratification, the more we want that in real life. We need to understand that human consideration, deep thought and business decisions need time. But you'd have to really consider continuing to negotiate with someone who you can't pin down, where the goalposts are always moving or if a bit of a stalemate has been happening for some time.

---

apply now

How is your confidence? What from Glen's negotiation list could you work on?

_____

_____

_____

_____

_____

Side hustles

This could be one of the easiest ways to make more money, if you have the time and energy, and are good at something that can bring you an additional income.

A side hustle might be managing a business's social media, doing floor and wall tiling on weekends, driving Uber or pouring beers after hours. Something you hustle to get more money on the side!

I'll always encourage people to step out to make more money, but I'd generally only encourage a side hustle for the following four reasons:

1. *To pay off consumer debt*

   Most of the time when people have consumer debt in their lives (credit cards, personal loans, buy-now-pay-later and other store cards), it generally means they have systematically spent more money than earned. A side hustle is a good way to create income for a short term to pay off that debt! Get in, get it paid off and keep out of debt!

2. *To save towards a goal*

   You want a once-off trip around the world, which will be a big financial commitment other than your day-to-day or year-on-year expenses. A side hustle is good for getting extra money in the door alongside your day job. You may want to save for your first home faster or build up an emergency fund or do it seasonally (to save for school fees for kids). This is also a short-term output of extra energy and time to meet a goal. A friend of mine once did Uber to save up for a few tattoos without the money coming from the household budget.

3. *To transition to your own business*

    Side hustles are a great way to put your toe in the water to see if you can get enough customers, sales or work to do your desired job on your own terms. If your work contracts permit and/or it's a different field, you can ease your way in and it can be a low-risk way to start your business. Then, as things take off, you can make the call to lean into your side hustle and turn it into your full-time gig!

4. *You just like the thing and it's not really about the money*

    You are content with your life, career and general money situation. You love making and selling ceramics at markets or you have a beehive and you sell honey to people. You put any money you make from your side hustle back into your hobby or into your investment account. The point here is that if the money from your side hustle stopped coming in, it wouldn't bother you. It still is a registered little business and you will need to do tax returns and so on, but you do it for the love or hobby of it!

I don't believe a side-hustle income should be used to supplement your weekly income, as I'd rather have you focus on your core career and build that. The issue with doing a side hustle to just feed money into your week-on-week expenses is that you're doing more hours and consuming the money—it's not going towards something to enhance or propel your life. It could end up backfiring as you may be accustomed to living on that income and you won't be able to stop. It's become a bit of a popular phrase in the recent decade but not everyone needs to or has to do a side hustle. If you need more money, you can work overtime, if that's available, or focus on your career as a whole—leaning into other parts of this book—to make more money from your career.

What reason side hustle reason is your priority? What side hustle could you try?

_____

_____

_____

_____

_____

Let's talk about pay, baby!

Shell in the driver's seat

Big businesses want to make money. Small businesses want to make money. And of course, you want to make money. So why do we have such a hard time talking about it? Well, for starters, it's a taboo subject. For so long, pay has been kept under wraps in the workplace. And although we're seeing this change more recently with organisations introducing pay transparency policies, it's still a difficult subject to broach.

Many people don't know how to have conversations about pay. They worry that if they talk about their pay expectations they're being selfish or greedy. We could not disagree more. Your career should be financially rewarding. And organisations want to reward, recognise and retain high performing employees—so they know this conversation matters.

> **Here's a tip for free:** to make more money, you need to get comfortable talking about money.
>
> Think about how often a business reviews its financial statements. Most businesses have those end-of-month financial processes where they reconcile their accounts and analyse the profit and loss. They have multiple conversations with their accounting team to look at the business's financial performance. In your own career, you need to be regularly reviewing your financial position. Don't be ashamed of that. That's what every business does. And your career is like a business. You're in it to help others, serve customers and of course, make money.

In this section, you'll learn how to make more money by having non-awkward conversations about pay. We'll also teach you the art and science of asking for a pay rise, communicating your salary expectations and negotiating pay during a recruitment process.

Negotiating pay for a new job

When is the right time to ask about pay in a recruitment process? The short answer: it depends. You don't want to ask too early and look like you're only in it for the money. But, you also need to know if the role is financially viable for you. Yep. It's a weird little dance that no-one wants to perform.

Here's our general rule: wait until you get to the interview stage to ask. If the hiring manager hasn't provided you with a salary range during the application process, we recommend asking for the salary range by the end of the first interview.

Before the interview, consider the pay you're hoping for. Do your research on comparable roles and salaries. Use this data to create a desired salary range you would want to achieve. The start of the range is the lowest you're willing to go. We call this your walk-away price. If they don't meet this, you're walking. The end of the range is the ultimate salary goal. You don't communicate your walk away price—keep that to yourself for now. You start at the higher end of the range and see where this fits with what they are offering.

Here are some messaging ideas to help you communicate about pay.

- How to ask about the salary range during an interview:

  I am excited about this opportunity. I think it's a great fit with my skills and experience. I'm keen to understand the salary range for this role. Can you talk me through the remuneration (HR speak for pay) and benefits?

- How to respond if they ask what your salary expectations are:

  My salary expectations are $X, based on my skills and experience, and the pay for similar roles externally. How does this align?

  Pause—wait it out, allow the breathing room

- How to respond if they say that's too high and you're keen on the role:

  I'm really interested in the opportunity to work with you, so I'm open to discussing the salary further. What were you thinking the role would be paid at?

These are nice ways to position the conversation. It doesn't come across as pushy, but it is confident, clear and concise—exactly how you want to come across when you're talking about pay.

You want to know the salary as early as you can without seeming to be too focused on money. Say you have three rounds of interviews for a role you're super keen on. You get to the end of the third interview, and finally dredge up the courage to ask how much the role is paying, only to learn the salary range is $20000 less than what you expected. Ouch! By asking at the first interview, you get that clarity up front and you don't waste each other's time.

Knowing your value and communicating it with confidence

One of the questions applicants find most challenging during recruitment is 'So what are your salary expectations?' You need to prepare a response in advance so you can communicate it with confidence.

One of my mentors asked me to practise my sales pitch in front of the mirror. He said I needed to observe how I communicated the cost of my services. It was a really interesting (albeit a bit awkward) experience. When I said how much money I charged for a service, my body language and communication would shift. I became tentative, hesitant and I'd flinch when I said the cost.

It wasn't a sign that my pricing was too high. It was a sign I needed to become more confident in what I was worth. So I practised my pitch over and over until I knew my value and could communicate it unapologetically. Now, I don't flinch about money. It's business baby, and I know my worth.

Don't baulk or flinch at the salary you're putting out there. It's important to know your value. Practise the conversation in front of the mirror until you can communicate it with confidence.

Requesting a pay rise in your current job

Remember, back in chapter 3, how we said that as people we don't really like to ask for help? Add money into the mix, and things get even more complicated.

Don't worry though, we're going to break the process down into three steps so you can get that ca$h money baby.

People often think there are only two possible outcomes to the pay conversation. Your boss is either going to say yes or no to your request. Getting a pay rise is not a one and done conversation. We like to think of it as more of a continuum—a journey, if you will.

Figure 9.3: the pay rise request continuum

Your employer's response to your request for a pay increase will sit somewhere along the continuum presented in figure 9.3. It's not an either/or scenario.

Your job is to move them closer to a *Heck yes!* Each time you have a conversation about your pay and performance, you have an opportunity to move them forward on the continuum. Your manager looks at your ongoing performance as evidence as to why you should or shouldn't receive a pay increase. So, it's important you see it as an ongoing process, not a one-time thing. This also takes the pressure off having a single, high-stakes conversation.

You're inviting your boss to come on this journey with you. Each time you meet, you're moving them closer towards the *Heck yes!* side of the equation. You're making it a no brainer to give you a pay rise.

So how do you bring your manager along the journey? First, you need to find out who is responsible for signing off on your pay rise. Is it your immediate manager or HR or the CEO? Once you know who makes the final decision, you need to look at the request from their perspective. Tailor your 'ask' to what the decision maker cares most about (which in most cases is the success of the business). Don't make it all about you and your entitlements. Make it about the business. Talk about how you've contributed to the business success.

In your preparation, find examples of how you have helped the overarching business performance, culture or strategy. It isn't just about getting more money in your back pocket—it's about being rewarded for the work you have done that's contributed real value to the company.

Okay, so now let's look at the three steps to going for that pay rise.

Step 1: Do your research

As humans, we have a tendency to overestimate our own abilities and when it comes to our work, this can often lead us to feel like we should be paid more. But, before we make 'the ask' for a pay rise (that's step 2) we need to check ourselves by objectively assessing whether we have genuine grounds to request one and what exactly that request might look like.

We begin this preparation by first asking ourselves the vital question: *How am I paid in relation to others performing the same role?*

Once we know what we are paid relative to other people in similar roles we will have a clearer picture of what we are working with when it comes to asking for an increase.

This isn't permission to go and conduct a poll of your team (that's a bad idea). Instead, do your research externally.

Check publicly available data from salary comparison websites (Glassdoor, salary.com payscale, Hays). You can also check out jobs advertised with remuneration information on LinkedIn and Seek.

Minimum pay rates in Australia: Fair Work

For readers who are employed in Australia, your employment may be covered by a modern award. A modern award establishes the minimum terms and conditions of employment.

You can find the award minimum rates by searching fairwork.gov.au. Often roles are paid above the award minimum, but you can find out more by checking your employment contract and looking on the Fair Work Ombudsman website.

As you build this picture, know that hitting the median is considered being paid 'on market'. So if you are being paid above the median, you are paid better than most people in your role. In other cases, however, you may find you're paid quite a bit less than people in similar roles. Either way, this is a helpful sense check and starts to give you clarity on what your role is worth.

Also take into consideration the location of your work. For example, similar roles in capital cities may be paid more highly than regional areas due to cost of living. So do your research across a number of locations as well.

---

apply now

Write down your current salary (all benefits included), your position and your location.

Salary	Position	Location of role
$		

Use the search tools mentioned in this chapter and list the ballpark of salaries for a role the same as or similar to yours.

Salary	Position	Location of role
$		
$		
$		
$		
$		

Salary	Position	Location of role
$		
$		

How does your salary compare? (circle)

Low   **Mid–Low**   **Mid**   **Mid–High**   **High**

What do you bring to your current role that is a unique value-add for the business?

List where you have:

- increased sales or revenue

- increased the customer or client base

- created or improved processes

- performed above and beyond company expectations.

_____

_____

_____

_____

_____

List a scale of percentage increases that you could consider bringing to your pay-rise meeting.

(continued)

Example

Salary: $52 000 gross (before taxes, superannuation, other payroll deductions)

Percentage increase	Amount salary would increase	Overall salary package
5% × $52 000 =	$2 600 (0.05 × $52 000)	$54 600
10% × $52 000 =	$5 200 (0.1 × $52 000)	$57 200
15% × $52 000 =	$7 800 (0.15 × $52 000)	$59 800
20% × $52 000 =	$10 400 (0.2 × $52 000)	$62 400
25% × $52 000 =	$13 000 (0.25 × $52 000)	$65 000
30% × $52 000 =	$15 600 (0.3 × $52 000)	$67 600

Now it's your turn:

Percentage increase	Amount salary would increase	Overall salary package
5% × your salary	$	$
10% × your salary =	$	$
15% × your salary =	$	$
20% × your salary =	$	$
25% × your salary =	$	$
30% × your salary =	$	$
Other	$	$

Taking all of this into consideration, what would be your preferred salary increase?

Percentage increase	Amount salary would increase	Overall salary package
% =	$	$

This data helps you determine how much more money to ask for. It will also help give you confidence in your request because you have a stronger sense for how you are paid in relation to similar roles. Now that you know what you're aiming for, you can start to prepare key points to justify the pay increase.

Step 2: Prepare your business case and make 'the ask'

Now that we have constructed a more meaningful picture of how you are paid in comparison to the market, you can prepare your business case and make 'the ask', which is the conversation where you make your request for a pay rise.

Getting to a *Heck yes!* means preparing a solid business case. You're asking your employer to make a sizable investment in you, so show them why it's a good decision. Look at examples where you've gone above and beyond in your past performance. Use these as positive indicators as to why they should invest in you. Communicate the return they can expect in future years. This is how you justify the increase to your pay.

Write down your talking points and practise them out loud until you can communicate the business case for why you deserve a pay rise with confidence. When you are ready, set up a meeting. This is definitely not a conversation that should occur via email, slack or text. It's a discussion. You don't want to catch the decision maker by surprise.

Speak to them first and highlight that you'd like to have a meeting to discuss your pay (you could raise this in a regular 1:1 meeting if you have them). Ask them when they're available and prepared to have the discussion. Then, follow up by setting up a meeting time, maybe in a week or so. By giving them space and the heads up, no bombs have been dropped. You're not springing it on them with no notice. This really sets the conversation up well. Big ticks for you.

Now it's time for you to make the ask! Before you get to what you're wanting, talk about the business *first*. Express what you've done in the past 12 months. Don't focus solely on the things you've done well in the past few weeks, or any recent spikes in performance. You need to show how your performance has been consistent over a longer period of time.

At this point, some people make it all about what is important to them—their key achievements or their personal circumstances—but fail to connect it back to the business value. Instead, find obvious links between business goals, strategy and the impact you have had on these things in your role.

What have you done in the past that has helped the business achieve its goals? Perhaps you have retained a key client, created a significantly measurable saving in expenses or driven efficiency through process improvement? Anchor your request in these specific, measurable examples.

As the conversation unfolds, avoid projecting any sense of entitlement. It is very common in conversations about pay for this mentality to seep into the tone of the discussion. Yes, you definitely could be paid more elsewhere, but the employer is not going to warm to people saying, 'I know I can get paid an extra $25 000 by the competitor down the road, so I deserve a pay rise.' This sense of entitlement doesn't move an employer towards a *Heck yes!* In fact, it is more likely to cause your employer to move towards the *Heck no* end of the continuum.

And remember, keep it focused on your role and the business. Don't use your personal reasons for wanting more money (that is, the new boat, Europe trip or home renos) as justification for a pay rise. Build a portfolio of evidence that you can use in 'the ask' to clearly demonstrate your value and your chance of success increases significantly.

apply now

Write down examples where you added value and contributed beyond what was expected.

List where you have:

- increased sales or revenue

- increased the customer or client base

- created, automated or improved processes and systems

- performed above and beyond expectations

- contributed positively to team culture.

_____

_____

_____

_____

_____

Pay-rise meeting checklist

☐ I have researched similar roles and their salary.

☐ I have selected an ideal percentage increase.

☐ I have prepared the performance examples I will bring to the meeting.

(continued)

Step 3: Accept with grace

You can't control the final decision, but you can control your response to it. So choose to respond with grace. Yes, it's disappointing if you don't get a salary increase, but remember, it's an ongoing conversation. Here are our recommended responses based on the outcome.

If your employer refuses your request for an increase:

- thank them for taking the time to consider your request

- ask them for any feedback as to why

- ask them what they would need to see from you in order to give you the increase. Are their any skills gaps you need to address in order to move up in pay?

- ask them if there are any other non-monetary benefits they would consider offering like training and development opportunities

- ask them if you can schedule in a review meeting in 6 months to reassess.

If your employer gives you a pay rise but it's less than you expected:

- thank them for the pay increase

- ask them if they can give you some feedback based on their review of the pay rate (for example, is it to do with the business budget or skills gaps?). You want to ask this question sensitively because you don't want to come across as ungrateful, but having this information is helpful as it will set you up well for the next time you ask for a pay review

- if appropriate, ask to schedule in a follow-up for 6 months' time.

If your employer gives you a pay rise:

- thank them for the pay increase

- follow up with an email to your manager or the decision maker thanking them for taking the time to think it through.

Gratitude goes a long way at work. Being thankful and gracious in your response will serve you well. Choose up front to respond with gratitude regardless of the outcome. It will position you well for future conversations.

Some final thoughts on pay

You have now conquered your awkwardness when it comes to pay conversations. What a win! The more confident and comfortable you become in talking about pay and money, the better positioned you will be to increase your income.

Here are a few more things you might like to take into consideration:

- Achieving a pay rise is a process. Your job is to move your employer towards a *Heck yes!* It is made up of big and small interactions that occur before, during and after 'the ask', even before it is on your radar!

- If you're working in a small business without formal performance management, wait 12 months before asking for a pay rise. Informally ask your manager out for a coffee to have the chat.

- Wait 12 months after getting a new job or starting a new role before you start considering a pay rise.

- If you've been undervalued for a long time and a pay rise has been refused, consider all of your options. Would moving externally benefit your career goals? Think through all the options available to you.

Marleen, 30
Bunbury, WA

I am an occupational therapist working in a country town, specifically focused on NDIS clients. I changed jobs due to unrealistic job expectations, and thankfully I joined a new company with a better work culture. But I worked exclusively from home and I struggled with social isolation.

I was approached by a company to join their local office. They offered more pay and with a local office it was an attractive offer. However, there were fewer career progression opportunities than with my current company, and fewer opportunities to work with NDIS clients, which I enjoy. So I decided to meet with my line manager to discuss what options there were in my current role, including how a pay rise could work into that.

I had the meeting with my line manager and national operations manager. In preparation for this meeting I wrote down why I enjoyed working with the company, what I'd brought to the role, what I saw as opportunities and where I had and could add further value. This was exactly what I'd heard talked about on *my millennial career*!

Thanks to my preparation and meetings, I got a 14 per cent pay rise by knowing what I was worth in the market, and I was able to draw on what I had brought to the company and the value I added!

I figured out that I started on a salary of $60k and I had increased that to $89k, which is not bad! And I am looking at starting my own business as I have found a niche in the market that my current workplace is not able to support!

Marleen pulled together the perfect business case to demonstrate the value she brought to the business. By assessing the market and highlighting the tangible benefits she'd brought to the business, she was successful in gaining her pay rise! Plus it meant she could remain in a role where there were more career opportunities available to her.

A final word

There are a number of ways to increase how much you earn. Which one is the next best option for you?

- Become a specialist = time to build some niche skills and experience

- Become a manager of people = start working on your interpersonal skills

- Move into sales = work on your self-drive and customer service skills

- Become a business owner = time to jump in with both feet!

- Pay rise = focus on your performance, and work on your confidence and negotiation skills

---

resources | **Scan the QR code for these resources and more.**

- Download a copy of the advanced income quadrant.

- Download a copy of the salary comparison framework.

- There are episodes about pay rises on the *my millennial career* podcast.

could
anything else
go wrong in my
career right now?

10

tl;dr

- Career crises, career change, burnout and redundancy are opportunities for growth and to replan your career road trip.

- Don't spin the Career Wheel of Fortune in the hope that any new job will solve your situation. Rest, recover and take ownership of your career.

- Painful experiences in our career are inevitable, but we can cultivate these experiences for post-traumatic growth.

- Working through your answers to part I of this book is critical to ensuring your career journey brings you the joy you're seeking.

Coming to a career crossroads

As with any good road trip, you need to prepare for the unexpected. You'll hit a roadblock, a crossroads, a dead end, get bogged, run out of fuel. Or maybe your career car will have a [nervous] breakdown that leaves you stranded on the side of the road, waiting for the tow truck, wondering where to next.

Career changes, career crises, burnout, redundancy, unexpected employment ends: each of these situations can feel like your career road trip has come to an abrupt stop. Emergency break activated.

If you've experienced one of these, I want you to know you're not alone (welcome to the career crisis club). As we process these tricky parts of our careers it can feel like we're isolated, lacking the knowledge or resources to move forward.

But we want you to think of this as an opportunity. It may not have been part of the plan, but sometimes your best moves come from sudden changes.

Can you make things better? Yes.

Is there still time to figure out what you want in your career? Yes.

Should we nap first? Yes.

When you hit a career crossroads, it is critical that you give yourself time and space. Time to reflect, rest, process how you're feeling. It's the moment to go back and work through parts I and II of this book, but only when you're ready to tackle it.

Remember the concept of 'antifragility' that Nassim Nicholas Taleb references in his work: unexpected and difficult experiences are a consistent part of our lives, and true happiness isn't found in avoiding these feelings. It's learning how to experience them, absorb them and become more capable as a result.

To demonstrate just how un-alone you are, I've written this chapter with a collection of personal stories from the m3 community. These are stories that show it can be done. Some things won't work out, but we learn, grow and try again. You can move sideways, turning left or right at the crossroads. Consider us your good mate, here to help you jump-start your car and get back on the road. You can re-evaluate your values, mindset, strengths, skills and risk—and start the car again.

Career crossroads 1: Changing careers

According to recent research by McCrindle, most Millennials and Gen Zs will have between three and five career changes during their working life. So, if you're feeling desperate to try something new, that's normal.

If you're 30 years old and you haven't had one yet, your time is coming (not to be the voice of doom or anything).

Expecting the unexpected is a sign of antifragility and maturity. There will be multiple times in your working life when you'll feel dissatisfied with the status quo and want to shake things up.

Knowing this before it happens gives you power (it also helps you to not have a major freak out when it does—an added bonus). Take Rach, for example.

Rach always knew she wanted to become a chef. Growing up, she'd spend hours in the kitchen cooking with her mum, experimenting with new recipes. By the age of 16, she had her dream job mapped out. She was going to become a chef.

Rach landed an apprenticeship at a local pub and her second shift fell on her 18th birthday. It was a fitting introduction into the life of a chef—but a bad omen of things to come. Over the next few years, Rach learned how much she'd have to sacrifice for her dream job.

Rach is one of those people who thrives off pressure. The adrenalin highs of a Saturday night service. The frantic energy of hospitality. People streaming through the front doors. Hundreds of dockets lined up. The head chef screaming orders. It was an exhilarating kind of chaos. 'The stress was huge, but there's nothing like the feeling of plating up the perfect meal.'

Two years and thousands of chicken schnitzels later, Rach needed a new challenge. The pub life wasn't cutting it. And like every young chef, she wanted two things: to work in fine dining and to travel.

At 20 years of age, she quit her pub gig, left her suburban hometown in New South Wales and crossed the border into Queensland. Rach was on the hunt for the perfect fine-dining job. And she found it, or at least she found the fine-dining part. Everything else was far from perfect.

Rach stared down at the menu. If she focused hard enough, maybe the words would somehow make sense. What the actual foie gras is this stuff? She cringes to think back on this time in her career. Like the best porcini mushrooms, she was growing in the crap. Bad money. Toxic culture. Crying the whole drive home each night. All for her so-called 'dream job'.

But over time, Rach became a damn good chef. Fuelled by ambition and talent, the next years raced by in a blur. She climbed the ladder, working at some of the best restaurants in Australia. And, she got to travel around the world with her job.

She was ticking off all her career goals. Fine dining, tick. Travel and adventure, tick. Career progression, tick. But, the work was slowly sucking the life out of her. Every night. Every weekend. Every 70-hour week.

Rach realised she was only travelling to escape work.

'It's how I survived. I'd work as hard as I could for as long as I could. Then I'd use travel to avoid burning out.' She'd work nonstop for a year and travel overseas for as long as she could afford, only to grudgingly return and repeat the cycle.

Seven years into her career it started to catch up with her. She had given up so much for her job. She'd missed birthdays and weddings. Never seeing her partner and friends. She lived in some of the most remarkable cities in the world, but never got to fully experience them.

Over time her resentment grew.

'I was constantly angry. After every shift, all I would do is complain about work.' Every day, Rach would feel nauseous and miserable. 'I kept telling myself, it's the restaurant, or it's the staff, or it's the money.' She would change restaurants, work with different people and get paid more money. And for the first few months, she'd love the job again because it was a new environment. But sure enough, the same issues would arise.

Rach had been a chef for almost 10 years and had worked at so many different restaurants. She'd perfected the art of ignoring her career problems. But eventually, she had to confront the painful reality.

Her time as a chef was over. But, she had no idea what to do next. So she gave herself time to figure it out. She used all her savings and took three months off work. It was what she desperately needed to reimagine her career and life.

She used this time to renovate her house with her partner. She found herself spending a lot of time in the back yard. She ripped up the concrete. She laid new grass. She redesigned the garden. She planted trees. She built planter boxes. And most importantly, she found her joy again.

'I loved being outside in the garden—I was really curious about it.' Rach had so many questions and wanted to find out all the answers about why things grow. She decided then and there she was going to study horticulture. 'I thought, if I don't get a job in it, at least I'll have all my questions answered.'

She started researching horticulture, and she came across the apprenticeship pathway. She knew she couldn't stay in hospitality, so she decided to sacrifice the money and try something new.

Rach googled every landscaping company in Victoria. She was on the hunt, looking for the fine-dining of landscaping. It was going to be tough to find a job. 'My resume was made up of all these restaurants and zero landscaping experience and I was 30 years old. Not your typical horticulture apprentice.'

After emailing countless landscapers, and getting no replies, Rach started volunteering at an agricultural plot to gain experience. She learned how much this work aligned with her values, strengths and personal priorities. She knew this was the right move for her. Now, it was about finding someone to hire her.

Three months passed, and one of the places she emailed had a job come up on Seek. Even though she'd heard nothing back from them originally, Rach wasn't put off. She threw her hat in the ring and applied for it. A week later she got the call-up for an interview.

'When you're a chef, you don't do interviews. You only do a trial shift. I had never done a proper interview in my life. I had no idea what to wear to a gardener interview. I didn't want to be too fancy that they thought I couldn't handle it. But not too underdressed that I didn't care.' Rach arrived at the interview in black jeans, a country road shirt and boots. Nailed it.

She was jittery, nerves in full force. But she had confidence in her interview strategy. She was going for all honesty and a willingness to learn. It worked a treat! Rach shared her career journey vulnerably: she was open about where she lacked experience, and her drive to grow and develop. She had a trial shift, and a few days later, she got the job. That same weekend, it was her 30th birthday. But unlike her 18th birthday, she didn't have to work. She spent a weekend with her best friends and family on a holiday in Noosa. A good sign for her new career.

Rach is now three years into her horticulture apprenticeship. In 2021, she was awarded Apprentice of the Year in Victoria for landscaping. But more than the awards and goals achieved, Rach is happy. She has found energy and purpose in her job. She doesn't work solely to go on holidays. On the tough days, she still finds her work fulfilling and meaningful. And that's what building a career you love looks like.

Here's how others in our m3 community have navigated a career change.

Casey, 30
Melbourne, VIC

When I was 15, I dropped out of high school in Werribee and bounced from casual job to casual job. School wasn't for me and I had little to no support from the faculty. So, I just worked. I found night shifts were more to my liking—think Pizza Hut, McDonald's, all the shifts no-one else my age wanted. Fast forward to 17. I was hired by one of the local

(continued)

dive pubs (Mum knew the owner; that's how I was able to work behind a bar before I was 18) and boy did it open a door! (enter: sarcastic tone). I found the next 4 to 5 years were spent in a drunken/drugged stupor. Pubs and parties—and, looking back, really toxic environments. I barely made my rent as I was living alone or couch surfing when I could, and putting myself (a young, naive girl at the time) in very real danger occasionally. I look back to this time and honestly can't fathom how I thought and did things the way I did and survived.

When I was about 23, my friend and I enrolled at the Australian Institute of Fitness in Certificate 3 & 4 of Fitness as a gag. I paid it off over time (as I was not eligible for any discounts). It took 6 to 8 months of going to classes three times a week in the city, working when I could to pay my rent over the weekends and night work still in TABs and bars. When I looked around me I knew I wanted more for my life. I quit the toxic boyfriend, job and friends and moved out of Werribee.

I rented in Melbourne, living there for just under 6 years, which was the longest time in my life I've lived in one house. I got a dog and a real boyfriend. I got a real life.

I completed my Certificate 3 & 4 in Fitness and enrolled at VU as a remedial massage therapist. I then enrolled for my Bachelor of Health Sciences online. I did all my studies while working and saving, and my partner and I were able to buy our first, small, humble, lovely home.

I am currently holding two jobs, one casual, in a very quiet, no-trouble bar, and one part-time two days a week in the health field, while I'm completing my Masters of Public Health.

I look back and see little-me and I am so proud of where I am. I am past 30 now and fully aware I'm not at the end—not even in a career yet—but I recognise not a lot of high school dropouts with a drug and alcohol history can say they are doing their Masters. So, all up, I've been studying for 7 years, and at the end of this year, when my Masters is finished, I will be applying for public-policy jobs around international law, aid and humanitarian issues. With my *Masters*. Whoo!

Career success for me means having freedom. Freedom to study/educate myself, as I am the best investment I can make. And that's what I'm working toward.

Casey could easily have continued on the road she was on, but she took a huge risk to change the direction of her career road trip. But the risk was worth the reward! Not only has she built a completely new career by dipping her toe in an area where she showed strength, and growing that (literally), she was also willing to reshape her whole personal life alongside it. She has every right to be proud of her achievements! This takes so much courage. The personal progress she has made from taking any night shift she could to completing a Masters is astonishing.

Kylie, 23
Sydney, NSW

When I left school, I moved to London for two years and while I was over there I had exposure to two industries, which helped me get to where I am now.

The first was teaching high-school classes with zero experience or training and I was barely older than the kids themselves. I got a Working with Children's Check, went for one chat and then off I went to different schools on a daily basis. It was wild.

The second industry was in events at a five-star hotel, managing corporate events and weddings. I had the opportunity to lead a team each night

(continued)

of waiters/waitresses, which was my first exposure to leading and managing a team.

My visa ended and I came home to Australia (20 years old) with the intention of going to uni, but being *broke as,* I decided to work first to pay off my debt before studying.

I mentioned to a contact of mine that I was considering going into sales as I had seen some entry-level jobs. In London I'd handed pamphlets out on the street and done all sorts of random cash jobs, which required me to be very outgoing. I researched recruitment and thought it could be a great fit as I enjoyed working with people and was interested in doing a commission style job.

All the job postings I saw at the time required a degree (which I did not have) or HR experience (which I did not have) or sales (which I also did not have). I spent a great deal of time redoing my resume. Once that was done, I applied for roles even if I didn't tick all the boxes. I received four different company call backs, ignored everything I didn't have and highlighted the different experiences and skills I had developed in the past and how I could make them transferable.

I ended up getting the job for $10k more than I had asked. Salary wise I had undersold myself believing I did not have all the skills required. Fast forward one year I had my base salary bumped up to $75k; fast forward another year I had received three promotions (two on fast track programs) and in my third year I made $150k total including commission.

I've been introduced to the world of tech, had the opportunity to manage my own team and now recruitment across an *amazing* sector (human-centred design—cool stuff).

I wouldn't have dreamed I'd be where I am now three years ago. I'm glad I took a chance on myself! I don't need uni or have a HECS debt. I have a great network across the tech and design community if I ever want to transition. I've had the chance to work with start-ups, government, not-for-profits, councils, enterprise and I've made some awesome colleagues and friends along the way.

I am *super* passionate about helping people get into their dream careers now, making sure people *don't* undersell themselves, giving general advice and transitioning into the tech space.

Kylie's story highlights how varied the process can look as you change careers—not all career changes are an abrupt shift from one industry to another. Sometimes it's about seeing an opportunity in a new area, taking small steps in that direction and then doubling down where your strengths and skills are performing at their best.

apply now

If you're feeling like a career change is what you need, what do you have in mind as your possible next step? We can test this against the career planning work we did with you in part I of this book. Gotta start somewhere, yeah? Write down your thoughts.

_____

_____

_____

_____

_____

Career crossroads 2: Career crisis

We'd define a 'career crisis' as knowing you can't stay in your current job, but having zero idea of what you want to do next.

If you're asking yourself, 'What the heck do I want to do with my career?' and can't seem to find the answer, you're right where you need to be. On behalf of Glen and me, welcome to our club. The career crisis club. The membership is free, meetings are Tuesday nights and we've all signed up at least once in our life. Joining our club is a good sign. It means you're on your way to sorting your crisis out.

Maybe your career was going to plan for the first few years, but it's not cutting it anymore. You found out being a lawyer is nothing like the show *Suits*. Or the dream you had to start your own business fizzled out like the five-day-old bottle of Coke Zero sitting in Glen's fridge (oof—not good).

Before we get to solving your career crisis, there's one thing you need to avoid at all costs: the career crisis Wheel of Fortune (see figure 10.1).

Figure 10.1: the career crisis Wheel of Fortune

For the love of all that is good in this world, do not spin this bad boy, hoping wherever it stops is the universe's way of confirming your next career move.

I'm bloody done with Electrical Engineering.

...

Step right up and spin the wheel for your next career move.

...

High-school teaching, here I come.

Jokes aside, when people are in crisis mode, decision fatigue takes over. In these moments, it's common to make rushed, poorly thought-out decisions. We're so desperate to get out of one bad situation that we make huge changes with the flick of a coin (or the spin of a wheel, if you will).

Solving a career crisis requires time. You need to carefully reflect on what's not working for you right now, which takes deep thinking. But it's difficult to do the deep thinking when you're having to show up to work every day. You're basically having repeated exposure therapy every week without the therapist for support. Not an ideal situation.

Remember Glen's personal story back in chapters 2 and 3? He's had three career crises, from telecommunications trade, to financial adviser, to podcast host and media business director. Each of these changes came from understanding what wasn't working in his current career, and reflecting on his values, strengths and skills, and risk tolerance to inform his next move. These big changes weren't a spur-of-the-moment decision.

Five steps to navigating a career crisis

Before we move on to the next career crossroads you might encounter, we want to share five steps to help you navigate a career crisis and make the right change for you. Consider this your 'get out of career crisis free card'.

Step 1: Take time to diagnose the problem

Remember the last time you were feeling unwell? Naturally, you type your symptoms into Google and 0.68 seconds later, voilà! A clear diagnosis: you've got 30 days left to live, so you better bloody enjoy them. Of course, you then book in to see your GP and it turns out you're just dehydrated and you need more than 3 hours' sleep a night.

When faced with a painful problem, we're all susceptible to misdiagnosis. We rush to figure out the solution without properly trying to understand the root of the problem.

There are all kinds of problems that can lead people to pursue a career change. And where there is a problem, there is a solution. But before you jump into solutions, stop. Tell yourself to slow down. Many people make a career change without understanding the problem first.

Design thinking is an amazing process for solving complex problems. It helps you identify the problem and come up with as many solutions as you can.

Perhaps you're considering a completely new career, but you're worried you might not like being a graphic designer any more than being a midwife. Or you've climbed the career ladder only to realise you hate managing people, but you're not sure if you can afford the pay cut that comes with changing jobs.

You might feel disengaged in your job and look to make a big career change to fix this, only to realise that it wasn't the career that was the problem—it was the culture of the business you were in that was the real issue.

Making a career change is equal parts exciting and daunting. It's a big call to make a change like this. So give yourself time to slow down and diagnose the core problem. You can think through the solutions and identify the risks later.

Here are our favourite questions to help you define the problem:

- What is it about my current role/career that I don't enjoy?

- How do I feel about the business I'm working in or the team I'm working with? Is that impacting my job satisfaction?

- How is the culture in my workplace? Could that be influencing how I'm feeling?

- What parts of my role do I enjoy, and can I do more of those activities or tasks?

- If I were the boss, what would I change about my job tomorrow?

Step 2: Brainstorm as many solutions as you can possibly find

Create a career ideas map. Or, better yet, call it your career ideas mood board. Now you're feeling way more creative, right?

Write down as many ideas for potential career changes or new roles as you possibly can. Think big. Use up all the blank space. Fill it with ideas. This is all part of the design thinking process. Go back to chapter 4 and revisit your strengths. Look for jobs and careers that draw upon your strengths.

Write down your career ideas here.

_____

_____

_____

_____

_____

Step 3: Narrow down your ideas

Once you've got your ideas out there, start searching LinkedIn or job sites to get a better sense of what these jobs require in terms of skills and experience. Do your research to learn what's involved.

Talk with people in your network who work in those fields about how they ended up there. Ask them to give you insight into what the day to day of that career looks like. You want to get into the nitty gritty of the role—what's behind the curtain. Event management might sound like an exciting role on the surface, but when you talk to someone in the role, you may realise it's not as glamorous as it sounds. This step is about gathering as much information as possible to inform your decision making.

Talk with your mentor or coach. Sound out your ideas with them. See what they think about the options.

From here, narrow it down to a couple of final options.

Step 4: Get a job preview

You're keen to pursue a career change, but first you need a job preview. Some tangible experience to work out whether the change is your best move. Think of it as watching the trailers at the movies. The previews help you work out whether you want to watch the full movie.

Getting an accurate job preview can help you determine if the change is right for you, before you go all in.

Say you're an engineer but you're super interested in website design. Here are a few ways to gain a job preview:

1. *Ask a website design agency if you could volunteer a few hours a week for a period of time.*

   You'd be surprised how many people land new jobs this way.
   Top tip: Aim for 3 months at a minimum; it needs to be valuable for them as many organisations find it time-consuming to have volunteers for short stints.

2. *Find someone in your network who would be willing to show you 'a day in the life of'.*

   Ask them for the full ins and outs. No rose-coloured glasses. You want to know the good, the bad and the ugly.

3. *Look for online courses from website designers where you can learn the basics.*

   Complete a few of these and see how you find it. If it's engaging and challenging in a positive way, that's a good sign!

Step 5: Take the plunge

You've diagnosed the problem. You've brainstormed solutions. You've narrowed down your ideas. You've done a job preview. Now you're ready. It's time to take the plunge.

This is where you start applying for jobs in your desired new career. Connect with people in your network and start having conversations to see what opportunities are out there. Remember what we talked about in chapter 5 on risk: the biggest risk is taking no risks.

So dive off the diving board.

And if you're still freaking out, that's okay. Be encouraged by these stories from the m3 community of people who took the plunge.

Naveesha, 25
Sydney, NSW

I have had a bit of a unique career pathway in that I've changed industries quite a bit since being out of uni — industries that were not at all related to what I originally studied!

While I was at uni I was working at a pathology lab. There were a lot of older people who had been in this role for about 20+ years, and I thought I was going to follow in their footsteps. Don't get me wrong, I really enjoyed the job, and continuing to work in this role until the day I die was definitely the path of least resistance, but I wanted to explore my options. I was confused about where my career was really going to head as I did a Bachelor of Science, and being a broad field of study, the endless career possibilities overwhelmed me.

On a bit of a whim, I attended a 'Careers in Science' event that my uni was holding for penultimate students. The keynote speaker was a partner at a Big 4 firm. He talked about his career path which, interestingly, began in almost the exact spot I was at the time — working in an entry-level lab role. After his speech, I was keen to pick his brain about his journey as I found it interesting that he ventured from science to business. I was extremely nervous and had to work up the courage to approach him. I went into it with no expectations but at the end of the chat, he ended up giving me his business card and told me he'd be open to discussing his career further over a coffee.

Two weeks after we caught up, he reached out to me regarding a graduate position at the firm, which I ended up interviewing for and accepting. I ended up staying for two years. I really enjoyed myself as the culture was amazing but at the end of the day, I was a scientist at heart. During my time there, I found that I enjoyed working with STEM clients which, ultimately, really made me miss science. This reaffirmed what I knew I wanted and allowed me to gain a wealth of experience in other areas. I decided to enter the clinical trials industry, specifically in pharmaceuticals, which is a field I developed an interest in while working with clients in that space. I have now been in the clinical trials industry for a bit over a year and have thoroughly enjoyed my time here. It was a roundabout way of finding out what I wanted to do, but I believe I'm now on the right pathway for me.

Naveesha's story is so unique—it's not the classic 'sad to happy' career journey. She tested the concept of a completely new industry to see if it really was the area she had strength in. And you know what? It wasn't! And that's okay. But it kept her moving forward, and ultimately she was able to intentionally craft how her career looked in her previous industry.

Kinsey, 28
Sydney, NSW

The culture in classical music is high performing and high pressure. I was taught to lean into my perfectionism and obsessive tendencies. Despite running a successful business teaching and conducting, my perfectionism and 'can do' attitude got the best of me.

At one point I was working full time, studying a Masters full time, went on tour to Spain to play for the Spanish Queen *and* decided 'for fun' I would learn the bagpipes (don't get me started). I was burning out hard.

COVID-19 hit and even though I had done all this work to improve my skills as a musician playing and growing my business, it wasn't enough in the face of a pandemic. I spent a lot of this time reflecting and walking (almost 8 kilometres a day) and had some real 'aha' moments, the first being that I had always felt inadequate and unrealised as a person in the music world. The second, that the bit I actually loved all along was running the business side of things. The hustle. It drew out my strengths in creativity and analysis. I was also able to spend more time being with people and communicating. Twenty years in a practice room by myself made me a great flautist but also made me really lonely!

I managed to pivot into the family business and I now run a motor racing company. The jump was scary and hard. I left an industry I had been in since I was 6 years old! I boiled down what my strengths and values were, which centred around creativity, stability and culture. I also got clear on what my transferable skills were, which was an incredibly eye-opening experience. It ended up making me so much more confident in myself and my abilities and allowed me to pivot with the trust in myself that I would adapt to the situation.

Kinsey's example is so on point—she took the time to stop and figure out options for where to go next. She re-examined her strengths and values, aligning an opportunity that met those to a T. It's stories like these that give us all hope that it is possible to come out the other side of a career crisis, but also to do it really well.

---

apply now

What's your career crisis? Vent about it here.

_____

_____

_____

_____

What are some potential areas of interest you can test against your answers from part I of this book? Jot down any industries or jobs that could be opportunities to explore here.

_____

_____

_____

_____

Career crossroads 3: Burnout

Burnout is too common a story. If you're here because of it, we feel you.

No-one performs well on empty, particularly when the empty sign has been flashing for months, possibly years. More than that, no-one can sustain working at 150 per cent day in, day out.

Step back for a minute. What even is burnout? According to the World Health Organisation, burnout is the result of chronic and unmanaged stress at work. It's characterised by feelings of extreme exhaustion, fatigue, cynicism, and mental or emotional detachment from your work. Burnout, aside from the physical effects and exhaustion, can have serious and long-term impacts on your mental health and wellbeing.

Burnout doesn't happen overnight. Similarly, recovery isn't as quick as we'd like it to be. Rebuilding your health takes time. Allow yourself the rest you need. Be kind to yourself. Your mind, emotions and body have been through the ringer, so turn the pace down.

Here are members of our community who have navigated their own burnout journey. These stories are ones that point to the road to recovery, and rebuilding a career you love.

Liz, 33
Brisbane, QLD

There's a quiet feeling of chaos and urgency in the room. We all know what is coming, and I'm approaching this with a mechanical mentality—I have three people lined up to do the relay race that is CPR. I have two nurses drawing up drugs based on a weight of 15 kilograms. I've called social work and no-one is available, so that role will fall to me. My other nurse is cracking open the paediatric airway trolley and we've already tested our defibrillator for the shift. And as team leader, I'm externally calm so that my team remains calm. Internally, however, I'm half dread half detached to what we are about to treat.

Because the child coming to us, lights and sirens, isn't breathing.

Twelve hours later this isn't the only horrible thing that's happened in the emergency department I work in. We go from one patient having the worst day of their life to the next. And we have a special way of instantly becoming your best friend as we must do things to you that require the highest level of trust.

I'd been working as an ED nurse for 10 years, and when people heard what I did for a living, 99 per cent of the time they'd ask the same thing:

'What's the worst thing you've ever seen?'

Now, I know what you're asking. You're asking for the weirdest injury or, even better, the wackiest thing I've ever seen jammed into a body cavity. I can't answer that question properly because you really aren't ready to hear the answer. And I'm not ready to tell it, as answering will mean I don't sleep for a week without night sweats and reliving it.

Our management told us about 'resilience' workshops we'd need to attend. Resilience: 'the capacity to recover quickly from difficulties; toughness'.

We are tough. And we are human.

I'm not a nurse anymore. Despite undergraduate degrees, multiple post-graduate degrees, years and years of experience and my absolute passion for teaching the new generation of nurses, I left the industry. I could have just changed specialties, but I was well beyond that. And for a while I mourned that part of my identity, because nursing isn't just a job, it's something that gets etched and weaved into the very fabric of your being.

(continued)

They call it burnout. Burn. Out. Two little words that encompass such a severe and isolating experience. A charring and scorching that singes the edges of every part of your life until it's consumed everything.

I now work as a finance broker. Completely different field, but I'm still utilising the skills that I gained after years as a nurse—especially that ability to immediately become your best friend and biggest advocate. It's like chalk and cheese; I've been there for you during your worst times, now let me be there for the best.

Changing careers has been the biggest and scariest thing I've ever done. And it has been worth it. I firmly believe that you are not a tree; you don't need to stay in a garden that doesn't water you.

Burnout is a slow burn. For Liz, her energy reserves were slowly depleted over 10 years as an ED nurse. That's why rest is so significant. You need time to heal, reflect and recharge. Don't rush this part of the process. Allow yourself the space you need to recover.

Kimberly, 36
Sydney, NSW

I have been practising as a lawyer for over 12 years. I have worked in private practice and in-house for several large companies across different industries. I am often asked to mentor junior solicitors who are paving their way forward in a demanding industry, which has a huge dropout rate after 3 to 5 years.

After spending quite some time early in my career feeling constantly burned out in the legal profession,

I believe I have now managed to find happiness and balance in my life, which gives me great personal and professional fulfilment.

My personal version of career success involves working in a role that is purpose driven and that motivates me, surrounds me with intellectual thinkers and pays me a competitive salary, all while providing flexibility and the freedom to enjoy my life outside of work.

After practising law for 5 years, I took a year-long career break to live in Thailand where I was training and fighting in Muay Thai. I also took quite a few contract roles early in my career in order to experience different industries which gave me the opportunity to go back to Thailand to train (and fight) once a contract was over.

After 10 years of practising law, I took a role in regulatory strategy, which was a move away from the practice of law, but also closely aligned to the practice of law. Transitioning into something which utilised my skill set and where all of my advisory skills were transferable, was the smartest decision I have ever made in my career. I have known many practising lawyers who stay in the profession for 15 to 20 years and don't have the courage to leave, but I knew my skill set was extremely transferable into different roles (and for a much more competitive salary!). Now I get paid for the experience I bring to the table, not for the hours worked. I work flexibly, which allows me to focus on my training commitments before and after work, and I continue to enjoy the pace and stimulation I get from the important work that I do.

Kimberley's provided a brilliant example of how to replan your career road trip after burnout. She took time off to do something completely different—something that energises her. She's redefined everything we work through in part I of this book, and reshaped a career that doesn't just take take take—instead it sparks joy in her. She's beautifully blended her strengths in a few different fields.

apply now

How full is your tank? Is it full, or are you running on empty?

How intentional are you in prioritising your health and wellbeing?

What activities re-energise and refill you?

How can you become more proactive in taking time out to rest?

_____

_____

_____

_____

_____

Career crossroads 4: Redundancy and unexpected employment endings

Redundancy or an unexpected end to your employment can be an extremely stressful experience.

One day you go to work believing that your role and what you contribute matters. Next minute someone says, 'thanks for your time; here are your things and there's the door'.

An unplanned employment ending like redundancy can leave you in a state of shock. It can rattle your confidence. In fact, many people describe endings like this as a grieving process.

It takes headspace and distance to work through the feelings of hurt and grief that come with these types of exits. It's important to give yourself grace and time to reflect before you move forward.

The truth is most people will have an unexpected and painful employment exit like this at least once in their career. While this doesn't necessarily make it any easier to navigate, if you're in this position right now, you're not alone. The work that you're doing through this book will help you to find the right next opportunity and rebuild your confidence.

Charli, 28
Sydney, NSW

I'd completed a Bachelor of Commerce, majoring in Marketing and PR. Despite the creative nature of this degree, I had always been great at maths, strong with numbers and great at decision making.

At the time of studying, I was working part-time at a bar. A patron told me I'd be a great flight attendant. Some airlines happened to be recruiting in town later on that month so I went to their recruitment days. At one of the events there were 155 candidates but only six roles were offered. I managed to score one, and off I went to Dubai, starting a career as a flight attendant.

Fast forward 4 years and the COVID-19 pandemic hit—planes were no longer flying, I had to re-skill ... but how?

I took up a part-time job at Woolworths to cover the bills while I got on the phone to recruiters and applied for anything and everything on LinkedIn.

(continued)

A recruiter I spoke with asked for my personal strengths, so that's where I focused on my skill with numbers and critical thinking. I was offered a job from a bank and re-started my career journey. It was not easy, with a $40k pay drop, but it enabled me to get my foot in the door to the world of finance.

I have since moved on to a new role within finance, and am beginning to specialise in markets.

My goal one day will be to have enough financial stability to return to flying part-time, and to enjoy spending time with my partner, taking him on some work trips. And maybe in my 50s, to see out my working life.

I have found that the key to beginning a new career is to find where your personal strengths lie!

Charli worked something that would absolutely have felt like a kick in the guts, into an opportunity to focus on her strengths. Instead of this being a dead-end experience, she transferred her strengths to a seemingly unrelated field. She was prepared for the risk of a pay cut too.

apply now

How has your redundancy or unexpected employment end left you feeling?

_____

_____

_____

_____

_____

What is the next best opportunity to explore?

_____

_____

_____

_____

_____

Work through part I of this book again. Redefine your values, mindset, strengths and skills, and your approach to risk.

A final word

You are not at this crossroads alone. Many from the m3 community have come to this point. The trick is to take the rest and time out you need.

Once you've had some space, you can come back, and get the car started again when you're ready. Work through part 1 and 2 of this book. Remember the idea of antifragility: each of these difficult moments is how you become stronger. You got this!

resources **Scan the QR code for these resources and more.**

There are episodes on *my millennial career* about changing careers, and navigating redundancy, bad employment endings and burnout.

reaching the end of the road

at the roundabout, leave your job (because it sucks)

11

tl;dr

- You need an exit strategy before you begin a job in any workplace.

- Aim to finish your job so well that you could be welcomed back. Don't burn your bridges—reinforce them.

- Don't resign if you simply need a holiday, have created a habit of job-hopping, haven't tried to fix the issues in your current role or you've dodged having a conversation with your manager.

- It *is* time to resign when the workplace is toxic (not Britney Spears' style), your values have stopped aligning with the business and you've achieved everything possible in your current workplace.

- Identify one primary reason for leaving and focus on that as you resign with grace. Leave your secondary complaints at the door.

- Try to prevent leaving altogether by having ongoing, healthy discussions with your manager about your career goals and how they could be fulfilled where you are.

- Write a resignation letter and hand it to your manager or boss in person in a meeting you pre-prepared (not in the hallway as they run to the toilet).

- Prepare *amazing* handover notes.

- Create a communication plan for once you've left.

- If an exit interview isn't organised internally, ask for one to be set up so you can provide feedback to the business. This feedback is vital for them. It is also not an opportunity for you to be unprofessional and get all dramatic and yelly. Sit down, be an adult and keep it calm.

You need an exit strategy

I've seen a lot of people resign from their job. Some finish well, and others ... not so much. Think passive-aggressive all-staff emails, stolen company computers and painfully uncomfortable farewell morning teas (I think the last one is my least favourite—arghh, the morning teas!).

There is so much focus placed on starting employment, or landing the next role, that we overlook an essential part of your career: your exit strategy. How you leave a job and employer is crucial. So you need to start with the end in mind.

One-hundred per cent of people will leave their job. True story. It's like the death rate. You will leave your job, and you will die. Let's wrap this book up now, shall we? What an ending.

But seriously, I can't stress this enough. From the outset of employment, plan to finish well. You can't always control what happens during your employment. Whether you choose to resign, or your employment ends because of a decision your boss made, you can control how you respond.

Have open discussions with your manager

Before we crack into the resignation process, I want you to think more broadly about your exit strategy. You can lay the groundwork to finish well years before you choose to leave. It all starts by building an honest relationship with your manager.

Be intentional about sharing your career goals and long-term plans with your manager, and do this regularly. This is helpful for many reasons. It lets them know how to support you in your bigger goals and identify internal opportunities. They might be able to prevent resignation altogether! Maybe there's a way to find your next career steps within your current organisation. But you won't know that if you don't try to work with your manager to make it happen. It also sets expectations early. So, if a role comes up externally that they know they can't offer, they won't be taken by surprise, it's not awkward and there's room for understanding.

How can you start this conversation?

In the early parts of your employment or relationship with a manager it might sound like:

'My long term career plan is to end up in _____ type of role. I'd love any advice or feedback you might have around how I could get there.'

By doing this, you're setting the scene early. You're giving your manager insight into your long-term goals. Once they know, they may be able to help you get there (remember, be patient: this is a long game and can take years) or they won't be shocked if/when you leave to pursue the long-term goal. It makes the transition a lot easier for everyone.

When you get an inkling you might need a change, but you're not exactly sure what that looks like, your conversation could sound like this:

'I feel like in the next 12 months or so _____ (read the list below). I'd love to talk more about this and get your input and advice.'

Possible inclusions in the above sentence:

- I may begin to feel a bit bored in this role.

- I can see myself needing more of a challenge.

- I feel I might need a bit of a change to my role or responsibilities.

By having this conversation, you can open up more opportunities internally, or if those options aren't available, it can make your decision to exit a lot easier.

Start building this space with your manager early on, and look to create it in every workplace you're employed.

---

apply now

What could you discuss with your manager now to prevent your resignation?

_____

_____

_____

_____

_____

Stay or go?

One of the most common questions we hear from people who listen to the *my millennial career* podcast is 'Should I stay or should I go?'

Tough question. Lots at stake. Potentially high emotion.

How the heck do you know for sure that it's time to leave your job? Do the stars tell you at night? Do you have a dream that confirms your concerns?

Let's put the dreams aside and put a framework together to understand whether it's time to exit your job well (we'll talk about how to leave 'well' shortly).

It's *not* time to leave when:

- *You simply need a holiday.*

  A holiday is often as good as a change. When was the last time you took time off? Time to sit by the beach, travel, visit friends, eat good food and drink good wine/kombucha? If it's been too long between breaks, then think through whether this is actually what you need, rather than a new job. And it doesn't need to be an elaborate holiday—sometimes kicking it at home in your own backyard with no work responsibilities is enough. Time to empty your mind and let it reboot.

- *You've created a habit of hopping job to job.*

  Recruiters don't love the look on your resume if you've had a number of short stints in multiple workplaces. It makes it seem like you aren't dedicated or reliable (even if you are!). Don't give up just yet—see if there is something within your realm of control to make your current workplace a place you really love.

- *There's something you can change in your role or workplace to improve the situation.*

  Is there something you could do to make your current role more fulfilling? Is there additional training or job responsibilities you could ask for that provide the challenge you're looking for? Or do you need to reconsider your mindset? Sometimes we can get stuck in cynical cycle which can lead to bad decisions. So, consider the mindset you're bringing to work every day.

- *You simply need a conversation with your manager.*

  Glen regularly says 'communication is often the problem and solution'. Wise advice. Have you tried to communicate with your manager about how you're feeling? If not, how will they ever help you craft your role into the shape you enjoy! If you don't speak, they won't know. So set up a chat with them and say something along the lines of:

'Hey, I think I'm looking for something more—is that here? What opportunities are available to me?'

'I'm feeling a bit stagnant in my role, I wonder if we could discuss ways to provide more engagement or challenge?'

'I'm looking for something new to sink my teeth into—are there any new opportunities or projects I could be considered for?'

Managers have more opportunities going on in the background than you're aware of and if you don't ask you won't know—so ask!

It's go-time when:

- *Your values stop aligning with those of the business.*

  See now why we started this book with values? That deep-seated feeling of 'me and my workplace don't align' can start like a simmer and brew to a boil—next minute it's bubbling over. Sit for a moment and take the time to assess what isn't aligning with you. Has the vision of the organisation changed? Have your values changed? If the tectonic plates have shifted, it could be time to find a new workplace that does align with your values.

- *You've achieved everything you can.*

  Even if you're communicating and checking in with your manager, sometimes there's a ceiling on the things you want to and can achieve in a workplace. That's okay. Acknowledge the amazing opportunities you've had, and the ones you're going to look elsewhere to achieve. Before you do this though, check you aren't making assumptions. Talk with your manager and see if there are opportunities you aren't aware of. If there's nothing available then bow out with grace (read on in this chapter about how to resign with grace).

- *The workplace becomes toxic.*

  No-one should sit back and cop a toxic workplace or boss. No bullying boss, gossipy office talk or illegal activity (it happens) should be withstood by anyone. Talk to HR, try to raise your concerns with the right people internally, but if nothing changes, get out as soon as you can.

  You have permission to walk out that door and never come back. Be professional, read our upcoming steps to resign with grace and find a healthier workplace.

---

apply now

Reflecting on what you've just read, what is happening in your situation? Is there a legitimate reason to head for the exit door, or is there something you can do now to refresh things?

_____

_____

_____

_____

_____

Resigning with grace

The litmus test of an effective exit strategy is that you leave so well you could always go back.

Here's how.

Mindset. Ahh, that ol' chestnut

And here we are again, in the land of mindset. We bring it up because it matters. Whether you're leaving for personal reasons, redundancy or retirement, your mindset should be to finish well. Your boss might have been a total jerk, but be the bigger person in the room.

No matter the circumstances of how things end, you're responsible for how you respond.

When people finish up badly, it can taint all the years of hard work. Don't undo the great work you did while working in the business by letting the final stretch become sour.

Also keep in mind that your choices now—the way you manage your exit in particular—ripple into the future. Your future job applications have a better chance of success if you can be recommended positively by managers or teammates from your past. You want your previous managers to say, 'They were great. I'd welcome them back here any time.'

Remember that people talk (especially in the land of HR), and your past behaviour can often be viewed as a signal of what your future performance will be like. Potential employers can see on your resume or LinkedIn profile where you've worked and they may make contact with that organisation (even if you haven't listed them as a referee) to ask someone about your time there. If you manage things poorly, whether while you work in the role or as you resign, of course they'll think that's how you work on an average day at work. Poorly.

Look to be thankful for what the opportunity has given you: the people, the projects, the skills gained.

Start your job with the end in mind. Commit to yourself that you want to leave so well that you could come back.

Reasons for leaving

You'll usually have a primary reason for leaving an organisation—this is where you want to focus your energy as you resign. Do not, however, tell your manager that you're leaving for one reason, then go and blab to your colleagues that it's actually for another reason. Be clear, stick to your story and don't place colleagues in the uncomfortable position of having to hear you rant about why you're leaving. Keep it straight and simple.

You will also have secondary reasons for leaving— things that also make you feel like it's time to go. Be honest and respectful about how you communicate these issues. Remember, your team and peers will still need to navigate any challenges in the workplace every day (hello micromanaging boss). So be sensitive about how you share your concerns with them. If you need someone to vent to, chat with a friend or family member about it.

What if I'm leaving because of my manager?

Ahhhh, bad bosses. It's got to be one of the most painful work problems you can face. Managers have a

The resignation process

Identify your primary reason for leaving.

↓

Write your resignation letter (see our downloadable template).

↓

Request a meeting with your manager to discuss your resignation.

↓

Have a meeting with your manager. Hand them your resignation letter in the meeting (inform them, discuss details and agree on how you want to share the news with your team and work besties).

↓

Write your handover notes.

↓

Leave with grace and a smile 😊

↓

Move into your new role!

disproportionate impact on your engagement at work. Every bad boss moment detracts from culture and job satisfaction. The impact is immediate. And the longer it goes on, the more destructive it becomes.

Before we can deal with it, you need to separate the problem from the person. When we label someone a 'bad boss', we subconsciously push the problem to the individual to solve. It perpetuates the fallacy that leadership is an innate talent. You either have it or you don't. You're either a good boss or a bad one.

Instead of using the 'bad boss' label, let's think of it as 'bad boss moments'. The truth is anyone who's led people has had bad boss moments. The job is not an easy one.

People train for the technical skills in their roles, often studying for years before ever working a day in their profession. But when it comes to management, it's a different story.

New managers are thrown into the deep end, and the implication is obvious: it's sink or swim. We expect people to learn how to lead people on the fly. And it's a recipe for management disasters.

If you're uncomfortable with your manager's behaviour, find out the channels to raise concerns. If it's not safe to address directly with the manager, take your concerns to HR or another leader for input and advice.

Beware the counter offer

You've jumped through all the nerve-wracking recruitment hoops. You land a new job and sign the contract (*yes!*). And you finally resign. Except then your employer comes back to you with a counter offer. Ugh! Plot twist.

The counter offer is one of those pivotal career decisions. One you need to approach with caution. Yep, it's very flattering to have your employer throw everything at you to keep you. The big pay increase. The company car. The extra holidays. The new job title. The promise of a better culture.

Our word of warning: beware the counter offer.

Counter offers are fascinating. If all of the things your employer is offering you to stay were possible, why weren't they given to you before now? Human behaviour is a weird thing. We're often more concerned about what we have to lose, than we are about keeping something awesome we already have. So before you accept, we want you to think this through.

First, think about your motivation. Why did you seek out another role in the first place? If it's purely about pay and your existing employer matches or exceeds it, then you may want to stay. But if the reason you started looking for other roles is different, then it's time to stop and assess.

The counter offer needs to address the underlying problem. What caused you to resign in the first place? Is there a toxic culture? Do you keep getting knocked back for promotions? Is your boss an evil tyrant hell bent on crushing your soul? Take time to genuinely consider if and how the counter offer addresses these issues. If the underlying problem is not solved in their counter offer, thank them and kindly decline.

Think about the wins

Resignation can feel like a negative experience. But it's important to recognise the good that has come out of all of your jobs, even if they have become toxic or it's time to go elsewhere. Take time to reflect on all the experience you've gained, the skills you've built and the amazing projects you've been involved in. These are things to thank your employer for in your resignation letter and when meeting to discuss your exit.

The resignation process

Before you text 'boy bye' to your manager and hightail it out of there, here are some simple steps to avoid a bad job break-up.

Read your contract

Your contract outlines the notice period you need to provide and any other requirements you need to meet to resign from your position. Check the notice provisions in the contract, and even run the dates and requirements past a friend or family member before you draft your resignation letter and set up a meeting with your manager or boss. You may not like your work or your boss, but you signed a contract and you need to follow the guidelines of that contract.

Prepare your resignation letter

At the end of this chapter we've provided a downloadable template for a resignation letter. This should be given to your manager following a meeting you have pre-planned with them. *Do not*—I repeat, *do not*—email this to them without first talking about it.

Meet with your manager face to face

Once you have determined that yep, now is the most appropriate time for me to resign, you should request a 1:1 meeting with your manager. If you work remotely and need to set up a resignation meeting, do it via video meeting or phone call at minimum, whatever your version of 'face-to-face' might look like.

Create a communication plan

In the meeting where you resign, seek to establish a communications plan. Chat with your manager about how the news of your resignation is best shared with external stakeholders (this could be clients or contractors) and internal staff (your teammates, the broader staff team). Don't go back to your desk and email @Allstaff with your news! Work through how communication will happen with your manager directly—work as a team on this.

Also think through how you'll respond when your colleagues hear the news and come over to your desk to chat. What will your answer be? Sometimes keeping things vague and high level is the best thing.

Prepare exceptional handover notes

So you've had a meeting with your manager and broken the news with a resignation letter and a chat. Now we need to prepare for your exit and what will happen within your team once you've left—you need to make the transition for everyone as smooth as possible. Preparing handover notes for those left behind is a crucial next step. There's a bunch of ways to prepare handover notes and it's essential you prepare them for your successor.

Ways to prepare the team left behind include:

- using online recording software to record you sharing instructions personally

- writing an easy-to-understand written document and emailing it to the relevant people

- having a few meetings to walk it all through

- offering your phone number once you've left.

You need to recognise you're leaving them with an empty position or a new person to train, so assist in that process.

The exit interview

Oooh, the old exit interview. Do you overshare? Do you undershare? Do you plead the fifth and sit in awkward silence? Arghh. Send help.

The exit interview is a chance for you to debrief your employment and give the employer feedback on how they can improve the workplace. They are typically arranged as a meeting on one of your final days at the organisation, and you might be asked to complete a feedback survey. Any healthy and growing business will want to know why you're leaving and what they can do to improve employee experience. But it can be tricky to know what you should share in this conversation. Do you a) drop all the truth bombs and vent the years of pent-up rage, or b) avoid saying anything constructive altogether?

The answer, of course, is neither. The best approach is to be simultaneously honest and kind. It's not either/or. You don't need to be brutal when you're sharing something honest. It's about telling your experience truthfully, in a respectful way. One strategy I've seen work well is when the exiting employee frames the conversation like this:

'I really care about the team here, and I want the best for this organisation. I think, like any business, there are things that are amazing, and things that can be improved. I'd love to share my feedback on what I think can be improved so that the organisation can be successful.'

By communicating it in this manner, you're reducing any defensiveness by showing that your intention is to see the organisation improve and thrive.

Many people assume their employer is acutely aware of all the internal people issues, but this is not the case. Your feedback might be the first time they are hearing the concerns, so remove any assumptions or generalisations. Avoid absolute statements or lobbying for your work besties. Simply share your story. The good and bad. Share examples that reinforce your feedback so your employer gets a clear insight into your experience.

Exit interview tips

- If an exit interview isn't organised by HR, see if one can be arranged.

- Prepare beforehand to make this meeting constructive and valuable. Bring your notes with feedback for your manager.

- Do not use this as an opportunity to rant; communicate with both honesty and kindness.

- Thank them for the opportunities you've had at the organisation.

What if my manager responds badly?

Yeah, they might respond poorly, but you can't control their response. You can only control your response. Stay your ground and remain professional—choose to respond with grace and maturity in the scenario.

Keep these tips in mind:

- Don't stoop to their level of rudeness, anger or pettiness.

- Acknowledge their point of view, but stay steady on your choice to leave.

- Thank them for what they've offered you—this can go a long way.

- Perhaps look to another person in the organisation to be your future referee.

The exiting must-haves!

- Tell your manager in person or over the phone (if in person is not an option).

- Prepare a professional resignation letter for your meeting (see our downloadable template).

- Follow your organisation's policy for resignation— in particular the number of weeks of notice required.

- Work diligently until you leave.

- Prepare rock-solid handover notes and processes (offer to meet, offer your number).

- Don't steal the office staplers (lol).

A final word

What's your exit strategy? When or why would you leave where you currently work? Take the tips in this chapter and apply them to your situation. Tick the checklists. Work with your manager. Be real about why you are considering the option of leaving. Keep your cool, and leave well.

Leave so well that one day, if you wanted to, your old desk would be waiting for you to return.

resources **Scan the QR code for these resources and more.**

- There are a number of episodes on *my millennial career* about leaving your job.

- Download our resignation letter template.

where to from here?

A note from Glen

You made it. Congratulations. Hopefully you have made a lot of notes and have been inspired!

Like any new information, course or learnings I think it's important to step back and really think about your career. I don't, however, want you to get so excited about your career after reading this book that you resign tomorrow (unless you're cashed up and it's a toxic place!), but temper that excitement to formulate a plan if you have not started to put one in place already.

Go back and re-read the chapters that stood out to you. Implement one thing at a time in your career. Test some things out. Get your resume up to date, even if you're happy where you are.

If you're not naturally confident, can you arrange a catch-up meeting with your boss or team leader at a cafe just to see how everything is, without any expectations? Work on that confidence muscle.

Perhaps you are wanting to step out and do your own thing? This book is the tap on the shoulder you need to make some serious plans to start to hit the road.

Have you been putting up with job apathy in your life? Do you love your career but you really don't enjoy your current workplace? Have you wanted to leave for a while now? Now is the time to put a plan in place.

It's been a pleasure to encourage you with your career. I'm glad you have invested into it as you are the number one asset in your life.

Cheers!

• • •

A note from Shell

Put the car in park. Turn off the engine. You made it.

What a wild ride. Your career will have its share of road bumps, crossroads and breakdowns (metaphorically and literally). But as you become more aware of your strengths and values, you'll have far fewer of them.

You'll find yourself picking up pace and building momentum. As you put good habits in place, opportunities you never expected will come your way. You'll also learn to take a risk. To be bold and go off road and figure out where the heck you're going along the way. You'll feel energised by your work, instead of exhausted.

These are the hallmarks of a career you love. We know you're going to build it.

If there is one final thing you take away from this book, let it be this:

You don't serve your career; your career has to serve you. If you've got this the wrong way around and you're a slave to your career, own it and then make the changes. Let go of the external pressure and decide what you want for your life and work.

A career you love is only a few decisions away.

---

resources   **Scan the QR code for these resources and more.**

- Check out the my millennial education portal for career related online learning from Shell and Glen.

- Check out Shell and Glen's favourite career books and add them to your reading list.

- Check out the *my millennial money* and *my millennial career* podcasts.

A thank you

We would like to thank Jess Knaus, who has helped us keep on track with writing this book. She is the project wrangler, words guru, stress reducer and all around legend. Thank you Jess.

Also to all the individuals who shared their career stories with us for this book. You may be the encouragement someone needed!

• • •

Sam, you're my bestie and the most amazing Dad. Thank you for holding everything together. Shell

index